ORGANIC No-dig, No-weed

Learn about a method that will make gardening ;
requires no digging, a minimum of tools and no more weeding

ORGANIC
No-dig, No-weed
GARDENING

A Revolutionary Method for Easy Gardening

Raymond P. Poincelot

THORSONS/RODALE

First UK Edition published 1988

British Library Cataloguing in Publication Data

Poincelot, Raymond P.
Organic no-dig, no-weed gardening: a
revolutionary method for easy gardening.
1.   Gardening
I.   Title
635   SB450.97

ISBN   0-7225-1521-9

Published by Thorsons Publishers Limited, Wellingborough, Northamptonshire, NN8 2RQ, England

Printed in Great Britain by Woolnough Bookbinding Limited,
Irthlingborough, Northamptonshire

1   3   5   7   9   10   8   6   4   2

CONTENTS

ACKNOWLEDGEMENTS

To my wife, Marian, and our three children, Raymond, Daniel, and Wendy, thanks for their love, patience, and support during my gardening and writing times. A special thanks to William Loefstedt, a friend and partner in horticulture. Without his ideas, support, and inspiration, this book could not exist. I also thank Anne Halpin for her editorial assistance and patience.

INTRODUCTION

I have loved gardening for as long as I can remember. From early childhood on, I had a garden. Oh, there were some interruptions here and there. When I went to college and lived in my first few apartments, I had no land. Then house plants were the closest thing I had to a garden. But I always came back eagerly to gardening when the possibility returned. To me gardening is a special part of life; it gives me a chance for personal satisfaction, a closeness with earth, and a feeling of naturalness.

I can't say that I have the same warm feelings about some of the work that goes with a garden. New gardeners sometimes drop by the wayside because of the labour involved. Old gardeners often are forced off the road when the burden becomes intolerable. A few years ago I found myself somewhere in the middle of the gardening road, having survived the start and wondering about the finish.

The work had not become intolerable yet, but it sure consumed a lot of my time. As such the gardening was competing with my family time and other interests. If only gardening were easier, I wished.

My view was shared by a gardening friend, William Loefstedt. He is always questioning the basics, or what we take for granted in horticulture. Bill is an octogenarian who still gardens. He, too, wished gardening could be easier.

Sometimes wishes become reality with enough thought, work and luck. That's what happened with Bill and me. We set out to create a form of gardening that was less work but still retained all the good results. We put considerable time and effort into the project, testing new ideas in our backyard gardens. Friends of ours also tried out some of the ideas. Other ideas were tested through my research at Fairfield University, where I also teach horticulture. Some ideas worked, others didn't. Our test gardens got better and the work became less.

We did succeed. This book presents a personalized approach to gardening. The approach is called, appropriately enough, no-dig, no-weed gardening. Why not take a load off your gardening back and give it a try? If you do, I think you will go a lot further along the garden road.

CHAPTER 1

THE NO-DIG, NO-WEED METHOD

Each spring, for more years than I care to think about, I literally busted my garden's soil clumps. One could add that in the process, I 'busted my gut' to prepare the garden for planting. But like most dedicated gardeners, I wasted little thought on the hard work I did and the subsequent blisters and aches I suffered. I thought it was just part of what gardening was all about.

At first digging the garden was a challenge, a macho activity that proclaimed that spring was here to me, my family, and anyone else who looked. Then a sense of personal accomplishment took over, the blissful satisfaction of looking at a finely manicured seedbed. In the newly dug garden, the soil surface was smooth and free of lumps and clumps, and looking at it gave me the same feeling of calmness and cleanness that I get when I look at an expanse of freshly fallen snow, unmarked by footprints. In fact, I would get mad if a stray footprint from a neighbourhood dog or cat marred the illusion. Heaven help anyone who walked on my garden after it was ready! I even regretted the fact that I made footprints when I planted the seeds. Sometimes I felt compelled to grab a rake and wipe out the offending footprints.

About four years ago, I began to question the hard labour involved in gardening. Whether my doubts arose as a consequence of age or wisdom, I don't know. But something inside me said gardens were for enjoyment and for provision of food for the soul and body. I didn't enjoy the enforced spring ritual of digging the soil, even though I had gone from a spade to a rotovator a few years before, and I didn't like weeding the garden, either. I thought of my options: give up the garden or develop a better method of gardening. I loved gardening, so I couldn't give it up. My choice was simple: look for the better method.

At that point either divine providence or lady luck entered my life. A phone call started me on the road to a better way.

In a previous job I knew an older man, William Loefstedt, an active octogenarian with a love for gardening and a mind that questioned all aspects of horticulture. Whenever our paths crossed, we would stop and chat about gardens. He had the unsettling habit of raising questions about gardening, the kinds of questions that seemed to have obvious answers, yet somehow didn't. When we parted he would say, 'Think about it. Maybe next time you'll have the answer for me. Of course, I'll have some new questions for you.' Some of the questions got answered, and others didn't.

Although I had changed jobs, I still got an occasional phone call from Bill. One day the phone rang and Bill asked, 'Why do we dig?' I replied, 'Funny you should ask. I was just wondering about that subject.' We agreed to get together over lunch to discuss the topic. Bill said, 'I also want to show you something then. Can you use a few pepper plants?' 'Sure', I answered.

The day arrived and so did Bill. The back of his station wagon was incredibly loaded with garden paraphernalia: plants in various containers, empty trays and polystyrene cups, buckets of sand, assorted garden tools, and many gardening magazines. There was hardly any room for Bill.

He stepped out with a smile and said, 'Show me where you need a few pepper plants. I'll put them into the garden without digging.' He handed me the pepper plants—they were growing in polystyrene cups that had several slits in them—and he picked up a bulb planter with a short handle.

We walked into the yard and entered my garden. I pointed out a small, empty area. In one swift motion Bill bent over and with a thrust, twist, and pull, removed a soil plug from the garden. Next he deftly slid the root ball of the pepper plant from the cup. As he did, I noticed the healthy white feeder roots that covered the ball. He inserted the root ball into the hole left by the planter. It was a good fit.

'How's that for a no-dig transplant?' asked Bill with a smile. 'Great,' I answered, 'but how would you plant seeds or onion sets?' Bill looked at me and said, 'Those are questions for you to work on. We're just starting on the idea of no-dig gardening. Let's go to lunch. We have a lot to talk about.' A thousand questions began to roll through my mind.

Over lunch we discussed the idea of a collaborative project on no-dig gardening. Bill wanted to find a way to garden without digging because digging was no longer an easy task for him. The idea

appealed to me because, while I am much younger than Bill, I realized that I no longer enjoyed digging my garden and felt that my time could be put to better use. We agreed to develop the concept of no-dig gardening.

Over a period of four years, Bill and I developed various procedures for a no-dig method of gardening. We had many lunch discussions together and tried out dozens of ideas in our test gardens. Some of the methods failed, some succeeded, and others changed as we experimented with them. In time we realized our concept had evolved into a no-dig no-weed form of gardening; hence, the title of this book was born.

We've been able to develop a system that works in any size garden and that produces good yields of vegetables and beautiful flowers, too. Our system will let you have a terrific garden for a fraction of the work involved in conventional methods. And in this book I'm going to share our method with you, and show you step-by-step how to turn your garden into a no-dig, no-weed success.

Let's dig into the subject by first asking the most basic question: why dig?

Why Do We Dig Gardens?
Why indeed? To answer that question we must go back in our history to the first farmers. For the farmers, the primary concern was farming. Gardens came second and were dependent upon adaptations of prevailing farm practices.

The prevailing practice was tillage, that is, ploughing, sowing, and cultivating. The farmers ploughed with a moulded plough, which cut deeply into the soil and inverted a substantial layer, crumbling the soil as it turned it upside down. Next the farmers harrowed the soil to break up the lumps prior to sowing the seeds. As the plants grew they cultivated to destroy weeds.

This approach to farming was popularized in a book published in 1733. The author was Jethro Tull, and his book was titled, *The Horse-Hoeing Husbandry: or an Essay on the Principles of Tillage and Vegetation*. Of course the machine drill, which Tull invented in 1701 for sowing seeds, was featured in his book.

Essentially, Tull invented the concept of row planting and advocated vigorous tillage (such as with the plough), preparation of seed beds by harrowing, mechanical planting of rows, and weed control through repeated cultivations.

But what did this tillage system have to do with digging gardens? As I mentioned before, farming came first and the luxury of home gardening followed. Farming methods served as the model for technology transfer into the garden. Vigorous tillage with a plough in turn inspired the spring digging of gardens. However, garden sizes usually did not justify the need or provide sufficient room for ploughing equipment.

What simple hand tool gave the same soil-turning action as a plough? The standard garden spade. And the hand tools needed for harrowing and cultivating were the rake and hoe. The habit of digging the home garden became an ingrained custom that almost everyone accepted.

The Seeds of Dissent

Although today most of us still dig up our gardens, farming circles have for some time been questioning the wisdom of vigorous tillage. The seeds of agricultural tillage dissent were perhaps first sown over 30 years ago, by a Japanese farmer named Masanobu Fukuoka. He abandoned the traditional agricultural concept of tillage on his farm in Japan. Instead of ploughing his fields, Fukuoka planted vegetables directly into fields of white clover.

Today we see variations of this method undergoing extensive investigation in certain segments of the agricultural community. These variations include the interplanting of legumes with sweetcorn, soybeans or vegetable crops and the use of living mulch systems. The latter involves the growing of vegetables in grass and clover sward. Researchers are examining these no-tillage planting systems at the Rodale Research Center in Pennsylvania. Growers in Lackawanna County, Pennsylvania, are actually using the living mulch system.

Other farmers, especially organic farmers, have adopted conservation tillage. This practice is essentially that of reduced tillage. The farmer does not use a plough. Instead he uses some other ploughing implement, such as a chisel plough, which tills the soil far less vigorously. Disk ploughing is also popular. The main point is that the farmer keeps soil disturbance to a minimum, but is vigorous enough to ensure weed control.

An extreme variation of the Fukuoka method is the no-till system. This way of farming allows no disturbance whatever of crop residues or mulches. The farmer plants the seeds by slicing or slotting directly through the surface residues. Herbicides rather than soil cultivation control the weeds. Although both traditional and organic farmers are increasingly practising conservation tillage, the organic farmers are not employing the no-till methods because using herbicides goes against their beliefs.

So, why do we gardeners continue digging our gardens while the agricultural community is questioning and even eliminating the practice? Most likely we do it out of habit. One gardener who broke the digging habit was the late Ruth Stout, the author of numerous articles and books on gardening without digging. Her method depended on a year-round mulch. My method differs somewhat from Ruth Stout's approach. I have replaced her digging trowel with no-dig tools. You can still try her year-round organic mulch, but you can also use a mulch about which Ruth Stout had few kind words—black plastic. Stout's method requires a mulch, but my no-dig method works just as well without a mulch. A no-weed garden is also possible without a mulch, it just takes longer.

But like Ruth Stout, I broke the habit, and I'd like to convince you to stop digging your garden.

The Case Against Digging

I don't think anyone will disagree with me when I say that digging a garden is hard work and consumes a lot of time. Bill and I agreed on this point, although his emphasis was a bit more on the hard work and mine on the time involved.

Is the work necessary? When I first thought about it, my answer was no. Let me explain why. First, think about the amount of dug and raked soil in your garden that is really used. Much of the prepared soil becomes either paths or the space between rows or beds. The actual soil you plant to seeds or transplants is only a fraction of the total area. My guess is that you use only 25 per cent or less of the total soil surface area in terms of seed contact or root ball contact with transplants.

Some gardeners might argue this point, claiming that perhaps prepared soil throughout the garden makes for better root growth from the seedling or transplant. I would counter this objection with the following observation.

Perennial beds surround my sideyard walk and greenhouse perimeter. These beds contain, among other plants, assorted spring bulbs, summer lilies and phlox and autumn chrysanthemums. A gap occurs after the bulbs blossom and before the summer perennials flower. The bulb foliage, which must remain undisturbed even when it yellows and dries, makes the gap between blooming times even worse. I keep the bed looking nice by filling the gap with colourful annuals. Because I don't want to disturb the perennials, I don't do any digging when I plant the annuals. Instead I scratch in some seeds or put in transplants with a trowel.

These seeds and transplants go into soil that has little or no digging. As the plants grow, their roots eventually reach out into surrounding soil that has had absolutely no digging preparation. Yet these plants grow and thrive. In fact, they look every bit as good as those flowers I plant among the vegetables in the fully dug and raked soil of the main garden.

I can hear the sceptics saying, 'Yes, but we know good reasons for digging garden soil. It controls weeds and improves the aeration and drainage of the seedbeds.' Of course, you can rattle their complacency a bit when you mention the Ruth Stout method. The sceptics have a tough time explaining how she managed to grow such healthy, abundant crops without ever digging her garden. Perhaps they slough off Ruth's garden as an isolated case or claim they didn't want to bother with an all-year-round mulch. After all, they may say, no-dig gardening only works with a permanent mulch. Perhaps they feel they can't use a permanent mulch because their soil is too wet or their garden has slugs or mice or some other recurring problem. To these sceptics I can reply that the no-dig method Bill and I have developed does not require a year-round mulch. It won't encourage slugs or mice to hide in your garden.

To further convince you that you can

have a great garden without going through the usual spring ritual of digging, I'm going to examine the supposed benefits of digging. Are they really so beneficial and necessary after all? Let's examine them one by one.

Weed Control

First, let's talk about weed control. It is true that turning the soil by digging buries any newly emerging weeds or ungerminated weed seeds lying near the soil surface. But I found over the years that my freshly turned garden quickly developed a luxuriant weed crop every spring, even though I cultivated it the preceding year. But I had a sparse weed crop in my perennial bed where I didn't dig or cultivate for weeds each year. Why did this happen? The answer lay in the soil.

Below the surface of any garden's soil lies a ticking time bomb: ungerminated weed seeds. Weeds produce prolific numbers of seeds. For example, the worst weed in my garden, purslane, can produce 190,000 seeds *per plant* in a single growing season. A plantain can produce 36,000 seeds and chickweed 15,000. You can imagine how weed seeds fill the soil.

Weed seeds can lie dormant underground for long periods of time. Most will survive for 10, 20, even 40 years. Some weed seeds have life spans of many hundreds of years. These seeds germinate whenever conditions become favourable, such as when you bring the soil below up to the surface during the digging of your garden.

The sceptics may say that, eventually, turning the soil followed by surface cultivation should exhaust the weed seed supply. I don't think so. I dug and thoroughly cultivated one garden of mine for an eight-year period. After each turning of the soil, I was still rewarded with a thriving jungle of newly emerged weed seedlings.

The problem lies in numbers. Firstly, most garden soil contains vast numbers of weed seeds, each with a long lifetime to wait for the right conditions to germinate. Secondly, no matter how thoroughly you cultivate, you will miss a few weeds here and there. Just a few missed weeds will add tens of thousands more seeds to the soil. Thirdly, wind, animals, clothing, or soil on shoes can transport even more weed seeds into your garden. Finally, other seeds can arrive in mulches, manures, and even in bird droppings. So much for the value of digging garden soil to control weeds!

The best way to control weeds is to *not* dig the soil and to use shallow cultivation or a mulch. In this way the deeper seeds remain buried, never to germinate. Those weed seeds near the surface eventually disappear as they germinate. If the cultivation is shallow, no new seeds will make their way to the surface.

Drainage and Aeration

We've just seen that one of the traditional reasons for digging the garden each spring is not really valid. But what about the other two? Does cultivation improve drainage and aeration of the seedbed? Again, the answer is no. In fact, the reverse is true. Digging the soil ultimately brings about a deterioration of drainage and aeration, and I'd like to prove it to you.

Turning the soil brings organic matter in the root zone to the surface where the levels of oxygen are higher. This condition increases the oxidation, or breakdown, of organic matter, because the soil microorganisms that decompose organic matter are more active in the oxygen-rich surface layers of the soil. Studies show that soils under cultivation lose about two per cent of their organic matter each year. These losses of the soil's organic matter result in poorer drainage, decreased aeration and less ease of soil workability (tilth), as any good book on soils can inform you. Ultimately, continued loss of organic matter leads to increased water and wind erosion. The latter problem has become serious for US farmers.

A second fact, revealed by Mark Kane in the September 1983 issue of *Organic Gardening* (published in America), is that tilled or dug soil is more susceptible to compaction. Compacted soils have poor aeration and drainage. Plant roots cannot get enough oxygen for good growth and stunted plants result. The conversion of organic matter to humus also slows, since the needed microorganisms fail in oxyen-poor soils. In turn this curtailment decreases the levels of available nutrients supplied by the breakdown of organic matter. Nutrient storage is lessened and leaching increased, since humus helps to retain nutrients. The bottom line is less fertility and lower yields.

Al Trouse points out in Kane's article that slight pressure of 3.5 pounds per square inch will start to compact well-tilled soil. The simple act of walking on soil exerts far more pressure, perhaps as much as 25 pounds per square inch. When you dig and rake your soil into seedbeds, you produce a well-tilled soil which is easily compacted by even light foot traffic. (For the record, Al Trouse retired from the USDA's National Tillage Machinery Laboratory. He studied the development of plant roots in compacted soil, among other things.)

The problem of compaction involves soil structure. Turning the soil by vigorous digging has a detrimental effect on its structure. Essentially, disruption of soil crumbs and particles is caused first by the slicing and tearing action of the spade or fork, and then worsened by force as the soil drops from the spade or fork and hits the ground. Structure breakdown intensifies further as you bring the organic matter to the surface, where the newly exposed organic matter is lost quickly at the oxygen-rich, microbially active surface of the soil. Soils with weakened structures are more susceptible to compaction, have less ease of workability and have poorer drainage and aeration.

Now are you convinced that digging your garden isn't necessary? As you can see, the digging of your garden actually damages your soil. You're probably ready now to throw away your spade and give up digging for ever. But what do you do instead of digging soil? How do you control weeds? That's what Bill and I wondered several years ago. Although we solved the problem, it wasn't easy. But you can benefit from our experience. First, let's turn to the tools that will convert you from a hard-working soil buster to a no-dig loafer.

Tools for No-dig Gardening

Do garden tools fascinate you? They fascinate me! When I buy a new tool for my garden, I feel like a kid opening a birthday gift. Once I have the tool at home, I can't resist admiring the complementary blending of fine wood and gleaming metal. And I have a lot of fun trying out the tool in my garden, where I look for good balance, comfort and efficient function. A tool with these qualities, that is, one that works well and feels good in my hands, makes gardening tasks go much more easily.

It was therefore with pleasure that Bill and I examined old and new tools for our no-dig garden. First, we had to shake our perceptions of the tools we traditionally relied on, the spade, fork and the trowel. Sure, these tools can prepare a fine seedbed or plant transplants, but their use requires a lot of physical effort and time. And for what?

The seeds or transplants fill only 10 to 20 per cent of the garden area we struggle so hard to prepare. Once we saw the spade, fork and trowel in that light, Bill and I changed our rigid thought patterns and started to look for new tools.

Our new-found insight helped us to focus quickly on finding tools that would simply and rapidly prepare seed furrows or transplant holes in untilled soil without digging. When we discovered that Bill (who, remember, is in his eighties) found the tools we chose easy to work with and my children could handle them with no trouble, the no-dig gardening method for all ages was born.

Tools for Transplants

First, let's look at the tools for planting transplants. Bill and I had to decide whether or not one tool could handle all kinds of transplants, no matter how they were grown. As you know, you can grow or purchase transplants either in individual containers or as several plants in one container. The plants can be large or small. Transplants present a range of different situations for a single tool to handle. But we found two tools that could handle just about any kind of transplant.

Our first choice was a bulb planter. You may remember that I mentioned Bill's short-handled bulb planter earlier.

Many of you probably already have a short-handled bulb planter and so you can use the transplanting technique shown in Chapter 3.

Bulb planters are compatible with larger transplants, including those purchased in individual containers, such as broccoli, cabbage, aubergines, geraniums, peppers, marrow and tomatoes. Transplants grown at home in individual containers also work out well.

Sometimes for reasons of economy or limited space, gardeners grow transplants in groups in deep seed trays or similar containers. Bedding plants such as begonias, marigolds, petunias and salvia are often grown this way. Many people like to grow lettuce in deep seed trays too. If you have an uncrowded deep seed tray and the transplants are medium-sized to large-sized, you can usually separate them with a reasonable intact soil ball. You can use the bulb planter for this task. If the transplants are small or have little or no soil ball, you will need another no-dig tool.

This additional tool is known as a dibber. Essentially, a dibber is a pointed stick with a handle. The better models have a metal-encased pointed end and a slightly rounded tip.

When you're looking for a dibber, the question is whether to make your own or buy one. You can easily make dibbers from the broken handles of tools. The broken handle of a spade or fork can become a short-handed dibber.

You can also buy some well-made dibbers for a reasonable price. One metal-encased short-handled version comes with a pistol-type handle, another with a 'T' handle. Prices vary, depending on the type of wood and metal used. These short-handled dibbers are all comfortable to use, regardless of handle shape. (See address for Wolf Tools on page 167.) Between these two tools, you can tackle any transplanting task that arises in your no-dig garden.

Tools for Seeds

OK, great, we've settled the matter of transplants, but what about seeds? How do you plant seeds without digging and preparing the soil? First of all, Bill and I found that we could plant some seeds, such as large bean or sweetcorn seeds that are planted in hills, with the bulb planter and dibber. Peas worked fine, too. (As an aside, these tools also made it easy to plant onion sets, garlic cloves and seed potatoes.)

But suppose you want to plant seeds in rows. Although planting seeds was the toughest challenge Bill and I faced as we developed the total no-dig garden, we did find a tool that let us make seed furrows easily, without digging.

Our initial attempts concentrated quite naturally on hoes. At first glance the hoe looks ideal for creating a furrow as you draw it through the soil. But in reality, the labour involved in making a furrow with a hoe is comparable to an exercise workout. The problem with hoes is in their design. They are great for cutting weeds and disturbing soil in small amounts, but cutting a furrow tends to build up a pile of soil at the blade front. This mound slows the hoe's movement and makes your muscles fight the hoe.

We quickly realized that what we needed was a hoe that behaved like a plough. This implement should cut through soil like a knife through butter, while throwing the removed soil to the sides of the furrow. Also, the tool should pull easily enough that anyone could use it.

We found such a tool in the 'ridger' made by Wolf Tools (see page 167 for address). The wedge-like blade is polished steel, the edges are sharp and the 'wings' are angled. The blade's sharpness and wedge-like shape help it to sink into and slice effortlessly through the soil. The polished surface stops the soil from sticking, and the angled wings prevent soil build-up by throwing it to the sides. The ridger cuts neat, broad V-shaped furrows in depths from shallow scratches to several inches.

Whether you need the ridger or not depends on what you plant and keep in mind that you can also plant seed potatoes with the bulb planter and even the dibber.

At this point I'd like to mention a multi-headed tool that can become, among other things, a ridger. It is made by Wolf Tools in the range called 'multi-change garden tools'. The range gives you the option of an auxilliary handle grip and the ridger comes as an interchangeable head for the tools. The benefit of the Wolf tools is that you can convert the handle to make other tools. You can save money by changing tool heads instead of buying several individual tools.

Bill and I have a final thought about no-dig tools for planting seeds. Suppose you just want to try the no-dig preparation of a seed furrow without buying a ridger. You can get a rough idea with a hoe.

Some hoes are better than others, but most will do the job. If you have one of the conventional square or rectangular bladed draw hoes, just turn it at an angle so that the corner of the blade cuts into the soil. However, the hoe is a poor substitute for the ridger.

Tools for No-weed Gardening

As you know, this book is also about no-weed gardening. Why, you may ask, do you need tools if you're not going to do any weeding? Actually, you have a choice between doing no weeding whatsoever and doing very little weeding. If you prefer never to weed the garden at all, just use one of the permanent or temporary mulching systems discussed in Chapter 5. If you find you have the need to handle some weeds, Bill and I think we can surprise you at how easy it can be.

We examined and evaluated over a dozen different hoes for weeding, looking for the right one. Our goal was to find a hoe that cut through the soil with ease. As I explained earlier, most hoes pile up soil, thus increasing your workload. Others are blunt, thick or heavy and hinder your effort. We also wanted a hoe that severed weeds effortlessly, not one that chopped like an axe. We finally found the ideal hoe. Suffolk Herbs sell a Swiss reciprocating hoe (for their address, see page 166.) The mount of the cutting blade gives this type of hoe its name. The mounting allows the blade to move back and forth as you push or pull.

Helpful Accessories

Some useful additional items can make the task of the no-dig gardener more comfortable and easier. Bill and I tried out several accessories along the way and believe that some of them are worthy of your consideration.

Regardless of whether you are young or old, the contact between your knees and the garden's soil is often uncomfortable. Soil usually feels hard after the first few contacts. Stones, twigs and crop residues add to the unpleasant sensation. If the soil is wet or cold, the ache in your knees seems to go even deeper. Soils in the spring, being both wet and cold, can be enough to discourage planting sessions with bone-chilling promptness. What's a no-dig gardener to do?

Even a no-dig gardener must kneel sometimes, such as when placing transplants. But this communion between soil and gardener need not be an uncomfortable event. It can be a pleasant sharing of the plant's environment, an opportunity to get close to the soil with a sense of appreciation.

The difference between pain and enjoyment can be as simple as a pair of sponge rubber kneepads. My inspiration finally to get kneepads came from watching my children rollerskate. Sometimes they fell to their knees on the pavement but were unhurt because they wore protective pads. The light clicked on in my head, as they say. Working on my garden soil has become a pleasure, thanks to my gardener's kneepads.

You can also buy a kneeling pad. The comfort level is the same, but I don't like picking up and carrying the pad every time I move elsewhere. The knee pads are no bother; you're wearing them, so they automatically go with you to the next area. However, a more sophisticated version of the kneeling pad should be considered if you appreciate a little help as you kneel or rise. The kneeling stool has a soft kneeling pad. In addition, two supports at the right and left sides provide arm-assisted kneeling or rising. If you get tired, you can flip the kneeling stool over and it becomes a bench! When you finish, you can fold it for easy storage. The kneeling stool is a blessing for older or disabled gardeners.

Another quite useful gadget is a garden straightline, or row marker. This unit consists of one stake with a windup top containing line attached to a second stake. You push the second stake into the ground and feed the line out to the desired length. Then, push the last stake into the ground. Now you have a way to make a nice, straight line. If you team up the straightline device with a ridger or bulb planter, you can make nice, straight rows. (The kneepads, kneeling pads, kneeling stool and straightline are available from most garden centres or by post from Dobies—for their address, see page 166.)

I found yet another application that makes this gadget useful. If you have ever tried to lay black plastic mulch, you know that the trench into which the plastic edge goes must be true. If you prepare your trench based upon the garden straightline, you greatly simplify the installation of plastic mulches. Using a garden straightline and a spade, just try the easy one-two-three steps of placing plastic mulch that I mention in

Chapter 5. I'm sure you'll agree the straightline is an indispensable accessory.

One last accessory deserves a mention. A row seeder can save you a lot of bending and stooping. Although most of us with smaller gardens do not really need one, proprietors of large gardens or older or handicapped gardeners may find the row seeder invaluable. My advice is to avoid the smaller hand-held units with 'click' features. These devices give good results if you are steady of hand and true of eye; however, your need for a seeder usually arises because you do not rate high in those traits. The better device is the wheel-type seeder with a long handle. You can push such units along with hardly any effort as you walk the row. Wolf Tools sell a sower in their multi-change garden tools range (for their address, see page 167).

Tool Simplicity

By now you have noticed that the no-dig gardener needs very few tools. If you are a gardener who works only with transplants, either purchased or home-grown, you can make do with only the bulb planter. You might need a reciprocating hoe for weeds, but if you opt for our total no-weed approach described in Chapter 5, you won't need the hoe. Even if you like to grow plants that are not conventionally recognized or available as transplants, you still need but a few tools. If you plan to plant seeds, you will need the ridger.

At most, then, you will need two tools for the no-dig, no-weed garden with full mulch. If you opt for no mulch or only a partial mulch, make it three. New gardeners need not invest a fortune, but established gardeners need not despair. Hang on to your tools. You may find new uses for them, such as using the spade to install plastic mulches. And don't forget, trees and shrubs will still need planting and lawns will need raking.

CHAPTER 2
BETTER TRANSPLANTS—
THE KEY TO SUCCESS

You can't beat transplants when it comes to getting a head start in your garden. So why is it that we don't use more transplants? Several reasons may pop up in your mind. You've surely heard them all. 'Some plants don't transplant well.' 'Growing transplants is too much work.' 'Transplants never take well in my garden.' 'I'll get quicker-growing, better plants with direct garden seeding.' 'Transplants cost too much.'

Bunk and baloney! That's what Bill and I say to these arguments. Transplants are a great time saver for gardeners. When they don't perform well, it's usually because the gardener doesn't fully understand how to handle transplants or is doing something wrong along the way. Let Bill and me tell you about our own way to grow the best-ever transplants with little work. You won't need a greenhouse or a lot of money to follow our method and you will be able to transplant even the most finicky plant. No transplant shock or slow recovery will occur. Your transplants will grow as soon as they enter the soil, and you'll love the results. First, let's look at why you should consider planting transplants.

Why Use Transplants?

Gardeners use transplants for different reasons. The most important reason they give is the head start transplants offer in the growing season. Transplants offer instant colour with annual bedding plants like marigolds, petunias, impatiens and geraniums. Of course, no tomato-lover would even consider direct sowing of tomatoes in the garden, since transplanted tomatoes yield fruit roughly two months sooner than directly sown tomatoes. This earlier and, hence, longer harvest is especially important to northern gardeners because of the shorter growing season.

Another big plus in using transplants is that they allow for economical use of space in the garden. Because transplants are started outside your garden, plenty of garden space is available for direct seeding of fast-producing early crops. After the harvest of early crops, like peas, radishes, spinach, chard and lettuce, you can fill in the garden space with transplants.

Another advantage of using transplants is the need for fewer seeds. Rates of seed germination are better indoors under controlled conditions, therefore fewer seeds are lost to the elements. Spacing becomes easier in the garden with transplants as opposed to seeds, because you can see just how much room each plant will need. With transplants there is no need for thinning, again due to more accurate spacing from the start. Seed packages seem to stretch further.

You can also use transplants throughout the season as reserves. As you harvest your crops, you can replace the old plants with new plants from your ongoing transplant nursery to fill the holes. Direct seeding during the hot, dry days of summer can be difficult, because the seeds need moisture and controlled warmth to germinate properly. On the other hand, transplant production can be a breeze at that time. (This topic will be covered in more detail later in this chapter.)

Another transplant plus is the significant advantage they offer in the fight against insects, disease, and unfavourable weather. The development of a plant from germination through seedling is a critical time. You must closely watch temperature and moisture conditions and insects plus disease can knock out young seedlings very quickly. While you can control these problems outdoors in gardens to some degree, producing transplants indoors borders on luxury conditions. Each resulting vigorous transplant will have bypassed early problems and will now be at a stage and time where outdoor garden conditions will pose much less hazard.

This last reason for using transplants is important to people who live in areas subject to, say cold, wet springs when most of the seeds rot before they germinate. You may resort to sowing many more seeds than you need and try to wait out the weather. Transplants, however, come through the miserable weather with flying colours.

I began to wonder if I could plant my entire garden with transplants, a reasonable thought considering the fact that I grow my own. Long ago I became displeased with commercial transplants and the very limited choices available, although I didn't blame the growers, who were forced to select cultivars based on saleability.

Bill and I began to discuss the possibilities of producing transplants for any vegetable or flower. We knew that it was easier to produce transplants for some plants than for others, but we didn't know why. For example, why not produce sweetcorn transplants because I had many sweetcorn seeds ruined by weather and devoured by squirrels? We reasoned that the growing of some plants as transplants was not economically feasible and the direct outdoor sowing of others gave satisfactory results. Some plants were thought to be difficult to grow as transplants, but were probably easier to raise if handled properly. Other transplants probably got the reputation for being difficult only through hearsay, while others were difficult to grow because of taproots.

Bill and I reckoned we needed to think beyond conventional approaches with transplants, as we did earlier with our no-dig techniques, but we knew that any new technique would have to satisfy certain conditions. The procedure would have to be inexpensive and easy, it could not require any special equipment, it would have to perform well under conditions available to the average gardener, it would have to produce transplants for any crop and it would have to produce transplants that would not experience transplanting shock. You might say it was a tall order, but Bill and I have succeeded in satisfying all the requirements. Our method, like any other, utilizes containers, growing media and certain cultural attention; however, some differences from traditional methods do exist.

You, the reader, now face a choice: whether to finish this chapter or to skip to the next one. If you grow or want to grow your own transplants, read on. If you are a diehard buyer of commercial transplants, you just might want to grow your own after reading further.

Transplant Containers

The problem with transplant containers is that they serve only one purpose when they really should serve two. They serve to hold the soil and roots of the transplant in a nice, tidy package, but they fail to allow for the production of the kind of roots that help transplants recover quickly from the shock suffered when you remove them from the containers to plant them out. To the original designers of planting containers, roots were roots. Surprisingly little has been done to improve containers since those first designs. Yet Bill and I know that the container makes or breaks the transplant.

I'm sure you'll agree with Bill and me that transplanting success depends heavily on causing little or no damage to the root system. However, a second key point overlooked by early container designers is that root balls need to have many, healthy feeder roots on their surface. These feeder roots, essentially smaller roots with fine hairs, are extremely important to producing the best-ever transplants. You see, feeder roots are the part of the root system through which the plant takes up water and nutrients. Technically, plant scientists call such roots *root hairs*. You can find these small root hairs near the tips of actively growing roots. To the eye, root hairs give the root tip a fuzzy, white appearance. If a transplant has an extensive, fuzzy covering of feeder roots on the root ball, all the better. Feeder roots, being tiny and delicate, are good indicators to use in assessing root ball damage. If root hairs are present on the root ball when you remove it from the container, you know you have an undamaged root ball that will recover quickly after transplanting. Also, the feeder roots respond rapidly to water and nutrients in the starter solution, so the plant is off and running quickly. The fuzzier the root ball looks, the better the roots soak up water and nutrients from the soil.

The location of the feeder roots is also critical. If the feeder roots are not on the surface of the root ball, but mostly concentrated inside the root ball, the response of the transplant to planting will not be as good. The reason the transplant does not take as well as one having surface feeder roots may not be obvious but should become clear after our explanation. We based our information upon our own experiments with watering combinations of garden soils and growing media and also upon the research of soil scientists.

If you've grown your own transplants in the past, you know that the soil in your garden differs from the material in which you grow your transplants. Mixtures for growing transplants are put together for one main purpose, that is, to produce better transplants than would soil. Therefore, these transplanting materials drain well, have excellent aeration, and are often rich in organic material. They look, feel, and weigh differently from the soil in your garden. Doesn't it follow, then, that when you put the transplant root ball into the garden, you join together two materials with different textures—soil and transplant potting compost? Because of this texture difference, these two materials don't mesh together as soil to soil would. It's essentially like trying to mesh together two zip tracks with different teeth spacing; they just don't go together. Scientists call the place where the two textures meet an interface.

Now let's add another element to the picture. Moving water seeks out the easiest path. Anyone who has a leaky cellar will agree with this observation. The easiest path through the soil and the transplant root ball is at the interface. Many spaces and gaps in this area speed the water right on by; therefore, water and nutrients tend to flow over the root ball and spread out under it;

Figure 1. Water will flow rapidly along the path of least resistance, that is, the point where the transplant soil and root ball meet the surrounding garden soil. Only at the bottom of the root ball does water start to spread out. Roots at the sides and bottom surface of the root ball are the only roots situated for taking advantage of the passing water.

less water actually enters the root ball (Figure 1). If the feeder roots are at the junction of the two soils, that is, the root ball's surface, they are in the water pathway. Their location, then, is ideal for gathering water and nutrients in the few critical days after the transplanting operation. Such surface-rooted balls give you a transplant that shows little or no wilting and rapid development in the garden.

Surface feeder roots promote not only initial growth but also later growth. Again we base our statement upon our personal observations and the comments of other gardeners. Transplants lacking surface feeder roots, when dug up at the end of the season, tend to show poor root balls. Roots are small and show very little outward spread from the original root ball. On the other hand, our transplants with lots of external feeder roots · exhibit much larger root balls and greater spread. Better leaf and stem growth and higher yields go hand in hand with the

bigger root ball. Such results are sure to bring smiles to gardener's faces.

A similar, confirming situation is familiar to those of us who have planted container-grown shrubs and trees. To encourage root development outwards, the gardener quarter-scores the root ball. Failure to do so usually results in a poorly developed shrub or tree that never reaches its potential or, even worse, dies. Upon digging up the shrub, the gardener would find limited development of the root system.

OK, you say, I'm ready to give it a try. How do I encourage feeder roots to form at the root ball surface? The answer is very simple: *localized aeration,* which translated means, give them air! Roots require oxygen to survive and to grow. Without oxygen, such as in over-watered soil, roots rot and die. They literally suffocate. Plants specifically need oxygen for a process called *respiration,* which is essentially the breakdown of food to supply energy for plant development. Roots tend to grow through the pore spaces in the soil: the feeder roots form at the growing tips of roots where oxygen, water and nutrients are present. In conventional containers, air enters through the surface of the growing mixture and spreads through the mixture. The roots in the centre get first crack at using the air while they grow. By the time the air reaches the edges, little is left for the surface feeder roots.

Logically, we wish to increase oxygen levels at the junction between the growing media and the container. You cannot find this favourable condition in the usual nonbreathing (nonporous) containers used to grow transplants. Even if we switch from plastic to a more porous material, such as clay, the slight improvement is not enough to warrant the greatly increased container cost. So what kind of container is the right kind of container for growing transplants? Only one type will serve our purpose: polystyrene coffee cups. Why? There are several reasons. Such cups are inexpensive, readily available, compatible with our no-dig technique, and are the easiest to modify for production of feeder roots.

What size cup do we need? Three sizes work out well with the no-dig hole left by the bulb planter, the 8 fluid ounce, 10 fluid ounce, and 12 fluid ounce sizes. How can all these fit into one hole? Quite simply, you just vary the depth to which you sink the bulb planter, putting a file mark on the bulb planter or drilling a small hole through it once you find the right depth.

The ultimate size of the transplant is a guide to cup size. For example, tomatoes, peppers and aubergines do quite well in the 12 fluid ounce cup and lettuce fits in the 8 fluid ounce cup. (Our recommendations for sizes can be found in Chapter 8, along with many other guidelines for growing individual vegetables.) You can use the 12 fluid ounce size for all transplants, providing you don't mind using a little extra growing mixture. You may have to grow some plants longer, such as lettuce, in a somewhat larger size cup than normal in order to complete external feeder roots, but the plants will still transplant easily. An alternative is to have two or three lettuce transplants in the large cup.

You can purchase the polystyrene cups at many places, such as supermarkets and discount shops. If you plan on using a large number of cups, or want to get the cheapest price, we suggest that you buy them in bulk. You can purchase in bulk by arrangement with supermarket or co-op managers or right off the shelf from a cash and carry.

Now let me explain the coffee cup modification or 'secret' that produces tremendous surface roots. We suggest that you do this in the winter months when gardening activities are not competing for your time. Actually, you will need very little time; one evening, afternoon or morning should suffice. First, make three holes in the cup's bottom such that they would form a triangle if connected (Figure 2). The holes must be ¼ inch to ⅜ inch in diameter to provide good drainage. You can use a drill bit, large nail, or even a screwdriver to make the drainage holes.

For the next step in preparing the cups you need a double-thickness hacksaw blade. I take a standard hacksaw blade, wrap it in a towel and break it in half. Next I glue the two halves together with a high-strength, fast-acting glue that works on metal. Be careful not to get any on your hands or elsewhere! Those of you who do woodworking can make some form of a wood handle for your home-made tool. I usually place the doubled blade in a vice to hold it steady while I guide the cups over it.

Punch ¼-inch to ⅜-inch holes in a triangular pattern, as shown, with a file, screwdriver, or drill bit.

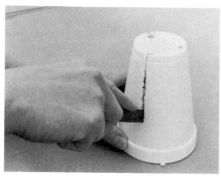

With a double-thickness of hacksaw blade or a keyhole saw, slice from the hole down to just short of the rim. Make this cut at each hole.

Halfway between each cut, put a new cut from just under the tim to about half way to the bottom. You now have three long and three short alternating cuts. For a short cut, put the six slits in first. Make sure the long ones cut into the cup bottom.

Next make the bottom holes by pinching with your fingers.

Figure 2. Here's how to prepare polystyrene transplant cups.

You may be tempted to use only a single blade, but Bill and I advise against it. We found that the root systems produced with aeration cuts done with the doubled blade were far superior to those done with a single blade.

Now take the doubled hacksaw blade and, starting at each hole, cut upwards to just under the cup rim (Figure 2). This provides you with three slits. Now make a new cut halfway between each existing slit, starting just under the rim and stopping halfway down the cup. This last step gives the cup three long and three short slits. The air that enters the cup through these slits bathes the surface of the root ball with oxygen, producing the magnificent feeder roots shown in Figure 3. Incidentally, the root ball slides very easily out of this kind of cup.

You may be wondering how the cup can survive all the cutting. The cup can take it and will not fall apart now or during the growing period. In fact, we found that we could reuse the cups for a second year; but we recommend against it because the leftover residues in the cup are not easy to clean, thus posing a threat of seedling disease. You may also be wondering how the cup retains the growing media. Commercial potting compost, or the potting compost that we use (see the next section in this chapter) will not leak through the cuts or holes. Finally, we suggest that you use inexpensive plastic trays to catch the drainage from these cups. You can readily purchase these trays at garden centres and discount shops.

Remember one more important fact. While these containers are fantastic at producing feeder roots, they can't do their job if you skimp or cheat on the soil mixture. The soil mixture must have good drainage, aeration and nutrient content. We will cover what makes a good mixture for growing transplants shortly; but before we do, I'd like to comment on producing transplants by other means.

In all honesty, a transplant produced in other containers by other methods, whether grown by you or purchased, will work with the no-dig method. However, these transplants will experience some transplanting shock and will get off to a slower start. For example, you might love peat pots. These pots fit nicely into the no-dig hole and produce transplants that show little or no transplanting shock; however, the plants that are produced in peat pots have fewer feeder roots and will not grow as quickly as plants started by our coffee cup method. You might like the ease and economy of growing marigolds or let-

*Figure 3.*Transplants grow beautifully in the polystyrene cups. Here's a close-up of the root ball on a tomato plant; note the excellent development of feeder roots.

tuce in conventional deep seed trays, but you should expect some shock and delay when you transplant the seedlings. Or perhaps you like the newer self-watering, greenhouse-type plastic deep seed trays. Whatever transplant container you choose, it will work with the no-dig method of gardening, as I will explain in Chapter 3.

Potting Compost

You have two basic choices with potting compost, whether to make your own or to buy commercial formulations. If you make your own you know exactly what went into it. Home-made potting composts are also less expensive than commercial types. The drawback to making your own is inconvenience. Commercial mixtures are convenient but more costly, although their prices are reasonably moderate. I'll cover both and you can select the one that's right for you. Remember, we will introduce a modification to improve drainage and aeration over existing mixtures.

Home-made Potting Compost

My experience with home-made potting compost is considerable. Over the years I have come to favour the following simple mixture:

⅓ sphagnum moss
⅓ vermiculite
⅓ perlite

Mix these three materials based upon parts by volume, not weight. For example, if you use a 2 pint jug filled with sphagnum moss, you would also add 2 pints of vermiculite and 2 pints of perlite.

The sphagnum moss should be shredded in a compost shredder, if you have one. Alternatively, you can substitute this home-made compost for worm compost, available from Turning Worms (for their address, see page 167.) Sphagnum moss has natural fungicides that fight the 'damping off' diseases that attack seedlings. With reasonable sanitation and clean containers, you won't have to pasteurize your finished produce. The vermiculite should be horticultural grade, and fine. Perlite should be coarse grade, with particles varying in size from ¹⁄₁₆ inch to ⅛ inch in diameter. These materials are available from most garden centres.

Perlite dust is a nasal irritant and you should spray or wet it prior to handling.

Perhaps you are thinking of using moss peat or compost as a substitute for sphagnum moss. If you do, you will lose the natural fungicidal action of sphagnum moss. Also, the mixture will need pasteurization or treatment with a fungicide to avoid damping-off diseases common to germinating seedlings.

If you prepare your own mixture, based upon the earlier directions, you will need to treat it differently than the commercial mixture. You can prepare the home-made mixture ahead of time and store it in plastic bags in a dry place. When you are ready to use the material, you will have to make some adjustment of pH. Add dolomitic limestone, since sphagnum moss is acidic. Commercial mixtures don't need this step, because the manufacturer has already corrected any pH problems.

To add the limestone, take a bucket with gallons marked on it. Each gallon of growing mixture requires slightly over ½ tablespoon of limestone (0.6 tablespoon to be exact). Three-and-a-half gallons of growing mixture would need about 2 level tablespoons of dolomitic limestone.

Both home-made and commercial potting composts need yet another addition. Bill and I found a material that promotes exceptional, rapid root growth through the ball. This material and the root mass help to hold the growing mixture together upon removal from containers and assure the quick appearance of feeder roots on the root ball surface. This 'secret' ingredient that really excites the root system is none other than the polystyrene 'peanuts' usually found as packing material in packages sent through the post. We save these packing materials in a large plastic bin bag as well as encouraging our friends to save some. If you know a shopkeeper, he or she may let you cart these polystyrene peanuts away for the asking. You may be wondering about the polystyrene 'chips' also seen as packing filler. These chips don't work well, probably because of their thinness.

We add the polystyrene peanuts at a rate of 1 gallon (by volume) to 4 gallons of home-made or commercial potting compost. Their addition not only improves drainage but, more importantly, also increases the aeration of the potting compost. The rooting results are dramatic, as you can see in the root ball section in Figure 4. The peanuts, coupled with the slitted polystyrene cups, will let you grow the best-ever transplants, no matter what vegetable or flower you choose!

If you can't get the polystyrene peanuts, you can substitute nylon screening cut into squares of 1 or 2 inches. Rather than mixing the screen pieces into the growing mixture, put three to four pieces in each 12 fluid ounce cup. The top edge of the screen should just break the surface of the mixture. The results are shown in Figure 4.

I just can't say enough about the combined aeration effect of the slit cups and polystyrene peanuts or screen. The feeder roots on the surface and the interior root growth are impressive. Just look at Figures 3 and 4 again! The roots even grow right into the polystyrene peanuts or through the screen, which really holds the root ball together. The feeder roots seem to thrive at the surface, most likely a result of excellent aeration and the diffusion of water and nutrients. Evaporation pulls the water and nutrients to the surface of the root ball. The slits admit air and help to increase surface evaporation on the sides of the root ball. You can't go wrong with our special cups and improved potting compost.

Figure 4. Above left This photo shows a root ball with visible polystyrene peanuts.
 Above right Nylon screen is a good substitute and helps to hold the soil ball together.

Commercial Potting Compost

But suppose you wish to use a commercially prepared potting compost rather than a home-made one. I have used commercial mixtures with fine results. Garden centres and many shops with garden supplies carry several brands of these potting composts. Also, seed companies carry their own brands. One point to keep in mind is that some commercial mixes contain chemical fertilizers or fungicides, which you may want to avoid. Check the content before you buy a commercial brand. But now let's move on to growing areas and techniques.

Growing Areas

I know a lot of gardeners who would like to grow transplants but don't because they haven't got a greenhouse. Take heart! You can grow transplants without a greenhouse. I know, because I have produced healthy transplants for several years in my home. All you need is a brightly lit south-facing window or some fluorescent lights. Growing transplants is easy, and you can't go wrong using our altered cups and potting compost, so why not skip that spring trip to the garden centre and grow your own?

Indoor Growing Areas

Do you have a south-facing window? Is it bright and sunny most of the day? South-facing windows usually are aglow with sun, unless some obstruction is present. Sometimes a roof overhang, another building, or nearby trees and shrubs block the sun. If you can't avoid the obstruction, don't let the gloom at your window discourage you. You can still grow transplants.

You can produce excellent transplants under fluorescent lights. Since you don't intend your transplants to flower or produce vegetables but only to reach a reasonable size for outdoor planting,

the choice of lamp is not critical. Any lamp will do. The cool white lamp used in fluorescent fixtures in homes or offices is a fine, economical choice. Should you have other lamps on hand such as daylight or warm white, or lamps designed specifically for growing, use them instead.

You don't need special fixtures either. The best bet for growing plants is the fluorescent fixture with a hood that accommodates two 4 ft fluorescent tubes. These fixtures are commonly sold as workshop fixtures for the home and even come with fluorescent tubes and wire clips designed for hanging purposes. Since they are intended for work areas, they are not fancy or costly. You can suspend the fluorescent fixtures by chains from hooks in the ceiling of your cellar, loft or any other spare space. You can raise or lower their heights by adjusting the chain.

Place an old table or door over two sawhorses situated under the lamp or lamps. Depending on how many transplants you need, you may want one, two or possibly three fixtures. Each fixture serves a growing area of 4 feet by 1½ feet, or 6 square feet. Such an area accommodates up to 70 of our 12 fluid ounce modified growing cups, if they just touch each other. If you use trays to hold the cups and allow for a little space around them, you will be able to fit about 60 cups under the lights. Eighteen standard plastic deep seed trays will fit into the area.

One fixture could easily supply the light for tomatoes, peppers, aubergines and a few flowers for a garden. Two fixtures are probably adequate for growing enough seedlings for the average garden. However, if you like working with transplants, you may go for that third lamp! The space at your south-facing window may no longer look quite as inviting.

Outdoor Growing Areas

Under some conditions you can produce transplants directly outdoors. I experimented with raising seedlings outdoors over the last few years because of a succession of cold, wet springs that rotted many of my directly sown seeds (such as beans, sweetcorn, cucumbers, melons and marrow). Now I sow these seeds in our containers and germinate them indoors. I quickly place the new seedlings outdoors at normal outdoor planting time under a plastic cover, which sheds rain and warms the seedlings slightly but not enough to require ventilation. I staple the plastic cover onto a wood frame, which I can transport anywhere I want. Figure 5 shows a plastic cover in place in the garden.

Admittedly, I could start such transplants earlier and grow them indoors completely to have a head start. However, my way circumvents the wet, cold soil and doesn't tie up room indoors that I need for transplants such as tomatoes, where a head start is critical. The results I obtain are more favourable than having rotted seeds and offer a more timely harvest than would the later, direct replanting of rotted seeds.

The Greenhouse

Lastly, if you have a greenhouse, you are blessed with luxury quarters for growing transplants. I did without a greenhouse for many years and still grew great transplants. In fact, I only grew transplants for a few years in my present greenhouse before a large collection of cacti and succulents crowded them out. Now I use a little space in a greenhouse where I work; however, I still keep my fluorescent lights handy for the overflow. Who knows, they may serve fully again should I lose my present greenhouse space.

How to Grow Your Own Transplants, Step by Step

If you are ready, I'll take you through the steps for transplanting; but first I'd like to make a few comments. I will be using general information here on timing, the need for bottom heat, light requirements, and so forth. I will give more specific details for individual crops under their respective entries in Chapter 8 and 9 on vegetables and flowers.

Firstly, make sure you buy your seeds as early as possible. You must start some seeds, such as geraniums (which are hybrids that grow easily from seed), as long as 10 to 12 weeks prior to outdoor planting. Most plants need 6 to 8 weeks of indoor growth before they're ready for transplanting, so I make sure I buy my seeds by mail order before the end of January.

Figure 5. Covers come in handy for starting seeds outdoors at normal planting times. Candidates for starting outdoors include crops like beans or marrow, where early starts are not important and seeds are easily lost during germination in abnormally cold and wet springs.

Secondly, make sure everything you need is on hand. Nothing is worse than interrupting your planting to run off somewhere for whatever you forgot. Use the list below as your checklist.

Seeds
Potting compost
Room-temperature water
Modified polystyrene cups or other transplant containers
Labels
Marking pen or pencil
Clingfilm or other clear material
Tray(s) to hold cups

You need the clingfilm to hold moisture during germination, because drying during that time is fatal to seedlings. If you have scrap pieces of window glass, pieces of rigid plastic such as acrylic or polythene sheeting, you can use these materials instead.

The plastic trays catch the water that drains from your growing containers. You can buy these at garden centres or DIY shops. You can also recycle old washing-up bowls, discarded baking tins and baking trays to catch the water.

Preparing the Potting Compost

The first step in preparing to plant your seeds is to wet your potting compost. I prefer to wet it in a plastic bag, whether it be the one in which the mixture was sold or another. The amount of water needed varies slightly with the composition of the potting compost. A good starting point is the ratio of 8:1, which works well with any of the mixtures described earlier in this chapter. Add one part of water to eight parts of dry potting compost in your plastic bag.

After you add the water, begin to knead the mixture like bread dough by alternately squeezing and releasing various parts of the plastic bag. Hold the bag closed and turn or shake it a few

times to assure that all the contents get moistened. Inspect the contents after a few minutes to see if all the material is wet. If it is not, continue kneading until the mix is moistened throughout. The mixture is wet enough if you squeeze it into a ball and it does not fall apart when you open your hand.

At this point I'm sure you have a few questions. Will the mixture keep? If you recently made the sphagnum mixture or stored it dry in a plastic bag, or newly opened commercial mixtures or those promptly resealed after use should be all right, assuming that you practised normal sanitation (use of clean scoops for removal of mixture or direct pouring from the bag, no return of wetted mixture to the bag and storage in a clean, dry place).

Also be sure to keep containers clean, because a dirty container could harbour the organisms which cause damping off of seedlings. If the containers are new, such as our modified polystyrene cups, you will have no problem. However, do not reuse the cups unless you rinse them with warm, soapy water and soak them in a bleach solution. You can make the bleach solution with ⅓ pint of bleach to ½ gallon of room-temperature water. Soak the containers for five minutes and then rinse them well. Personally, I think the cost of the cups is so low that I don't bother to reuse them. If you are using any scoops, tools to make rows, or recycled plastic containers to start seeds, you should also treat them with soapy water and a bleach soak as described above.

Using the aforementioned precautions, you should have only remote chances of seedling diseases. I have not had any trouble as long as I have followed those guidelines.

Since you should not return excess wetted compost to the bag, you should only make enough wetted mixture for your immediate needs. But you may be wondering just how to determine the amount you need. Here's a rule of thumb to help you to gauge the right amount of mixture. 2 pints of wetted mixture is enough to fill one standard 6½ inch by 7½ inch plastic deep seed trays or 3 of our 12 fluid ounce modified polystyrene cups.

But now you may be wondering how many deep seed trays or cups you will need. Firstly, if you use only our cups for the whole process of growing transplants, you will need one polystyrene cup for each plant. Thus, if you want one dozen each of tomatoes, peppers, aubergines and marrows, you will need 48 cups. With smaller plants you can put more than one transplant in a cup, if you wish. For example, you can plant four lettuce or beetroot transplants in one cup. I have suggested specific numbers of plants per cup for various kinds of transplants in Chapters 8 and 9.

Suppose you want to start your transplants in standard deep seed trays and then transplant them later to the cups. You will usually need one deep seed tray for each crop, since the standard tray can accommodate 300, 200, and 100 seedlings from tiny, medium, or large seeds, respectively. These figures assume even broadcasting of seeds and transplanting once the true leaves (leaves that follow first seed leaves) of

transplants touch each other. The use of rows in a deep seed tray cuts the number of seedlings it can accommodate by one-half to one-third. At the worst, each tray will accommodate 33 tomato seedlings—probably more than the average gardener wants.

The topic of using trays raises an interesting point. Do you really need to use plastic trays prior to our cups? Not necessarily, except in the case of very fine seeds, which can be easier to sow in trays. You may elect to raise transplants completely in trays, but I suggest not to do it. The no-dig transplant method works best with transplants that you grow in individual containers, although I do suggest a no-dig method for transplants from trays in Chapter 3. To repeat a point, the best and earliest crops come from single-container transplants. Difficult transplants, such as sweetcorn, fare very poorly in trays.

Let's move on now to the sowing of seeds to produce transplants.

Sowing the Seeds

Fill the containers you are using for starting seedlings to within ¼ in of the top with potting compost. Gently level the mixture with a flat stick that fits within the container, or gently pat the mixture flat with your hand (Figure 6). If you are using peat trays or pots, make sure you have moistened them first. Dry

Figure 6. I level the potting compost in my deep seed trays with a home-made 'T-bar'. To make it, I took a wood dowel, slotted it and glued in a wood slat. If you make the slat slightly narrower than a standard-size deep seed tray, you can use it to make rows for seed planting, too.

peat containers can act as a wick and suck moisture right out of your growing mixture.

If you decide to make rows, use the eraser end of a pencil or a wood dowel (Figure 7). For example, in a stardard tray (5½ by 7½ inches), run your rows starting about ¾ inch from one side and spacing them at 1¼ inch intervals. Depending on the length, you can have four long rows or six short ones. For larger seeds, you can also poke individual holes into the mixture with the pencil or dowel. I prefer to use this approach for tomatoes, aubergines, peppers and marigolds. I usually make about one dozen holes for each tray or one hole for individual containers like the modified polystyrene cups.

It's a good idea to sow more seeds than the actual number of transplants you want to produce, because some seeds won't germinate and you can always pinch out weak seedlings, leaving the best. I usually throw in two or three seeds per hole and I still end up with leftover seeds. Save these leftover seeds for reserves in case of seedling failure. If you have no problems, store them in a cool, dry place and use them to start next year's transplants.

Next, by pushing in the potting compost from the sides, cover each seed to a depth of one or two times the thickness of the seed. Do not cover seeds that require light for germination, such as begonia and petunia but, rather, press them gently into the soil. Spray the surface with a fine spray of lukewarm water. An old spray bottle from a kitchen cleaner will do nicely, but be sure first to rinse it very well.

Another way of sowing seeds is to broadcast them. Although I prefer making rows when I use seed trays, some seeds are too fine to be sown in rows. Broadcasting gives you a much better spread with fine seeds, such as begonia or petunia. I also suggest sowing fine seeds in trays and transplanting them to individual containers later rather than directly planting them in individual containers. You can cover broadcast seeds with sprinkles of dry growing mixture. Again some seeds, especially fine seeds, require light for germination, therefore you should gently press them into the mixture. Make sure you lightly spray them with water to moisten the surface. Watch for dry areas if you used dry mixture to cover the seeds. The surface of the growing mixture should be evenly moist, but not wet.

You may be wondering what to do with pelleted seeds or seed tapes. Some fine seeds, such as petunia, are given a coating that produces an enlarged pellet that is easier to handle. Sometimes the

Figure 7. My 'T-bar' is great for making rows or you could make rows with your finger or a pencil.

pellet material has additives, such as traces of plant food or fungicide. The packet usually lists such additions. Whether or not you need pelleted seed is a personal choice. If you dislike the task of working with fine seed and don't mind a slight price increase, go for the pellet. Plant the pellets but do not cover them with growing mixture. Pelleted seeds already have their 'cover', so just press them gently into the growing mixture.

Seed tapes are another device you can use for easy handling and, especially, to ensure correct spacing of seeds. Seed tapes differ somewhat from pelleted seed, since you can find small to large seeds in the tape form. Again, the choice of whether or not to use seed tapes is yours. If you do use a tape, cut it to fit your rows and cover it with potting compost as for seeds. Lightly spray the surface of the growing mixture with water. The tape will eventually dissolve and will not interfere with germination.

Next, label what you planted. Don't trust your memory, unless you plant only one packet of seed. 'Gardener's Delight' tomato seedlings look just like 'Harbinger' tomato seedlings. Cos lettuce looks just like cabbage lettuce when it's small. You can use your marking pencil to place the cultivar name and date of sowing on a label. Noting the sowing date will help you decide whether the seeds need more time for germination or whether you should suspect something went wrong. You will find the number of days required for germination of individual crops listed in Chapters 8 and 9.

I usually lay the label down in trays, because I will be covering them. But when I'm using individual containers, I label the plant name directly on the container. You will need to use two or more labels if you plant two or more kinds of seeds in one tray. Be cautious if you do mix seeds; make sure they are compatible with one another in terms of light and temperature requirements, as well as days to germination.

Covering the Containers

Next, cover the containers (Figure 8) with clingfilm or with scrap pieces of glass or clear plastic. An alternative to these covering methods is to place the containers in a plastic bag. If you have several trays or lots of cups, you will find that the plastic bags that come with dry-cleaned clothes make good covers. To ensure that the bag does not contact the potting compost, place a few upright labels in each container or some bent coat hangers to hold the bag above the soil. Some of the newer containers

Figure 8. Cover your tray or cups with clear plastic. Lay your labels on their sides for now. This step will greatly improve germination and eliminate watering for several days. The top of a refrigerator supplies warmth for faster germination.

come with clear plastic lids that fit neatly over the container. You can cover seeds that require absolute darkness with several sheets of newspaper or scrap cardboard. Do not neglect to cover the containers, because the seeds are critically dependent upon moisture during germination. Dryness at that time can kill or essentially result in a crippled seedling that never fully recovers. Also, watering at this point, unless done with care, can dislodge or uncover seedlings. We busy gardeners have enough to do without having to resow seeds. Fortunately, the clear cover over the container relieves the gardener of the constant worry and drudgery of checking for dryness.

Providing Warmth and Light

To use bottom heat or not, that is the question. Seed germination does depend upon temperature. Each seed has an ideal temperature at which germination occurs fastest. Temperatures above this ideal temperature result in no improvement and temperatures below it result in slow germination. Of course, temperature extremes will kill the seeds. You can find the favoured temperatures for each crop in Chapters 8 and 9. For economy of money and time, commercial growers of transplants usually use a soil-heating cable or mat to warm the bottom of their trays. But what's a private gardener to do? Firstly, most seeds germinate in a reasonable time at 70°F, a temperature you can find in your home, especially in the kitchen. You say you lower your thermostat at night or when you're at work to save energy? No problem. The top of your refrigerator is always warm. Put a few sheets of newspaper on the refrigerator's top and place your containers there. Do not put trays under the containers yet, because you won't need to water if you are using the plastic tray

covers. The newspaper underneath the containers traps any slight traces of moisture or dirt but it is still thin enough to allow heat transfer. The top of an upright freezer can also be warm.

Other warm places you may want to consider are near your water heater, but you must be cautious if you use one of these areas. Place your container nearby but not on top of or in contact with the water heater. Do not put newspaper or any flammable materials under the containers, in fact, it's best not to put anything under them. Propagation mats and propagators are available from suppliers listed in the Appendix on page 166.

Above all, do not place your containers in direct sun at this time. The plastic will trap the solar energy and heat the potting compost to temperatures fatal for most seeds. Only seeds that tolerate germination temperatures in the 80° to 85°F range will survive.

Another choice for providing proper germination temperatures is to purchase a heating mat specially designed for germinating seeds. I recommend this purchase only if you are seriously interested in raising substantial numbers of transplants. Most gardeners can get by with the previously mentioned, less expensive options.

Before we leave the subject of germination temperature, I should point out that a few seeds actually require cool temperatures for germination. The strawberry, for instance, has seeds that germinate best at 55°F. At 70°F, germination is not very successful. The best place to germinate seeds that need cool temperatures is a north-facing windowsill or the cooler concrete floor on the north side of your basement.

What about those seeds that require both coolness and light for germination? The sunny window is obviously out. Luckily, light needs for germination are nowhere near those for growing plants. Indirect light from a window, light from an incandescent bulb in a lamp or overhead or a fluorescent lamp will all suffice. These lights need not be on at all times; you can turn them on and off to suit your daily routine.

You should check your containers once a day for dryness, mould or seedling growth. If you spot dryness, water the potting compost right away, but dryness is unlikely when using a plastic cover. If dryness does occur, use bottom watering to correct the problem. Place the container in a tray of lukewarm water (water level below top of container) until the surface of the potting compost appears moist. Remove the container at once, drain the water and replace the plastic cover. Condensation on the cover is normal, therefore, you can ignore it (Figure 9). If mould appears, remove the cover once or twice a day for 15 minutes.

Caring for Growing Seedlings

Once seedlings start to appear, you must move into action. Remove the cover and transport the seedlings to your light source. Remember, as we discussed earlier, the light source can be either a sunny south-facing window or fluorescent lights. Turn the seedlings every few days at the window to get even growth on all sides of the plants. Start your lights at a height of just a few inches over the seedlings, raising them as the seedlings grow. Don't worry about the closeness of the lights to the plants as heat from fluorescent lights is minimal. If the leaves curl downwards, raise the lights; if the seedlings are thin and spindly or light green in colour, lower the lights. Don't worry about temperature as an ordinary room or basement temperature is fine, even if you drop the temperature at night to as low as 60°F.

Your seedlings will now need tender, loving care. Water and fertilizer will be

Figure 9. Use bottom watering for recently planted seeds prior to germination (left) and for small seedlings (right) that are not yet tough enough for overhead watering.

the main concerns at first. As your seedlings grow, thinning or transplanting will also become important, especially for seedlings not in individual containers. But let's not get ahead of ourselves.

Watering the Seedlings

First, make sure your young seedlings do not dry out. At the first sign of surface dryness, use bottom watering as described previously. With some plants that grow fast, like marigolds or tomatoes, you will only need to use bottom watering for a few weeks. Tiny, slow-growing plants like begonias will need bottom watering for a longer period of time. Use bottom watering only until the seedlings develop enough of a root system that overhead watering does not uproot them. Overhead watering is usually safe when seedlings are 1½ inches tall and are starting to develop their second set of true leaves. Now you will also need trays to collect the excess water as it drains from the plants. Be sure you discard the excess water. Letting the containers stand in a trayful of water could cause root rot. Trays also make it easier to carry the deep seed trays or containers.

After a few weeks, allow the surface of the growing medium to dry out to a depth of ½ inch or so between waterings. The degree of dryness improves aeration of the soil, which in turn promotes root growth and helps prevent root rot caused by overwatering. Allowing some dryness to exist also helps to toughen up the transplant for the harsher outdoor environment in your garden. Of course, if you see the plants wilting when the soil surface is dry, water them right away.

The time of watering isn't too critical, as long as foliage does not remain wet through the evening. There is greater risk of disease when leaves stay wet at night. Let the water that you plan to use on your transplants sit overnight in clean covered buckets or other containers. If you have city water, leave the covers off the buckets. Allowing water to sit brings it to room temperature. Water from the tap is usually too cold for the good of young seedlings, (temperatures often range between 40° and 50°F). If you use water straight from the tap, the temperature of the potting compost can easily drop 15°F, and several hours may pass before the temperature returns to normal. This

Figure 10. Once seedlings are well established, you can use overhead watering.

temperature drop decreases root and shoot development, so your transplants grow more slowly. When you later transplant them into your garden, you will have lost some of your head start.

At this time I'd like to explain further my suggestion to keep the covers off buckets of city water. Several cities have quite high levels of chlorine in the water, which can adversely affect some tender, young seedlings. Allowing the filled water bucket to sit overnight without a cover will allow some of the chlorine to escape. A simple step such as this protects the investment of time and money you have in your transplants.

Fertilizing the Seedlings

Besides water, your tranplants need nutrients, so you'll need to add fertilizer soon after germination. (Remember, our home-made compost does not include fertilizer.) The seed uses its nutrient reserves during germination so you must supply new nutrients for the growing plant. If you have a commercial potting compost, the label will tell you if any nutrients were added. Some mixtures even have enough nutrients to last through the entire production of transplants. Whether you use a commercial potting compost with no nutrients, small amounts of nutrients, or extended reserves depends upon your personal decision as an organic or conventional gardener. The nutrients in most commercial formulas are not supplied in organic forms.

When it's time to begin feeding the seedlings, organic gardeners will opt for organic, water-soluble fertilizer. My favourite is a product that combines fish emulsion* and seaweed extract. You can buy fish emulsion and seaweed extract separately and use them side by side. The fish emulsion supplies nitrogen in suitable amounts but supplies only small amounts of phosphorus and potassium. The seaweed extract supplies suitable amounts of phosphorus and potassium.

Seaweed extract also has numerous trace elements of value to growing plants. It contains gibberellin and auxin, natural hormones in plants that promote growth. Indications are that seaweed extract may also work to keep seedlings from getting 'leggy' and possibly may ward off spider mites. Some plants also show increased resistance to light frosts when treated with seaweed extracts. If you use seaweed extracts, perhaps you can worry less about that unexpected cold snap after you set out your transplants in your garden. Disease protection for seedlings is another plus offered by seaweed extract. (Two products worth trying are SMS from Chase Organics and a seaweed extract available from Maxicrop—for their addresses, see pages 165 and 166.)

Apply the Farmura and seaweed extract mixture to the plant as a foliar spray, that is onto the leaves. The plant's uptake of fertilizer and the growth response of the plant occur more quickly using a foliar spray than when fertilizing through the root system. The fertilizer runoff from the plant foliage supplies enough solution for the root system. Adjustable leaf openings called *stomata* quickly take in the solution on the leaves. When spraying the plant, try to get some of the fertilizer on

* At present there is no exact UK equivalent of this product but you can try replacing fish emulsion with Farmura Liquid Organic Fertilizer, available from the HDRA or Cumulus Organics (for addresses, see page 165). It is not an exact equivalent because it contains potassium and phosphorus in addition to nitrogen, which, in fact, makes it a more balanced fertilizer. Obviously some experimenting may be needed before you achieve optimum results, but it is well worthwhile.

the underside of the leaf, which usually has more openings than the top surface. Essentially, foliar feeding is like intravenous feeding of nutrients to hospital patients which makes the nutrients available more quickly than the patient's digestive system could.

Follow the route of more frequent but less concentrated applications of fertilizer. Transplants respond much better to this frequent but light diet. Follow the recommendations on the label, but double the dilution and frequency of application. Look for rates indicated for seedlings. If seedling directions are not present, use the directions for houseplants or even flowers. Remember, use twice as much water, and double the frequency of use.

Whatever you do with your fertilizer, watch your transplants for signals that you may need to raise or lower your fertilization rates. For example, if the transplants are light green and spindly (stretched-looking), they probably need more light. If, however, the plants look sturdy but are light green in colour, they probably need more nitrogen. Ex-

tremely dark green plants (leaves normal position, not curling downwards as with too much light) could indicate excessive nitrogen. A lack of phosphorus usually shows up as red-purple colour on stems, leaves and veins, although you may have difficulty noting this condition with a bronze-leaved wax begonia. Don't worry too much, though. I have never encountered problems with phosphorus or potassium and only on rare occasions with nitrogen. The beauty of using organic fertilizers is that extra, slow-release punch they provide that carries the plants through lean times!

Thinning and Transplanting Seedlings
Now on to the two Ts: thinning and transplanting (Figures 11 and 12). If you started your seeds in deep seed trays and do not intend to transplant the seedlings into other trays or individual containers, you will have to thin your transplants to a reasonable number. For example, a standard tray might hold four but no more than six tomato plants. Marigolds or peppers might

Figure 11. Above left Once seedlings touch, as these celosia seedlings do, you must either transplant or thin them.
    Above right These thinned celosia now have a while to grow before they're ready for transplanting.

These dahlias are ready for transplanting, as they have touching leaves.

Cut or separate a good root ball with each plant. Put some potting compost in the bottom of the cup. Note the polystyrene peanuts.

Place the transplant in the cup and fill in with potting compost.

Label the cups.

Figure 12. These photos show how seedlings are transplanted into the special cups.

approach eight to ten plants per tray. Actual numbers of plants per container depend on the size of the container, the size of the plants, and the amount of time they stay in the container. Remember, the more plants per container, the more tangled the roots and the more difficult the transplant. With individual containers, where your sowing produced more than one plant, thin out the plants to leave only the strongest. Should you want more than one plant, such as three lettuce plants, in one of our polystyrene cups, thin the plants to the desired number.

The next 'T' is transplanting, which you won't have to do now, if you started with individual containers. You will need to transplant from trays once the plant's true leaves touch. You can transplant some of the extra seedlings into another tray or into individual containers, which we recommend (and discussed earlier). If you can transplant only some of the plants to individual containers, make those the vegetables that need an earlier start, such as tomatoes. Remember, once the true leaves touch, transplant soon as the neglected, crowded plants will soon become stunted or poorly developed and will result in poorer quality transplants.

Transplanting of seedlings need not be difficult (Figure 12). Of course, every individual container with which you started means less work now. Usually, the rule is to look for the stronger seedlings and discard the weaker ones, a rule that holds well for vegetables. An exception to the rule occurs with several annuals, such as begonias, dahlias (small bedding types), impatiens and petunias, where the weaker seedlings often have more unusual colours or forms not found with stronger seedlings. With mixed-colour annuals, then, you might just want to include a few of the weaker seedlings for interesting variety.

Use the same potting compost for your transplants as you did for your seeds. A teaspoon makes a fine tool for removing seedlings. Remove medium to large seedlings with the spoon end and smaller ones with the handle. A small spatula or the end of a pointed label or lollipop stick is also helpful when removing tiny seedlings. Handle the seedlings with care and gently shake them to remove any excess potting compost from each plant. If you have to hold the transplant, pick it up by the leaves and not by the stem. A damaged leaf is a minor matter but a broken or bruised stem is usually beyond repair.

With a dibber or a spoon, open a hole in the potting compost for your seedling transplant. Place the seedling and some potting compost in the hole, and adjust the planting level. Do not sink the seedling deeper than it had been planted in the previous container. Water the seedling with the dilute solution of seaweed extract mentioned earlier and keep it out of direct sun for one day. If you use fluorescent lights, you can replace the transplant directly under the lights without a one-day wait. The seaweed extract will usually speed up the recovery of the transplant. Don't forget to label your new containers, and make sure you continue with watering and fertilization as explained before.

Moving Outdoors

You must now prepare your transplants for the move outdoors to the garden. An abrupt move from indoors to outdoors in the garden will most likely kill your transplants. They will need an adjustment period of two weeks to toughen, a process we call *hardening off*. You are faced with two choices concerning where to harden off your transplants: the luxury approach, otherwise called the *cold frame,* or the economical way, called 'making do with what you have'. If you have a cold frame, great, your choice is made. Should you not have a cold frame, you could elect to build or buy one or to do without. You can use cold frames for hardening off transplants, growing cool-loving transplants like cabbage and broccoli, and for providing salad greens into early winter. If your only interest is hardening off transplants, you should probably save your time and money.

You can purchase a ready-made cold frame and buy an automatic window opener or build your own cold frame. Make sure, though, that the lights lift rather than slide and that the glass is not too heavy for the automatic opener or else it will not work! Scrap wood and windows or even purchased wood should give you a reasonably priced cold frame. Solar power (no electricity needed) activates the automatic window opener to open at the temperature you set it to. This device relieves you of the constant checking of temperature and window adjustments so essential to the success of transplants in a cold frame. Believe me, it's the only way to go! Automatic window openers are available from most garden centres.

Here's how to harden off transplants in the cold frame with the help of the automatic window opener. Place the transplants in the cold frame about two weeks before you plan to place them in your garden. Allow your transplants to dry out a little between waterings, but watch out for wilting. Don't forget to fertilize your transplants. Don't worry about temperature and window adjustments except if frost threatens. If a frost looms, cover your cold frame with either blankets or straw. An alternative to covering the frames would be to bring the trays and containers indoors for the night. The odds of a frost occurring two weeks before it's time to set the plants in the garden are low in most

areas, but nature sometimes does surprise us.

If you don't have a cold frame, you can use this 'no frills' method to harden off your transplants. This is the method I use. I start on a Saturday about two weeks before the time I will be ready to place the transplants in the garden. I put the transplants in trays outdoors in a sunny area for three hours from 11:00am to 2:00pm then I bring them back inside. On Sunday I return them outdoors for about five hours (11:00am to 4:00pm), and then bring them back inside. On Monday I take them outdoors before I go to work and bring them in on my return. On Tuesday, I take them out, and leave them outside for the rest of the two weeks, unless a frost or temperatures below 40°F threaten. If so, I bring them back indoors for the night. Don't forget to water and fertilize the transplants during this time. If you are lucky, rain will help you with the watering.

After hardening off your transplants, you can plant them in the garden. If your schedule gives you trouble, you can hold off planting after the two weeks of hardening off. However, don't delay beyond one or two weeks at most. Longer delays eat into your head start and container limitations start to stress your transplants, causing further complications. The actual process of placing transplants in the garden using the no-dig method will be shown and discussed in the next chapter.

Growing Your Own Transplants Outdoors

Earlier I mentioned that growing transplants outdoors was a good idea in areas subject to cold, wet springs when the direct sown seeds are likely to rot. The procedure I'm about to describe solves this problem. I germinate the seeds of beans, sweetcorn, cucumbers and marrows indoors in our modified polystyrene containers using the same procedures described before for conventional transplants. The main difference is that I start these seeds indoors at their normal outdoor planting time. At the first sign of germination, I move the seedlings outdoors to the wooden frame with a plastic roof described earlier (look back at Figure 5 on page 31). These seedlings develop normally outdoors, except that the plastic roof and frame sides protect them from wind and rain. Of course, I add water, fertilizer and tender, loving care. When the transplants reach the proper size in two to three weeks, I place them directly into the ground with the no-dig approach. No more rotten seeds! Using this method I have grown some wonderful

vegetables after years of defeat by the cold and wet springs.

Bill and I also developed an outdoor transplant nursery. Essentially it's a simple, rectangular, wood frame that is portable (Figure 13). I usually place the frame in a corner of my garden and use it for all my leftover transplants. Yes, I always grow a few extra transplants just in case one fails or I want to give some to someone else. Besides, I don't have the heart to discard them. You can hold these plants for a few weeks to fill any holes that pop up when you have harvested earlier crops, such as radishes and peas.

I keep the transplant nursery going by planting a few seeds every once in a while, using the modified polystyrene cups. Sometimes I'll plant one cup with

Figure 13. My outdoor transplant nursery is a square wood frame with no bottom. I can put it in any unused corner of the yard and keep it filled with extra or ongoing transplants. The little stuffed animal in the foreground was placed there by my children because they said a 'nursery' must have toys.

several lettuce seeds and thin it to three or four plants. Others may hold individual broccoli, bean or beetroot transplants. This way I'm always prepared for any empty spaces that arise in the garden. Maybe you should become the parent of a transplant nursery, too. Instead of direct planting the midsummer crops that will produce autumn har-vests, such as broccoli or turnips, start them in cups in your nursery. It sure beats the hot, dry soil that gives summer germination a hard time!

You've waited long enough, patient reader. Now we will move on to no-dig techniques for planting and maintaining the garden.

CHAPTER 3

PLANTING THE NO-DIG GARDEN

Are you ready to say goodbye to that spade or fork, and your aching back and blisters? Once you become a no-digger, you'll wonder why you put up with the annual rearranging of your garden's soil. Perhaps you are about to become a first-time gardener and you're hesitating because of the thought of digging soil. Well, new and veteran gardeners, this chapter is for all of you.

Testing the Soil

I think the best piece of advice I can give any gardener, even no-dig gardeners, is to know your soil. Good soil is the foundation of a good garden. The one and only way to understand your soil is to study the results of a soil test and then make whatever soil corrections you need, such as adding fertilizer or lime. Before you do anything in the garden, and especially before you mulch or plant, take the time out for a soil test. It is a wise investment of your time, because a few minutes of testing can lead to a much more successful garden later.

You can conduct soil tests in two ways. The first method involves buying a soil-testing kit and testing your own soil. You can buy the kits from garden centres. These kits are good for testing the pH of your soil but for a complete analysis, get in touch with Elm Farm Research Centre (for their address, see page 166) as they can give you a complete picture and their service is suited to organic gardening. Elm Farm will supply a fact sheet about soil analysis giving details of how to take soil samples and label them. Home soil tests are similar to the sort of tests done with swimming pools. Basically you follow 'cook-book style' directions and you get a coloured solution that you compare to colour charts. From these colours it is a simple matter to decide what and how much of the various nutrients or limestone you need.

Which method is the best for you? Some gardeners use both kinds of soil tests and compare the results to check whether or not the tests are reliable. Some gardeners do a few soil tests of their own later after they receive the full report to check their soil's progress and find out if the soil needs additional correction as the plants grow.

Preparing the Garden for Planting

I will explain how to prepare for no-dig gardening in several different garden situations, so skip to the one that best describes your case. I will look first at established gardens, then new gardens and finally problem gardens. This last category includes gardens with soil so compacted that it seems like concrete, soil so rocky and stony that you could open a quarry, and soil with hardpans (compacted, often clay, layers of soil that are impenetrable by roots) or such poor drainage that the garden becomes a pond after the slightest rain. If your garden soil has one of these problems, go straight to the section on Problem Gardens, on page 48.

If you're not sure if you have a problem, consider these two questions. Can you drive the bulb planter into the soil and remove a soil core? Does the ridger scratch into the soil? If you answered yes to both questions, then you don't have a problem garden. Even if some stones interfere so that your bulb planter makes a slanted hole or you have to move it around to a slightly different location, you still probably have a garden that is not a problem.

Preparing Established Gardens for No-dig Planting

Any established flower or vegetable garden that you have dug or tilled and cleaned up the previous year, whether it's an organic garden or not, can easily become a no-dig garden. Most of you reading this book probably have gardens that fall into this group. These gardens will be transformed into no-dig gardens quickly and easily. How you go about achieving a no-dig garden depends upon how your garden looks now. Take a good look at it. Did you clean up the plant remains from last year? Was your garden relatively weed free last season, that is, were the weeds controllable with only sporadic weeding? If you answer yes to both of these questions, go directly to the section on no-dig planting techniques, beginning on page 52. Did you answer no to the first question and yes to the second? If so, first clean up your garden by cutting and raking off last year's debris, then skip to the no-dig techniques. Perhaps you answered no to both questions. Well, clean up your garden and continue reading here. And if your garden needed more than sporadic weeding last year, read on.

Weeds got you down? If that's all that stands in the way of your no-dig gar-

den, don't despair. This year you will destroy weeds and weed seeds in the top few inches of your garden soil, either by mulching or weeding. If you opt for mulching, make sure you read Chapter 5 to learn how to mulch the easy way by using black plastic. You can apply black plastic or organic mulches either before or after you plant, although applying them before is probably better because your crops will not need weeding before you mulch (as they would if you laid down the mulch later on). Before you lay down any mulch, it will be important to have your soil tested, as I described earlier in this chapter. Also, be sure to apply your fertilizer and/or limestone (as described in Chapter 4) before you mulch.

If you want to mulch at conventional times, that is, when the plants are several inches tall, you'll have to use your Swiss reciprocating hoe to keep weeds under control before the mulch takes over. Of course, you can also control weeds throughout the growing season with your Swiss reciprocating hoe. The severity of your weed problem will dictate which method of weed control is best for you.

Keep one thought in mind. Weeds, once controlled with black plastic, organic mulches or hoeing, will probably become a thing of the past. Remember, our no-dig techniques do not disturb soil, therefore no new weed seeds are brought to the surface. Once those top few inches of soil are weed free, half your work is done!

Preparing New Gardens

Are you planning a first-time garden? Did you skip gardening last year but decided to give it another try this year? Either way, whether the site was never a garden or was once a garden, you should treat the plot as a new garden.

Most likely some plants, either green

or dormant brown, cover the garden-to-be. The area may be grassy, perhaps even part of a lawn. Maybe the overgrowth is weedy, like an abandoned lot. The first step to preparing your new garden is a manicure. Use your lawn-mower on its lowest cutting level and go over the area well. If the overgrowth is too high for your mower, first cut it down to size with either a strimmer or hand sickle and then go over it with your mower. Make sure you wear appropriate clothing (high-top work shoes or boots with non-slip, ribbed bottoms and sturdy work jeans) and exercise caution.

Now you have a choice to make, assuming your garden-to-be is not a problem site. You must kill the remaining roots and stubble of the mowed plants so that they do not compete with your crops. There are two ways to solve the problem. First, you can rent a rotavator or hire someone to till under the surface vegetation. This digging step will be the first and last time you will have to dig or till your garden. If the area is bumpy and requires minor levelling, you can easily level the turned soil with a rake.

Your other choice for killing the roots and stubble is to use black plastic or other mulch, which you must apply before you plant. You can quite easily do the actual planting directly through the mulch for transplants or seeds, using the bulb planter, dibber and ridger. I will cover the technique for direct planting through mulches later in this chapter.

If you apply loose mulches to the garden too early in the year, the soil may be slow to warm up and planting times will have to be delayed. You will not have this problem if you mulch with black plastic and apply it shortly before normal outdoor planting times, because the black plastic absorbs heat and trans-fers some of it to the soil. You can actually measure this heating character-istic with a soil thermometer, which I did. I saw no delay in the warming of the mulched soil – if anything, the soil was slightly warmer than normal.

Preparing Problem Gardens

In this section you will learn what to do if you couldn't get the bulb planter to work in your garden because the soil is severely compacted or you hit rocks wherever you tried to push in the planter. This section is also for you if you could get the bulb planter into the ground but drainage problems from underlying hardpan kill or cripple everything except water lilies or marsh grass. If your ridger made only a scratch in the garden soil after lots of hard work on your part, well, you do have a problem garden, but Bill and I have solutions. Let's look at them and help you pick out the right one for you.

Compacted Soil

Let's examine the problem of compaction first. Soils that you dig up, as we saw in Chapter 1, are susceptible to compaction by ordinary foot traffic. Heavier traffic, such as tillers or wheel-barrows, makes the problem even worse. Compaction hinders root development, because there are few air spaces between soil particles for roots to grow in and roots are deprived of oxygen. Consequently, crop yields go down. Continual traffic at the same depth, such as occurs when you use a tiller year after year, can eventually produce a hardened, compacted soil layer, which we call hardpan. Roots cannot grow through hardpan and water drains through it very slowly. If you see standing water after rain and your crop harvests aren't good, you probably have a hardpan. A quick soil check can confirm the problem. Slowly push a pointed metal rod about ¾ inch in diameter into the soil until you feel slight resistance. Note the depth and repeat the test in several different spots. If you come up with resistance at about the same depth everywhere, you have hardpan. If you find no resistance down to 24 inches, you can count your blessings.

We have two possibilities that could be the cause of resistance. Either you have soil compaction but no hardpan yet or you have compaction to the point of hardpan. Let's look first at compaction. How bad is your compaction? Does your soil drain reasonably well and are your harvests respectable? Can you push in the bulb planter or open a furrow with the ridger? If your answers are yes, your compaction problem is not serious, and you can go ahead and follow the planting directions on page 52. I would suggest that you restrict traffic in the garden to small paths only and use raised bed or band plantings as described later and in Chapter 7. Remember, no-dig procedures do *not* cause compaction. You will also be adding organic matter to the garden (see Chapter 4), which will gradually reduce the slight compaction in your garden.

If your soil drains poorly, your harvests are poor and you found it difficult to push the bulb planter into the soil, you need to take steps to correct the compaction problem before you become a no-digger. The best way to alleviate compaction is to work a considerable amount of organic matter into the soil with a rotavator. This garden tilling will be a one-time event and will soon only be a memory when you become a no-dig gardener. Believe me, the work you save with the no-dig method will be well worth a bit of extra effort to correct the problem now. The kind of organic matter you work into the soil is not important. You can use whatever

you have or can get easily: manure, leaves, moss peat or compost. However, for reasons of economy, you might want to consider my choice: leaves. My garden had somewhat compacted soil from years of traffic and rotavating. The autumn before my 'no-dig spring', I spread 2 to 3 inches of freshly fallen leaves all over my garden. I turned the leaves into my garden with several increasingly deeper passes of the rotavator until I reached its depth limit. In went the leaves, out went compaction. Tilling leaves into soil effectively lightens its texture. Just don't do it on a windy day! A soil test in the spring is especially important here because the decaying leaves will use some of your soil's nitrogen reserves.

If you have soil compaction with hardpan, you may have one or two problems to correct prior to becoming a no-dig gardener. If your hardpan is 12 inches down or deeper and is not causing a drainage problem, you can ignore the hardpan and correct for compaction with organic matter as I just explained. But if you have serious hardpan woes, you must disrupt the hardpan layer or rise above it. The best way to disrupt hardpan is through subsoil tillage. Generally, the subsoil is loosened by the tedious method of double digging. Again, this step is a one-time correction, because no-dig procedures will not cause compaction and hardpan problems.

Other ways to correct hardpan include constructing raised beds (which I will cover in a moment when I discuss stony or rocky soils) and growing alfalfa in sections of the garden. Alfalfa has a deep, strong taproot, which will help break up the hardpan. At the end of the season, turning under the alfalfa will increase your soil's organic matter and nitrogen content. Raised beds, while more work, are a quicker option for small gardens. Also, you don't lose any of your gardening space or time with raised beds as you do with alfalfa.

Another problem you may have in your garden is stony and rocky soil. No-dig gardening can work in such gardens, depending on the severity of the problem.

I can use the bulb planter in my stony soil, although sometimes I may have to give up on one hole and try a new one close by. Sometimes I can slant the bulb planter on an angle and bypass the stone. The transplant may have a funny angle for a while, but it does eventually grow straight. My ridger also works fine. Sometimes I simply draw the ridger and it pulls out the smaller rocks, while other times I may have to zig or zag. These minor problems are nothing when compared to the back-breaking wholesale digging I used to do.

However, I will admit that at some point a soil can be so stony or rocky that it interferes with no-dig gardening methods. Should you have this problem, you may have solved it already with raised beds. If you don't have beds, you can construct some right on top of your present garden and never have to worry about rocks again. You will fill the raised beds with a fine, rich soil mix that will produce beautiful crops for

you. No-dig gardening works just fine in raised beds. We'll examine two ways to make raised beds — you can think of them as 'economy' and 'luxury' models. Keep in mind that the length of your raised beds is your choice, but the width should be such that you can reach the middle easily from the side. A good width is 4 feet.

Bill and I found that it's easy to make raised beds with inexpensive wire border fence and newspaper (the economy-model beds). Usually this kind of fencing somes in folding sections 12 inches wide, of various lengths, and about 18 inches high. You can join these fences together to create whatever lengths you need. To make our simple beds, first, push the wire border fence into the soil to form the outline of the raised bed (Figure 14). Pushing the wire legs into the soil anchors the fencing nicely. Next, take several thicknesses of newspaper, around 10 to 12 sheets, and line the inside of the fence with them (Figure 15). Do not use any newspaper with coloured inks, because there may be lead present in some of them. Now fill in the bed with your soil and you have an economy-model raised bed. (Where did the soil come from? We'll get back to this question in a moment.)

Admittedly this bed is not perma-

Figure 14. After you place the wire border fencing in the outline of your bed, hammer a pipe or other support at each inner corner.

Figure 15. Instead of newspaper, I lined this bed with sides from cardboard boxes for longer life.

nent. It will last one year at least, perhaps two, depending on weather conditions and the treatment that the bed gets. However, such a bed costs little and gives you the opportunity to observe its results. Chances are that the raised bed will outperform your problem garden soil severalfold. If you like the bed idea, you can always replace the sides with more permanent materials at the end of the season.

You may, however, want to start off with one of the luxury models of raised beds or at least consider them later. For the sides of these raised beds, you may choose to use railway sleepers, planks or breeze-blocks. Be careful when using wood, though, and especially with the railway sleepers. Sometimes wood is treated with preservatives, such as creosote, that are toxic to growing plants. If you are unsure or can't find out what preservative was used, buy untreated wood, then you can treat the wood yourself with a safe preservative, such as linseed oil or a special commercial formulation for plants. Green Cuprinol, for example, contains a special wood preservative (copper naphthenate) that is safe for use with plants.

You can hold the wood sleepers or planks in place by nailing them to wood stakes or attaching them to pipe stakes with screws and U-bolts. The height of the bed should be at least 12 inches, but 18 or even 24 inches is better. In most cases, the amount of available soil will probably determine your bed height.

Now to get back to an earlier question, where will you get the soil to fill the raised beds? It's not an unreasonable question, since your soil was a problem from the start. Well, only two courses of action are possible; you can buy the soil or make it. If you buy topsoil, you will obviously save some work, but it will cost you dearly. Make sure it's good soil and if at all possible, try to get samples and have them tested. Your other choice is to make your own soil mix. Blending an improved soil for use in your beds involves a fair amount of work. But sometimes its the best way to ensure an excellent growing medium for your plants. Consider, too, that you don't need to make enough soil to fill a garden, just enough to fill one or more raised beds. The richer soil in the beds will let you plant intensively. You will be able to grow as much in these raised beds as many gardeners do in conventional row gardens two or three times larger!

To make your own soil, you can either start with some lower quality, existing soil and add ingredients to it to make it better or you can start with basic ingredients and build a soil (actually a soil substitute) from scratch.

If you're lucky, you may have an area,

such as a hill or low knoll, from which you can remove some soil or you may be able to get a truckload of inexpensive, lower quality soil. To this soil, add an equal volume of a mixture composed of 50 per cent builder's sand and 50 per cent compost. If you don't have compost, you can substitute leafmould or moss peat. Mixing everything by hand will probably be quite a chore, so I suggest that you hire a cement mixer for the day. You can mix the materials while they are moist; but if they are too wet, you could damage the soil structure. Don't overmix, either. When the ingredients are evenly combined, fill your raised beds. Save some soil for a soil test, which we covered earlier in this chapter.

How much soil do you need? If you multiply the width times the length of your raised bed and then multiply this figure times the desired soil height, you get the volume of the soil you need. For example, a bed that measures 4 feet by 8 feet by 1 foot needs 32 cubic feet of soil. Using the recipe given above, you need 16 cubic feet of soil to which you add another 16 cubic feet of the sand/compost mixture.

To prepare soil substitute from scratch to fill the same bed, you need enough materials to make 32 cubic feet. Some measuring containers will be most helpful when you're mixing up a batch of soil substitute. A basket holds about 1.3 cubic feet, and a standard 5-gallon bucket with handle holds 0.3 cubic feet of dry material. You can make a soil substitute from scratch with moss peat and vermiculite (horticultural grade, either number 2 or 4). Mix 12 baskets full of each with 5 pounds of dolomitic limestone and 5 pounds of an organic fertilizer containing nitrogen, phosphorus and potassium. This formulation give you about 32 cubic feet of soil substitute. Don't worry about

which fertilizer to use. Any of the general-purpose organic fertilizers described in Chapter 4 will be fine. Incidentally, a 2-pound coffee tin will hold about 5 pounds of limestone or dry fertilizer.

And now here's a last option for correcting problem soil. Although your soil may be stony or have hardpan and be difficult to work using no-digging methods, it may still be tillable with a rotavator. Your best bet is to hire a rotavator or contract someone who owns one to do the job for you. You can then create raised beds quickly and easily with the rotavator, using your existing garden soil enriched with sand and compost. Once you have finished the beds, you can wall them in and become a no-dig gardener.

You even have a choice on how to make raised beds with a rotavator. One approach is to till your soil to the maximum depth of the rotavator. This depth varies, but 11 inches is possible. Next shovel and rake the loose soil from areas that will be paths between beds. Heap the loose soil on the beds-to-be. You will get raised beds nearly 15 inches high, assuming you use 4-foot-wide beds with 18-inch paths between beds.

Now that the soil is in good shape, you're ready to plant.

Planting the Garden

Planting time is the best time of year for gardeners. There's nothing like the happy, hopeful feeling you get as you tuck the young plants into the ground at the start of a brand new growing season. Besides, it's spring and it's just wonderful to get outdoors in the warm sunshine. Planting times for crops in your no-dig garden will be much the same as in a conventional garden. If you have put down a black plastic mulch, you may be able to plant a week or two earlier. You will find recommended planting times for specific vegetables and flowers in Chapters 8 and 9. Those chapters also have information on plant spacing and placement in the garden. A good way to test whether your soil is dry enough to plant in is to scoop up a handful and squeeze it into a ball by clenching your fist. As you release your hand, the ball should crumble and fall apart. If it sticks together, the soil is too wet and probably too cold to plant anything in it. You should figure out where all your crops are going to go before you start any planting. Some gardeners like to draw a garden plan on paper and others prefer to plan the garden in their heads and get out there and plant. Whichever way you choose, just make sure you know where you want to plant when you step into the garden.

When planting day arrives your first instinct, especially if you've gardened before, will probably be to look up in the sky and see if the weather looks right for planting. If you grew your own transplants using the method I described in Chapter 2, you don't need to worry too much about the weather. Our method produces strong, well-rooted transplants that are tough enough to go into the garden without danger of transplant shock. If the weather is more or less normal for this time of year, you don't have to wait for an ideal day to do your transplanting. However, if you purchased transplants or grew them by methods other than ours, you should transplant on a cloudy, calm day to lessen transplant shock.

Now we are ready to pick up our tools. Let's look first at the bulb planter. The first thing a transplant needs is a no-dig hole which you will make with the bulb planter. You can either prepare all the holes and then place the transplants in these holes, or you can make one hole, put in the plant and then repeat the process. Bill and I tried both methods and we thought it was easier to make all the holes in one continuous standing movement. After all, when you're on a roll, why stop? When we were putting the plants in the holes, we found that one stoop usually brought us into the reach of around four holes. At this rate we figured the method of preparing all the holes at once had about one-quarter of the stoop-and-stand action as did the method of making one hole at a time. The continuous up-and-down motion of the latter method tired us out more quickly.

Transplanting with the bulb planter is as easy as one, two, three. First, place your bulb planter on the soil where you wish to put in a transplant. While holding onto the handle firmly push the bulb planter down into the soil, with your right foot. Let the planter sink down until the hole is as deep as the height of the polystyrene cup or other container that holds the plant. If you encounter a rock, tilt the bulb planter and angle past it. Don't worry about the slanted hole; the transplant will straighten up in a few days. Large rocks pose no problem, if you move the hole to any side. Pull the bulb planter out of the soil.

Suppose you had decided to put down black plastic early to kill extensive weeds or turf, as mentioned earlier in this chapter. Just place your bulb planter on the plastic mulch and push it firmly right through the plastic. The bulb planter will neatly slice a hole through the plastic and into the soil (Figure 16). If you have an organic mulch on the garden, just push it aside and sink the bulb planter into the soil.

Removing the soil plug should pose no difficulty, if you are doing your planting at the proper time of year. If you try to transplant too early, the soil

Figure 16. After you make a no-dig hole, fill it with organic rapid starter solution.

will be too wet and will stick, causing you some annoyance. Remember the squeeze test for determining when soil is ready for planting. To get the soil plug out, just turn the bulb planter upside down and grasp the handle outside of the metal corer section containing the soil plug. Rap the handle of the bulb planter on the ground. The soil plug will fall out cleanly onto the ground without hitting your hands or feet. Once in a while I have to give a hesitant soil plug a little push with my free hand. By the way, don't worry about the mound of soil. Leave it and move on to the next position to make another hole. If you can't make straight lines by eye, you might want to use the line guide mentioned in Chapter 1.

The next step is to pour an organic rapid starter solution into each hole, filling it up to the top (Figure 16). Organic rapid starter solution contains kelp and Farmura (as described in Chapter 4) and it will give your transplants a quick start. If you grew your transplants our way, as discussed in the previous chapter, you will get a double quick start! Unlike conventional transplants, ours have lots of super-strong feeder roots to take up the organic starter solution ever so quickly.

Now gather up your transplants and place them near the planting holes (Figure 17). You should use recently watered transplants, so the root balls are moist but not soggy. Bill and I like to place them in groups of four in positions from which we can reach four holes. Do you plant in a squatting or kneeling position? We find a kneeling position most comfortable for planting, especially when we wear a pair of foam rubber kneepads. If you grew your transplants as described in Chapter 2, take the polystyrene container in your working hand, then place your other hand over the cup keeping the plant stem between your fingers. Invert the container and give the bottom a gentle rap. The soil ball should easily slide from the cup (Figure 18), as our seedling growing mixture allows for easy removal. You may be tempted to remove some of the drainage and aeration materials from the root ball, but don't! You will damage the roots if you do and besides, these materials will go on improving drainage and aeration in your garden soil if you allow them to remain on the root ball.

Planting Home-grown or Purchased Transplants

If you grew your transplants by some method other than ours or if you purchased them and the transplants are in individual containers, you can treat

Figure 17. You can assemble your transplants in groups of four near the planting holes, or lay out an entire row of transplants near the holes to save time.

Figure 18. To remove the transplant from the cup, place the stem between your fingers and invert the cup. The transplant will usually slide right out and the soil ball remain intact. Tap the cup bottom or gently squeeze the sides if a transplant seems stubborn.

Figure 19. Plants grown in trays can also be transplanted into no-dig holes. When planting a transplant from a plastic compartmentalized tray, like the marrow plant *left*, add soil to fill in gaps around small root balls or round off the edges on larger soil squares.

To transplant from a tray, first remove the soil block from the tray, as shown with the marigolds *left*.

Next, use a knife to cut the soil block into cubes that will fit the no-dig hole, as shown *left*.

them the same way as described above for our transplants. If your transplants are in paper or peat pots, you have to take one precaution. Make sure none of the paper or peat pot is above the soil line when you set the transplant in the hole. If it is, the pot edge can act as a capillary wick and evaporate moisture from the root ball, which can lead tos- lowed recovery, slowed growth and even death for your transplants. I usually feel better when I remove the top inch or so of a paper or peat pot before I bury it.

If your transplants are in trays, take a sharp knife and cut the soil into cubes, with a plant at the centre of each cube. If you are careful, you can also break the soil mixture apart by hand. The cube's length or width should not be any larger than the diameter of the garden hole, but it can be smaller. Remember, if the transplant looks quite small when

compared to the hole, you should prob- ably make your planting holes with the dibber, as I will explain later.

Next, place the transplant's root ball or the cut cube of soil into the hole. If you used our method for growing transplants, you'll find that the root ball fits perfectly in the no-dig hole (Figure 20). If you have other kinds of trans- plants, you will probably need some soil to fill up the hole. You can use the soil plugs left nearby from the no-dig holes, you can push in soil from around the hole's edge or, better yet, you can fill in the hole with our special mixture of soil and compost, called seedling helper (see page 73). You can keep a bucket of this mixture close at hand for filling the holes. One final note: if the soil cube or root ball is a litle wider than the hole, just place your fingers on the inside of the hole and pull to stretch the hole a little larger. At this point you will notice

Figure 20. When you prepare a no-dig hole for a transplant make it as deep as the container with the transplant. One excep- tion is with transplants in peat pots, where you want the hole to be 1 inch deeper. This extra depth allows you to cover the rim of the peat pot with soil, which will prevent it from wicking away soil moisture and fatally drying out your transplant. Plants from our polystyrene cups fit perfectly into no-dig holes, as shown with this pepper plant, *above right,* being planted through black plastic. If you cut the hole to the right depth, the plant will fit in just right. You can also use no-dig holes for either circular or square peat pots, *right.* If the square pot fits poorly, round it by squeezing carefully with your hand or stretching the sides of the hole with your hands.

that you did half as much work in half as much time compared to when you transplant with a trowel.

I'd like to give you a word of caution here. When the transplant is safely in the hole, resist the urge to press down on the root ball or the soil around it and do not water the transplant. Pressing causes compaction, which reduces the drainage and aeration of the soil. In turn, the compacted soil results in poorer root systems and slower growth.

As far as watering transplants, if you think back to the start of this section, you'll remember that we said to start with *recently watered* transplants, so the root ball is wet already. If you add more water, the root ball will be soggy and wetter than the surrounding soil. This condition defeats the purpose of putting our starter solution in the hole before planting the transplant. We want the soil around the root ball to be wetter than the root ball itself so the feeder roots will be encouraged to grow outward into the garden soil, seeking out the water. Of course, if the root ball dries out over the next few days, by all means water it then and afterwards as needed.

If your garden soil is in excellent organic health, you are done. The organic enrichment methods I'll explain in Chapter 4 can speed you to this goal.

However, if you are still working on getting your soil in top condition, you can assure a bountiful harvest from the transplants with one last simple step (Figure 21). Use the bulb planter to make a no-dig hole about 4 inches to the right or left of each transplant. Dump the soil aside as before. Fill each hole with some garden compost or leaf-mould amended with organic nutrients. Bill and I suggest you try our recipe in Chapter 4 for organic oases. These organic oases will be a favoured watering hole for your transplants' root systems after they deplete the starter solution. If your soil is in poor health, you might want to put two, three, or even four organic oases around each transplant.

If you have any leftover soil plugs when you have finished planting, you can just leave them or, if you plan to lay down a plastic mulch to keep away weeds, scatter the soil plugs with your foot or a rake.

Planting Smaller or Leftover Transplants

How can you handle those much smaller transplants in trays or the transplants that arise when you thinned extra seedlings from the containers? Using a sharp knife, cut the root ball into little cubes, with one plant at the centre of each

Figure 21. Use the bulb planter to make one or more holes around your transplants and fill with enriched organic matter, such as this leafmould mixed with organic fertilizer. The edge of the organic oasis should start roughly 4 inches away from the transplant. Use one oasis for each transplant in average garden soil, more if the soil is poor and neglected.

Figure 22. The bulb planter, when sunk just 1 or 2 inches into the soil, can be used to plant larger seeds in soil or black plastic (*above right*), as can the dibber (*below right*). Seed potatoes, onion sets and garlic can be planted with either tool.

cube. Next make a series of holes in the garden with your dibber. Make sure the holes are a little larger than the soil cubes. Rocking the dibber back and forth enlarges the hole. Now add the same liquid seaweed and Farmura starter solution recommended before with the larger transplants. Fill the hole twice, since its volume is small. Now place your transplant cube or your seedling in the hole. Put a little compost amended with organic nutrient or a little soil in each dibber hole so that the cube's top is even with the soil line when you place it in the hole. Fill any gaps with the same mixture. Again, do not press on the soil or water the new transplant until the soil around it starts to dry out. If your soil is not in good organic health, amend it for the short

term with the organic oases used with the larger transplants.

Other Uses for the Bulb Planter and Dibber

The bulb planter and dibber have other uses as well (Figure 22). The dibber is fine for planting onion sets, onion transplants, garlic cloves and small seed potatoes. You can use the bulb planter to plant larger seed potatoes. By cutting a bulb planter hole or dibber hole to the proper depth, you can also plant some large seeds, such as beans, sweetcorn, cucumber and marrow, in hills or groups. Of course, you can plant all of these equally as well in a row made by the ridger, which we will be discussing next.

Let me remind you that you don't *have* to use a bulb planter or dibber to plant onions (sets or transplants), garlic cloves, seed potatoes or large seeds. You could use the ridger instead, if you prefer. There is, however, one case in which a bulb planter or dibber will indisputably offer the greatest convenience.

If you have a black plastic mulch in place, it's easier to plant large seeds or various bulbs with the bulb planter or dibber. These tools slice nicely through plastic, but other tools, particularly a ridger, would only tear it. There *is* a way to plant rows with the ridger and still use black plastic mulch, but we'll cover that later on.

How to Use a Ridger

The other tool you need in the no-dig garden is a ridger. This tool, as you recall, is what you use to plant seeds of fast-maturing crops directly in the garden. How do you use it? First place the point downwards and work it into the soil. The angle made by the soil surface and the handle determines the depth of the furrow. Standing upright will let you create the largest possible angle and the most shallow furrow. As you bend at the waist, the angle decreases and the furrow cut goes deeper. Walking backwards, draw the ridger towards you. If you have a good eye for rows, you

will get a nice straight furrow; if you do not, use the row guide discussed in Chapter 1. Make sure you cut the furrow 1 to 2 inches deeper than the required seed-planting depth. You can easily cut a deep furrow in one pass. If, however, you find this furrowing too strenuous, you can make the task easier by cutting the furrow increasingly deeper using two or more passes with the ridger. The depth for seed potatoes, for instance, might require more than one pass for some people.

To prepare your furrow for seeds, place enough soil mixed with compost and organic nutrients in the bottom of the furrow to decrease the depth to that which is needed for the seeds (Figure 23). You can use the outdoor seedling helper recipe in Chapter 4, or you can buy ready-made mixtures. This material will help the seedlings get off to a great start.

Now you are ready to put the seeds into the furrow. If you are a kneeler and like to get close to the soil, please remember to be kind to your knees. Kneepads (discussed in Chapter 1) will be a great help. Not only are they comfortable, but they stop the chill and dampness that arise from contact with spring garden soil. Or perhaps you like to stand. I know that I can stand and

Figure 23. Add the seedling helper to the bottom of your furrow. Put in enough so that the seeds will sit at the proper depth.

drop large seeds, such as sweetcorn and beans, quite neatly into open furrows, but small seeds give me trouble. One puff of wind and I find that my straight line looks like a path through a maze. For small seeds, you might want to use a mechanical seed sower. Some of the seed sowers we covered in Chapter 1 fit the bill, in terms of both sowing ease and cost.

Now you can sow your seeds using the method of your choice (Figure 24). Of course, you can also plant onion sets and plants, garlic or seed potatoes in your furrow. Next, cover the seeds. Do *not* use the soil on the sides of the furrow unless it is friable (easily crumbled) and in good organic health. Left in place, this little ridge of soil will also trap and retain rainwater in the furrow. If your soil is not up to par yet, you can cover the seeds with a soil and vermiculite mixture called soil helper. You can find the recipe for this soil helper in Chapter 4.

Do you want super seedlings in a hurry? If you are like Bill and me, you do. Take your watering can and fill it with our rapid starter solution of liquid seaweed and Farmura for seeds (see Chapter 4). Now water your freshly covered seed furrows with the solution. The nutrients and growth promoters in this solution will improve both germination and seedling growth. A head start is a good start! Later when these quick-acting nutrients have gone, the slow-release nutrients in the soil/compost supplement (or seedling helper) underneath your seeds will continue feeding the growing seedlings.

What if you want to use black plastic or other mulches, but still use the ridger? With loose organic mulches, the ridger will work just fine. You can cut right through the organic mulch and into the soil, like a hot knife through butter. Black plastic, on the other hand, requires a somewhat different approach. One way to solve the problem is to leave roughly 12 inches of space between each sheet of black plastic. Use these earth strips for your seed rows. This method, however, has two disadvantages. Firstly, I find it difficult sometimes to plan ahead for row placement. My ideas change or a new packet of seeds comes my way. The other problem concerns the width of the plastic mulch versus the distance I want between rows. The two sizes are hardly ever the same, thus I end up trimming plastic and installing far more edges than I really need.

The better way to install black plastic involves using the widest available

Figure 24. Sow your seeds on top of the seedling helper.

width. This approach helps cut down the number of edges you need to install. Butt each of the edges up close together, leaving very little soil showing between sheets. Wherever you need to place a seed row, slit open the plastic (stop short of buried edges) with a knife or scissors (Figure 25). Now draw your ridger through the soil exposed by the slit. Don't worry about the plastic edges. The soil thrown to the sides by the ridger will bury the plastic edges as you make your furrow. If you are unhappy with the edge burial, you can pin down the edges with U-shaped pieces of coat hangers or place a few stones along the edges. Make sure you use the same procedure for furrowing and sowing as described earlier for bare soil; that is, cut a deeper furrow than

needed, place some seedling helper below the seeds, put in the seeds, cover them with soil helper and water them with rapid starter solution.

Raised Beds, Hills and the No-dig Method

If you have raised beds, the no-dig method will adapt readily when you plant the beds. If you want to plant your seeds in rows, use the ridger. If you are planning to plant transplants, use either the bulb planter or the dibber. You can also plant larger seeds using the dibber to make individual holes. You can find more information on these special cases under the various vegetables and flowers discussed in Chapters 8 and 9.

Perhaps you plant most of your crops

Figure 25. If your garden is mulched with black plastic, you can plant seeds if you slit the plastic as shown and then cut a furrow through the slit. The soil thrown to the sides holds the cut edges of the plastic down. Of course, you must cover the seeds with some fresh soil or soil and vermiculite.

directly into the existing garden soil, but you still like to plant a few special crops – like sweetcorn – in hills. The no-dig way of gardening works just as well with hills as with raised beds. It doesn't matter if your hill is just a simple mound of soil or a more formal raised mini-bed. Choose the dibber if you plant seeds for your hills of sweetcorn, marrow or other plants. If you have transplants, use the bulb planter. Just follow the steps given on page 53.

You may want to make some formal mini-hills like Bill and I use. We love using them because our hills, combined with black plastic and cloches (transparent plant covers), give us extra-early marrows. Gardeners in the South may not care about this result, but we northern gardeners are very happy to get early crops. Here's our method.

First, prepare 36-inch-square frames from pine or chipboard shelving. You can buy this board 6 feet or 8 feet long by 12 inches wide by 1 inch thick. Actually, the true dimensions for the width and thickness are more like 11 inches and ¾ inch, respectively. If you wish to reuse this frame for many years, stain it with a wood preservative that's safe for use with plants. For example, Cuprinol markets a formulation for use with wood greenhouse trays. Building this frame is a good winter task, when the call for garden work is minimal.

When spring arrives, you can put the mini-hills wherever you want them in your garden. I suggest that you drive in a wood stake or metal pipe at each inside corner of the frame. This step will securely anchor the hill frame. Now fill the mini-hill either with soil or the soil substitute described earlier in this chapter. At planting time (Figure 26) you can use the dibber for planting seeds or the bulb planter for planting transplants. Make sure you read about the use of the drinks bottle fertilizer feeds for hills and raised beds in the next chapter. And don't forget to check out early hill crops with black plastic and cloches, which I will discuss in Chapter 7.

Before we leave planting techniques, let's talk about planting patterns. The old standby is single row planting. The bulb planter, dibber or ridger easily makes a single row of holes or a single (row) furrow. However, if you want greater yields from the same area, you are better off with beds and bands. These planting patterns give increased yields because they use space more efficiently and cause less yield-robbing soil compaction.

You can plant beds with any of the tools, depending on whether you are using transplants or seeds. Beds should be 4 feet wide, so you can easily reach plants in the centre from either side, and

Figure 26. After you build your mini-hill, fill it with the best organic soil you have or can make. This photograph shows a completed mini-hill with plastic drinks bottle feeder.

be any length you want. Space the no-dig holes or the multiple furrow rows at the closest allowable distance (see Chapters 8 and 9) for intensive planting. You can place the transplants side by side or thin seedlings to the same pattern, essentially a compressed row concept. However, if you stagger the plants in the alternate rows (see Figure 46 in Chapter 7), you get even more plants in the bed than with row-type patterns.

Bands are somewhat narrower than beds (see Chapter 7) and perhaps more suited for smaller, intensive plantings like lettuce or carrots. Here, too, you can prepare transplant holes or multiple, tightly spaced rows with the bulb planter or ridger. Another no-dig approach with bands for small

seeds is to rough up the surface of the soil with either a rake or reciprocating hoe. Next broadcast or scatter the seeds and cover them with a light sprinkling of soil. Later on you can thin the seedlings to the efficient pattern and spacing of your choice.

Well, dear reader, I hope you are as excited as Bill and I are about the ease and versatility of no-dig gardening methods. You undoubtedly want to skip right to Chapters 8 and 9 now, but try to resist the urge. Our next chapter on fertilizing and adding organic matter to your no-dig garden is important. Remember, healthy plants and wonderful yields depend on organically enriched soils; no-dig gardens are no exception.

CHAPTER 4
FEEDING THE NO-DIG GARDEN

Many gardeners don't realize that digging the soil is the key culprit in the loss of organic matter. Digging brings deeper organic matter to the soil surface. There air-loving microorganisms quickly break it down, wasting much of the soil's organic matter before plants can make use of it. Of course, this sets off a whole chain of events that eventually ruins your soil as we already discussed in Chapter 1. No-dig techniques, however, conserve organic matter, so much so that you can maintain levels simply by leaving roots from previous crops in place and perhaps occasionally adding an organic amendment to the soil. Naturally this statement assumes your soil already has an acceptable level of organic matter, which is probably not true of many gardens with a history of heavy digging and cultivation. But don't worry. If your soil test indicates low organic matter content, there are ways you can quickly improve it (I'll offer some suggestions later in this chapter). Once you have improved your soil, it will be easy for you to maintain the level of organic matter in the no-dig garden.

A no-dig garden also requires less supplemental feeding of nutrients than other gardens do. In plain talk, the money you spend on fertilizer gets a lot more mileage in the no-dig garden. Part of this saving relates to organic matter. Any fertilizer, even organic fertilizer, has some part of its nutrient pool in a water-soluble form. This nutrient amount may be small, as with organic fertilizers that release nutrients slowly, or quite large, as with water-soluble chemical fertilizers. Plants can use only a certain amount of water-soluble nutrients in their day-to-day development, therefore, some excess nutrients are present. True, with organic fertilizers the amount of excess nutrients is reasonably small but, even so, the soil can either waste or store the nutrients not needed by the plants. What happens depends heavily on how much organic matter is present in the soil.

Organic matter has the ability to capture and hold nutrients until the plants need them, a process scientists call *chelation*. If organic matter is not present, water carries the nutrients downwards into the water table where they are lost to plants. This process is known as *leaching*. The no-dig garden has higher levels of organic matter, therefore, the no-dig garden soil has superior ability to capture and hold nutrients. Nutrient losses through leaching are minimal, therefore your fertilizer goes further and you need less.

Certain practices associated with our no-dig garden methods also greatly improve fertilizer efficiency. Normally you apply fertilizers by broadcasting or evenly scattering them over the garden before you sow seeds or place transplants. This approach to fertilizing is inefficient, or nutrient wasteful, for a number of reasons. One, a lot of nutrients end up in areas where the plants won't be able to use them. For example, the nutrients in the fertilizer that fall on the paths will probably be lost by leaching. Even if the soil stores the nutrients there, the degree of compaction present means the nutrients will probably never be used by plants. Foot traffic on the paths compacts the soil, driving out air and destroying soil structure to the point that roots will not grow into the soil in the path areas. It's not hard to see that if there are no roots, there will be no need for nutrients and they will be wasted.

Timing is also an important factor in fertilizer efficiency. Some nutrients land in good soil, but it is soil where the plant roots are not yet present. By the time the roots arrive in that area, leaching will have robbed the soil of some of its nutrients. The plants will eventually use the nutrients stored in the organic matter, but any nutrients outside of the organic matter holding area will disappear.

So what's the gardener to do? You should apply fertilizer at the right time and place so that you are sure you have utilized it as efficiently as possible. Bill and I use localized, intensive fertilizer applications, which I will explain. If you recall the transplanting procedure outlined in the previous chapter, you'll remember that we used an organic rapid starter solution. This starter solution goes directly into the transplant hole, so we localize the nutrients where the feeder roots can absorb them quickly. The solution quickly releases some of the nutrients for immediate use, while it releases other nutrients more slowly for later uptake. Thus, we have an intensive availability of nutrients for the transplant. A somewhat similar situation occurs when we use the rapid starter solution with seeds.

Bill and I use this same idea of localized, intensive applications as the plant develops from either a seed or transplant. We localize the fertilizer application by using foliar feeding and the leaves then directly absorb the nutrients. Any runoff at the plant's drip line also goes right to work, because this is where the feeder roots are found. The feeder roots capture the nutrient runoff, so the plant is actually fed twice. This is another kind of intensive fertilizing.

Of course we do use some slow feeding techniques, too, such as the seedling helper or the organic oases I mentioned in Chapter 3. These techniques, which I will describe in detail later in this chapter, help to maintain a steady, slow stream of nutrients to the plants.

Let's turn now to fertilizers and fertilizing techniques for your organic no-dig garden.

Water-soluble Organic Fertilizers

I have settled on two products as the mainstays of my foliar feeding programme; Farmura and seaweed extract. You can use them combined or separately. Their price is right, they go a long way, and they produce remarkable results. I use them on everything — vegetables, flowers, fruit trees and shrubs. First, let's look at the products themselves.

We keep coming back to seaweed extract and its value, above and beyond its benefits as a fertilizer, so let's talk about it now. Apart from nitrogen, phosphorus and potassium, liquid seaweed contains all the trace elements plants need. It can be used as a foliar spray, a seed treatment and a rooting solution. There are numerous claims being made for it. Reputedly, liquid seaweed will improve plants' resistance to disease, insects, and frost as well as improving their intake.

But let's take an even closer look at these claims. I mentioned that I use seaweed extract for foliar feeding. But is there a scientific basis for its use? Plant physiologists don't agree as to exactly how nutrients in solution penetrate leaves. They may enter through the adjustable pores in leaves (called stomata), the leaves' waxy cuticle layer or both. But scientists do have proof that nutrients do enter leaves in water. Nutrients also leach out of leaves during periods of heavy, continuous rain, but these nutrients eventually enter the plant through the root system. Foliar feeding is, then, indeed efficient.

There are many other pluses to foliar feeding. If the leaves, rather than the roots, take in the nutrients, the beneficial effects to the plant occur more quickly. Foliar absorption can be up to 20 times faster than root absorption and nutrients entering through the leaves produce beneficial results with a smaller amount of nutrients than when they enter through soil routes. In some instances with trace elements, foliar feeding may give quicker but similar results at feeding rates as low as one-twelfth the rate of soil feeding. This last point is especially important. It's the heart of our localized, intensive feeding programme and explains further why we use so much less fertilizer than gardeners who use conventional fertilization. The enhancement effect of foliar feeding is real, but a few reasons might better convince you.

For example, let's look at phosphorus. We're always adding phosphorus to the soil, so it seems as though most soils must be deficient in phosphorus. Wrong! Most soils have plenty of phosphorus, but it isn't available to plants because soil chemistry tends to keep it locked up. With foliar feeding, we can bypass this chemical lock, therefore, we need much less phosphorus. In effect, much of the phosphorus put into the soil is in an effort to get past the chemical lock, so that only a little of what we add goes to the plant. This problem of soil chemistry also affects trace elements added to the soil. Most become unavailable to the plant because of chemical attack in the soil. But foliar feeding provides an excellent bypass route.

Let's look at another aspect of foliar feeding versus conventional feeding: competition. The nutrients we add to the soil don't always get to the plant. Microorganisms in the soil and weeds steal some for their needs and some nutrients leach downwards to the water table. Conventional feeding is certainly inefficient, since we have to add extra nutrients to compensate for losses. Direct feeding through leaves bypasses these problems and results in more efficient feeding from a smaller amount of fertilizer.

One last point deserves a brief mention. When you encounter an unseasonable period of dry weather, it's impractical to apply fertilizers to soils, because the nutrients must be dissolved in water in order to enter the root system. Foliar feeding works even when the soil is dry. Again the foliar feeding solves a gardening problem.

Solid Fertilizers and Soil Amendments

I would now like to consider a few solid fertilizers. You may need them if your soil test shows that your soil isn't up to par. However, you may only need them for a few years, until you put your garden on an exclusive seaweed and Farmura diet. I'm recommending solid fertilizers on the basis of their effectiveness and availability. In the past, organic gardeners placed a lot of emphasis on rock powders such as granite dust. These products are hard to find, so I'm suggesting others instead.

Seaweed Meal

First let's turn to seaweed meal. Don't confuse seaweed meal with the previously discussed liquid or powdered seaweed extract. The extracts, whether in liquid or solid form, are hot-water or alkaline extracts of seaweed that are highly water-soluble and have immediately available nutrients. Seaweed meal is not an extract, but is ground-up seaweed itself (for addresses of suppliers, see pages 165-167.) It differs somewhat from the extracts.

One way in which seaweed meal differs from seaweed extract is that its nutrients are not readily available to the plant or soil. Microorganisms must first break it down to release its nutrients slowly. Unfortunately, if nitrogen levels in the soil are low, some nitrogen robbing from plants could occur initially. However, the nitrogen will eventually return.

One advantage of using seaweed meal is its residual effect. The nutrient release and growth enhancement effects go on for two or even three years. A second advantage is that it acts as a soil conditioner. Seaweed meal improves water retention and soil structure to a greater degree than do extracts. If your soil isn't up to organic expectations, a one-shot treatment with seaweed meal may be just the right ticket!

Home-made Fertilizers

You can also make your own organic fertilizers in various strengths. An easy one to make is a mixture of coffee grounds, bone meal and wood ashes in a proportion by weight of 4-1-1. This mixture will have an N-P-K (nitrogen-phosphorus-potassium) ratio of roughly 2-4-2. While this N-P-K rating may sound low, it's probably equivalent to a 5-10-5 chemical fertilizer. Remember, because the mixture is an organic fertilizer, it will release its nutrients slowly over a period of time.

Another fertilizer you can make consists of dried blood, bone meal, and wood ashes in a 2-1-4 ratio. This mix has an N-P-K value of 4-4-4 and might be similar to a chemical 10-10-10 fertilizer.

Another interesting product, worm castings, is available commercially. Manure worms (Brandlings) are fed on various raw materials such as animal manures and their castings are sold for use as a general garden fertilizer and for putting in seed drills. (For suppliers of these products, see pages 165-167.)

Leafmould

The last fertilizer and soil amendment I'll suggest, compost, is the most economical. You can easily make it yourself and it will be quite effective to use if you follow the hints that I'll give you. Compost, once called artificial manure, is roughly equivalent to manure in terms of its nutrients, but it sure smells better. Of course, compost is a wonderful soil conditioner. It improves water retention, aeration and nutrient storage and release in soils.

Let's start with the easiest approach to making your own compost. You can make an excellent compost with an easily available waste at a convenient time, when garden tasks are winding down for the year. The waste is those autumn leaves that you never quite know what to do with. If you bag them, you feel guilty. If you make them into compost, you help both the environment and your garden. An autumn leaf pile without any added nitrogen will produce compost sometime late the following summer. You can speed up the process by adding nitrogen, which will give you leafmould by late spring to early summer. The one exception to this statement is if your leaves are largely oak or pine. These two types of leaves take twice as long to form compost. You can mix oak leaves or pine needles with other kinds of leaves, but don't use them heavily.

Now you are ready to start forming your compost heap. First decide where you are going to place it. Pick a sunny, level, well-drained spot. If shade is all you have, go for it. Some people like to construct a retainer bin from wood or breeze-blocks, while others like to use chicken wire fence on poles. You don't need these 'leaf holders', though. Since you must keep the leaves moist, you shouldn't have to worry about their blowing away,

Now start raking leaves. If you have a big garden and a long way to go, rake the leaves into an old bed sheet. Pulling the four sheet corners into your hand, drag it to where you plan to construct your compost heap. As you make your leaves into a pile, keep certain points in mind. The leaves should be moist – if they are dry, you must wet them down as you make the heap. I like to make my leaf heap a day or so after a rain, because I save a step and don't have to drag out the garden hose.

The best and most effective shape and size for your compost heap is a 7-foot-square base that tapers to a 5-foot-square top. The ideal height is 5 feet. Don't aim for perfection, because approximations will work just as well. If you are using blood meal, sprinkle some on the leaves at 1-foot intervals. If you have a lot of leaves, you don't have to make a second heap. You can just make a longer heap, but keep the width and height the same.

Forget all those other compost recipes that you've seen or heard about. All you need is the leaves and moisture (see Table 1 overleaf). You do not have to add soil or buy the so-called compost starters. Supposedly these two additives enrich your compost with the right microorganisms so that your compost heap gets a quick start. In reality, the microorganisms you need are already there on the fallen, damp leaves, so don't waste your money on compost starters.

A concern you may have is whether or not to add limestone. I suggest that you don't do it because the pH of your compost will be fine without adding limestone. The finished product will have a pH of near neutral to slightly alkaline, the correct pH for most flowers and vegetables. Of course, if your leaf mixture is heavy in oak leaves and pine needles, the pH will be slightly acidic. If you do add limestone, you will create conditions that favour the production of ammonia. The ammonia will release into the air, taking your precious nitrogen with it. You will end up with nitrogen-deficient compost and a smelly compost heap. Don't waste your nutrients like this; avoid adding limestone to the composting process.

Essentially, once you make your leaf heap, you have finished your work. With an hour of work, you get rid of your leaves and have a rich compost as a reward. Do check the heap once in a while to see that it remains moist, because drying can distrupt the composting process. There's generally adequate precipitation in autumn and winter so I have never needed to wet down my leaf heaps after the initial wetting. You don't have to turn the heap either. Turning it may speed up the composting process, but it's hard work.

Perhaps one caution relating to composts is in order. Your heap will warm up in a few weeks. Within a month or two it will heat up considerably. The temperature of the heap goes over 140°F and often reaches 158°F – temperatures that will scald your hand. Do *not* poke your hand down into the heap. The outside may feel cool, but the

Table 1. Useful Compost Materials

Material	Source of	Nitrogen %	Phosphoric Acid %	Potash %
Bark	C	L	L	L
Bone meal	N	2	2-3	—
Coffee grounds	N	2	L	L
Eggshells	—	1	L	L
Fish scrap	N	2-8	1-6	L
Food wastes	C/N	2-3	L	L
Fruit wastes	C/N	1-2	L	L
Garden plants/weeds	C/N	L-2	L	L
Grass clippings	N	1-2	L	L
Hair	N	12-16	L	L
Hay	C	1-2	L	L
Hoof/horn meal	N	10-15	1-2	L
Leather meal	N	10-12	L	L
Leaves	C/N	L-1	L	L
Manure	C/N	1-5	1-2	1-2
Meat Scraps	N	5-7	L	L
Paper	C	L	L	L
Sawdust	C	L	L	L
Seaweed (washed)	C/N	1-2	L	3-4
Wood ash (unleached)	—	L	1-2	4-10
Wood chips	C	L	L	L

Note: In column 2, C stands for carbon and N for nitrogen. A material listed as a source of C/N contains a good ratio of carbon and nitrogen. It will easily compost alone, or can be counted as a source of either nitrogen or carbon in a mixed compost pile. In columns 3-5, L indicates a low content — less than 1 per cent of the given nutrient.

inside may be scalding hot. I have broken open what appeared to be a frozen heap on the outside only to find hot, moist steam escaping from the inside. All you really have to do is sit back and let the microscopic compost organisms do their job.

How do you tell when the compost is ready to use on your garden? You can check its readiness by digging out some of the compost with a spade. The material should look dark and crumbly. The compost temperature should be about the same as the air temperature. If the compost feels warm to the touch, it needs a little time to complete its cool-down period. I'm sure, though, that

it will feel either cool or about the same warmth as nearby soil. If it does, your compost is ready to use.

Carbon/Nitrogen Balanced Compost

If you want more compost than your leaf heap produces and have additional time to commit, you can increase production with a garden compost heap. The key to success is to use organic materials in a mixture that gives you balanced amounts of carbon, nitrogen, phosphorus and potassium. This nutrient balance makes the difference between a true compost and what I call a rubbish heap.

The microorganisms that make compost require a certain proportion of carbon to nitrogen if they are to do their job efficiently. The waste materials that we use as the carbon and nitrogen sources also contain sufficient amounts of phosphorus and potassium. We can divide the waste products we need into two categories: carbonaceous wastes, which are rich in carbon, and nitrogenous wastes, which are rich in nitrogen. As a rule of thumb, carbonaceous wastes are lightweight, dry and tan to dark brown in colour. Nitrogenous wastes are usually heavy, wet and green or dark brown in colour.

But how do you provide these wastes to your compost in the best proportion? You build your heap with alternating 8-inch layers of carbonaceous wastes and 4-inch layers of nitrogenous wastes. The heap size and shape should be just like the one described for leaves. (Look at Figure 27 if you are in doubt.) If you do not have enough material to make a heap as large as this, try the layering technique in a conventional compost bin.) The right carbon-to-nitrogen ratio is easy to achieve. To find out which

compost materials are carbonaceous or nitrogenous and which ones are good sources of phosphorus and potassium, look at Table 1 (on page 70).

The nice part about using this method is that you can build your heap as ingredients become available. If you have all your materials present at once and have a good eye for proportions, you can just mix everything together without using layers.

Again, as when you make leaf compost, I recommend you don't use soil, limestone or commercial additives with your compost. Work with moist materials and keep your heap moist at all times. Anytime the material feels drier than a damp, wrung-out sponge, you must add water.

You may be wondering whether or not to shred the compost materials. Shredding the compost materials will definitely speed up the composting process. With a bit of shredding you could have the compost in three months. You can shred the compost material by making several passes over small heaps with your rotary power mower. Not shred-

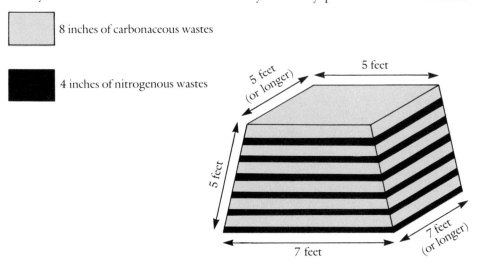

8 inches of carbonaceous wastes

4 inches of nitrogenous wastes

5 feet (or longer)

5 feet

5 feet

7 feet (or longer)

7 feet

Figure 27. Garden compost heaps work well, if you have the right ratio of carbonaceous to nitrogenous wastes.

ding will probably add a few months' time onto the composting process.

You may also be wondering if turning the compost heap is helpful to the process. Turning aerates the heap and speeds up the composting process, but as I mentioned earlier, it's hard work. If you do decide to turn the compost, turn it six weeks after you build the compost heap and then again four weeks later, both times using a spade.

Again, as with leafmould, there will be a heating phase followed by a cooling off period. Once the compost has cooled down, it's safe to use in your garden. The cooling period will usually vary from three to six months, depending upon the material you utilized and whether or not you shredded and/or turned the compost. If your heap fails to heat up within two to four weeks of building it, something is wrong. Lack of heat usually means there's not enough nitrogen in the heap. To correct it, add a nitrogen source such as green grass clippings to the heap.

If you notice an ammonia-like odour emanating from the compost heap, your problem is excess nitrogen. You can either add some more carbonaceous wastes or ignore the smell, which will stop. Next time you make compost don't use as many nitrogen sources, because the ammonia odour is actually nitrogen wasted into the air. You may also have a rotten egg odour. This stink comes from lack of air in the compost heap, which can result from prolonged, heavy rains filling the air spaces in the heap. Turning the heap should correct the problem. You can also wait until the heap dries out a bit and the smell will disappear.

Here are a few more troubleshooting suggestions for your compost heap. Don't add any meat scraps to your heap. If you must add some, bury them deeply so animals can't smell them. If

you carelessly place meat scraps near the heap, don't be surprised if you find dogs, cats, mice or even rats on the scene.

Do you have a cat? If so, I urge you *not* to add the used contents of your cat's litter tray to either your garden or compost heap. Cat wastes may harbour the microorganism that causes toxoplasmosis, a disease that attacks the central nervous system. While unpleasant for adults, this disease is really bad news for infants. Although it is rare, it's wise not to encourage the microorganisms. And under no circumstances should a pregnant woman handle the litter tray or areas contaminated by solid wastes from cats.

I would be equally cautious about sewage sludge. Two dangers concern me. First, many sewage sludges contain heavy metals, such as lead or cadmium, which result from industrial discharges. Heavy metals are especially hazardous if they enter the food chain and if you eat them with your garden vegetables. The only way to check sludges for these metals is with sophisticated analytical tests done in laboratories. The test results can be evaluated to determine whether or not the heavy metal content poses a hazard. Ignorance in this case is not bliss, but danger. Second, some sludges, if improperly treated, can harbour pathogens that infect humans. Again it's not wise to take any chances with their existence in your compost.

One last thought concerns the use of diseased plant material in the compost heap. If you compost correctly, you will destroy disease-causing organisms. Essentially, you must expose all the compost to temperatures over 131°F for roughly three weeks. This means it's important to attain good heating through using the correct heap size, proper balance of carbon and nitrogen-containing materials, sufficient moisture and enough air. You must frequently mix all outside materials inwards to expose all materials to the proper temperature. Remember, the outer edges of a compost heap are cooler than the middle. A far simpler solution to the problem of destroying disease-causing organisms exists: Don't put diseased plant remains in the compost heap.

Special Helpers

As you recall, I mentioned a few starter solutions and seedling helpers in Chapter 2. These fertilizers are easy to prepare from the previously discussed materials. Do take a few minutes to make them, because the results are well worth the effort. Your transplants and seedlings will take off rapidly and leave untreated plants behind in the dust.

Rapid Starter Solution

Firstly let's consider the rapid starter solution. This water-soluble, organic fertilizer is a combination of Farmura and seaweed extract. It's the same formula I suggested earlier for foliar feeding (see footnote on page 39). The hormones (mostly auxins) in the seaweed extract may promote rapid rooting of the newly placed transplant. At the same time, the nitrogen, phosphorus, potassium and trace elements contributed from both the seaweed and the Farmura nourish the transplant quickly, giving it a head start. With seeds, the reputed antibiotic properties of the seaweed keep soil-borne disease at bay, thus greatly improving the percentage of successful germination. The hormones may even help to speed up the germination process, then the combined nutrients quickly accelerate your seedlings into the fast lane for growth.

Organic Oasis Mixture

Remember the organic oases used earlier around transplants? These oases provide a rich nutrient bank and aeration chimney for the transplant roots. The organic matter helps aerate the soil and improve drainage while keeping the nutrients trapped until the plant roots arrive. The preparation of the oasis mixture is relatively easy: I simply mix some organic nutrients with my compost. Into each standard bucket of compost, I add, first of all, 2 tablespoons of either dried blood or hoof and horn meal for nitrogen. Next I add 2 tablespoons of steamed bone meal for phosphorus and a similar amount of unleached wood ashes for potash. If the ashes are wet, they have lost some potash, so double the amount. Mix all the ingredients thoroughly into the compost and use the enriched compost to make organic oases for your transplants.

Seedling Helper

The outdoor seedling helper is similar to the organic oasis mixture. The difference is that the seedling helper goes underneath seeds in furrows, while the organic oases go alongside transplants. Also, because seedlings are young and have small root systems, they do not benefit as much from nutrients as do robust transplants. Indeed, too many nutrients may harm the seedlings. Therefore, I prepare the seedling helper by cutting the organic oasis material in half with either garden soil, potting soil or even sand. Incidentally, you can use the worm castings described earlier in this chapter in place of the seedling helper.

Soil Helper

The last special mixture I will mention is optional and not really a fertilizer or soil conditioner. It is really a soil helper and you will find it useful if your soil is not in good condition. For instance, if the soil covering your seeds becomes concrete hard after a rain, you definitely need the soil helper's help. To make it simply mix some of your garden's soil or sand with vermiculite in a 1-1 ratio and cover your seeds with it. Of course, the long-term answer to the problem of concrete-hard soil is to improve your soil, which we'll talk about next.

Step-by-Step Soil Improvement

Now that you have the basics for feeding your no-dig garden, you must learn how to put these basics to work to create a well-nourished no-dig garden. Let me be your guide as we improve your no-dig garden step by step.

The first thing we need is that soil test report you now have, assuming you followed my advice in the previous chapter. If you didn't, you still have a chance to obtain one, but don't delay. The soil analysis report is going to be your road map, your guide to a better soil. What does the report say about pH? Ideally, we want a pH value near 6.5 for a vegetable or flower garden and, depending on your geographic location and garden history, you will either be close or way off. If you have an established garden and have adjusted the pH in the past, you should be reasonably close and need only minor corrections.

Whatever the pH, your report will offer the necessary remedy for your situation. If your soil is too acidic, the correction will be to add so many pounds of ground limestone (preferably dolomitic form) per so many square feet. Don't add more; in this case, more is not better, it's worse. Alkaline soils will require correction with powdered sulphur.

If your no-dig garden is new, first mow it, then follow up the mowing with either a rotavating session or covering the mowed vegetation with either black plastic or an organic mulch. If you use the rotavator method, sprinkle the limestone (or sulphur) over the tilled soil and water it in. If you are going to mulch instead, broadcast the limestone and water it into the mowed vegetation. Don't apply the mulch just yet, because you may need to add some fertilizer first. If so, wait at least a few days after watering in the limestone, then add the necessary fertilizer (as explained below). Now you can put the mulch over the mowed vegetation. Make sure you read about the easy way to apply black plastic in the next chapter, if it is your choice of mulch.

If you have an established garden with no mulch, just broadcast the limestone and water it in. If you have an all-year-round organic mulch, sprinkle the limestone over the surface of the mulch and thoroughly water the limestone into the soil until little or no white shows.

Nutrient Levels

Next, look over the soil report's level of the various nutrients, such as nitrogen, phosphorus, potassium and calcium, that your soil contains. Some nutrient levels may be low. If so, you will need to add some fertilizer to correct the deficiency. If calcium and/or magnesium are low, you took care of the problem when you added dolomitic limestone to correct the pH. Chances are your trace element concentrations are fine but if they are not, you will need to correct these. Consider for this organic fertilizers, such as dried blood, fish and bonemeal.

You can broadcast these fertilizers over your soil, organic mulch or mowed vegetation a few days after you add the limestone or you can wait longer if you wish. You can also scratch the fertilizer into the soil with a light raking or water it through the mulch. If possible, add the fertilizers one week prior to planting your garden so that your plants do not lose out on the quickly available part of your organic fertilizer. If you fertilized over mowed vegetation, don't delay on installing the black plastic mulch, otherwise you'll be feeding the mowed vegetation instead of your crops.

If you want to use rock dusts and various organic meals in an unmixed form, feel free to do so. For example, if your soil is nitrogen deficient, you can correct this problem by using leather meal (10-10-0) or dried blood (15-3-0). My suggestion is to use leather meal, because it has a good balance of both quickly and slowly available nitrogen. You can apply it at rates up to 8 pounds (roughly 8 pints) per 1,000 square feet. I suggest you use dried blood at rates of about two-thirds those suggested for leather meal. For sources of these products, see page 165.

Also you can correct phosphorus deficiencies with rock phosphate or bone meal. My suggestion is to use rock phosphate, because bone meal releases phosphate too slowly. You can safely apply rock phosphate at rates of 10 pounds for every 1,000 square feet.

A word of caution is in order. Do not routinely apply any of the recommended fertilizers each year. If you do, you'll probably end up with nutrient imbalances. If you can afford to, get a soil test each year and use the report's suggestions for a fertilizing guideline. In reality, the no-dig gardening method and the use of seaweed extracts and Farmura for foliar feeding during your garden season will help maintain soil fertility. You may only need to add other fertilizers every two or three

The HDRA and Cumulus Organics sell a complete organic fertilizer with an N-P-K ratio of 5:5:5. These suppliers also stock rock potash – for their addresses, see page 165.

years. A few minutes invested in an annual soil sample can save you a lot of money and reward you with the best-ever garden.

Organic Matter Content

Up to now I haven't said anything about organic matter. Your soil report may or may not indicate a problem with organic matter content. If you are starting a new garden in a sodded area or if you are an organic gardener using good practises, you probably have enough organic matter in your soil. Enough organic matter now means you'll have enough later on, too. Remember, as I explained in Chapter 1, no-dig methods conserve organic matter. Essentially, the remains of the plants' root system plus the addition of small amounts of organic matter with the bulb planter or ridger will maintain good levels of organic matter.

But suppose the soil test indicates a need for organic matter. How do we quickly get to the point where our garden requires only low maintenance? We can achieve this by one of two methods. The first method involves a one-time rotavating of organic matter, while the second is a no-dig application of gradually decreasing amounts of organic matter over a few years. The choice is yours, but let's look at the two methods to help you make your decision. Remember, once you reach a decent level, you can very easily maintain organic matter with our no-dig procedures.

Firstly, if you decide to improve the soil in a hurry, the best bet is to hire a rotavator or hire someone who owns one to till the organic matter, using either manure, compost or leaves. If you use fresh manure, you should till it under at least four weeks prior to planting or during the autumn. If you use fresh, moist horse or cow manure, apply anywhere from 25 to roughly 50 pounds per 100 square feet. If you use poultry, rabbit or pig manure, cut the rates in half. If you use manure to raise your organic matter levels, don't forget that it contains nitrogen, phosphorus and potassium and therefore, you'll need less fertilizer, possibly as little as one-third or less the normal amount. To be sure of your needs, have a soil test done after manuring, preferably close to planting time.

You can also apply compost in place of manure. Using finished compost apply it between 1 and 3 inches deep on your soil. Like manure, you should till it under at least four weeks prior to planting activities or in the autumn.

A last alternative for providing organic matter is to use leaves in the autumn. This plan does not allow for any other time frame because the supply is on hand only in the autumn and the leaves will need a while to decompose in the soil. While leaves decompose, they use nitrogen. Plants grown while leaves are decomposing lose out in the nitrogen race and become nitrogen deficient. In addition, some chemicals produced during leaf decomposition don't seem to agree with plants. I suggest you use 2 to 3 inches of leaves sprinkled with some nitrogen-containing fertilizer at the rate of 3 to 5 pounds (3 to 5 pints) for every 100 square feet. Next rotavate the leaves into the soil using your hired tiller or tiller operator. If possible, get a soil test in the spring prior to planting your garden; you must know and correct the nutrient status of your soil after leaf decomposition, if needed.

The second approach to achieving and maintaining organic levels involves the no-dig addition of organic matter only in the vicinity of the plants. This approach gives you efficient returns on your organic matter investment, helps to reduce amounts of material needed and lessen work. In fact, the no-dig garden procedure will eventually produce an even distribution of organic matter that you can maintain quite easily. But for now, let's worry about the immediate shortfall of organic matter.

My choice of organic matter for a quick build-up with no-dig methods is either garden or leafmould, aged and well-rotted manure or commercial dehydrated manure. If you don't have or can't purchase any of these materials, you can substitute moss peat. I do not suggest fresh manure or leaves, since these materials will be applied at planting time. Fresh manure or leaves are not compatible with seedlings and transplants.

The plan is very simple. For transplants make four holes with the bulb planter at the corners of an imaginary 12-inch square that has the transplant at its centre (Figure 28). Fill each of these holes with one of the suggested organic amendments. If you use the moss peat, sprinkle a few teaspoons of limestone over it to correct for acidity. Essentially, you are creating four organic oases for each transplant.

For seeds, make a furrow between every two rows, or a couple in each band or bed, using the ridger (Figure 29) to a depth of around 3 or 4 inches. Now fill the furrow with one of the organic materials. Again, if you use moss peat, cover it with a light dusting of limestone. You can leave the soil ridges or rake the soil over the organic material. If you live in a somewhat dry area, leave the ridges as they will help capture water in the bottom of the furrow. If too much rain is your problem, rake the area level. Essentially, you have created fertile furrows or organic matter strips for your row, band or bed crops.

How long do you continue with this

Figure 28. For a soil low in organic matter, make four holes with the bulb planter as shown, on a 12-inch square. Fill them with organic matter. This procedure is only for the rapid build-up of organic matter. Don't confuse it with the organic oases around transplants. Organic oases differ in that their intent is to maintain organic matter, once the proper level is established. They are usually used one to a transplant, contain organic matter mixed with nutrients and are placed 4 inches away from the transplant.

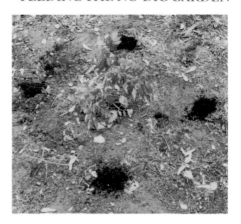

Figure 29. Surround your seed furrows (centre) with furrows or no-dig holes of organic matter if you need to build up organic matter in a hurry.

Figure 30. The easiest way to foliar feed your garden is with a hand-pressurized sprayer.

treatment? It depends on your soil type and the deficiency of the beginning amount of organic matter. The only way to know for sure if you have corrected the problem is to check your next year's soil report. If the report calls for more organic matter, repeat the procedure. If it doesn't, commence with the minimal maintenance procedure for organic matter, which I will cover later in the chapter. Incidentally, leave the root systems of all plants in the soil, except those of root crops. The root systems left in the soil will contribute additional organic matter to the soil. Based on my experience, the build-up of organic matter will most likely take only a few years. Remember, no-dig gardening conserves organic matter and does not burn up organic matter as does the conventional digging of soil.

No-dig Soil Maintenance

Now let's turn to methods of no-dig maintenance of nutrients and organic matter during the garden season. What

The HDRA and Cumulus Organics sell a complete organic fertilizer with an N-P-K ratio of 5:5:5. These suppliers also stock rock potash – for their addresses, see page 165.

we have accomplished so far is to give our seedlings and transplants a great start in the garden race. Like any runner, your plants will need some water and nutrients along the way, if the fast pace is to last.

Foliar Feeding

My mainstay for nutrient supply is foliar feeding with the combined Farmura and seaweed extract described earlier (Figure 30) diluted at the rate of 3 tablespoons to 1 gallon.

To get the most from your foliar feeding, you must get as much of your nutrient supply into the leaves as possible, which depends largely on your spraying technique. Obviously, if the spray does not stay on the leaves, it's not likely to get into the plant. You therefore need a product to help the watery solution stick to the leaves without harming them. I solve the problem by adding four to five drops of liquid soap to each gallon of Farmura and seaweed solution. You can use mild liquids intended for washing either dishes or clothes.

Several other factors also determine how much spray enters the plant. Generally, the smaller the spray droplets, the better. Remember, many of the droplets will enter through pores (stomata) in the leaf, which are quite small, so the best sprayers for applying foliar feeds are those with adjustable nozzles. Make sure you adjust the nozzle for the finest mist-like spray. Also, make sure you spray both the top and bottom of the leaves because both sides of a leaf have stomata. In fact, the bottom often has more stomata than the top. By spraying both leaf sides, you assure a larger number of entry points for the spray.

Spraying time is also important. Stomata start opening with the first light in the morning, the best time to spray, and gradually close in the afternoon. They also close rapidly when the plant is wilting, when it is very hot and when it is windy. Of course, on windy days, much of what you spray on the plant will blow off target anyway, so you would be wasting the spray in terms of foliar nutrition. Also, never knowingly spray prior to rain. The spray must remain on the plant for at least several hours if the feeding is to be effective.

The spraying schedule is yet another important consideration. You don't want to overfeed the plant and be wasteful. On the other hand, a nutrient starvation diet isn't good for the plant either. I usually start my first foliar feeding of transplants two weeks after setting them out. By then the plant has used up the rapid starter solution. With seedlings, I usually wait to foliar feed until three weeks after germination, because by then the nutrients added with the seeds are running low. From that point on throughout the gardening season, I repeat my foliar feeding every three weeks. This schedule need not be exact. If three weeks arrives along with rain, postpone the feeding until the next day. Should it rain within 12 hours after a leaf feeding, repeat the spraying because the rain will have reduced its effectiveness. If you're worrying because you'll be on holiday during the next due feeding, don't. You can either have someone else spray the plants or let it go and do it when you return.

Before I move on to the next topic, I'd like to mention a few things that I have experienced regarding foliar feeding. When you spray, make sure you spray to the point of foliage runoff. Once the leaves start to drip, stop spraying. I find the best results occur when I observe this pattern of spraying. Don't worry about the drops – they will soak into the soil, will help to improve it and nourish the plant through the root system.

Another of my observations concerns insect control. Before I began spraying with the seaweed and Farmura mixture, I had trouble with spider mites on my transplants grown in greenhouses. However, I found little trouble in my garden when I started spraying with the seaweed and Farmura mixture. While the evidence is circumstantial, I like to think it not only feeds the plant but helps in pest control as well.

Supplemental Fertilizer Treatments

Is this seaweed extract and Farmura treatment my entire fertilization approach during the gardening season? Not quite – I do use a bit of extra fertilizer along the way. About once a month I side-dress my vegetables and flowers with a little solid fertilizer, such as blood, fish and bone.

I usually start the first treatment about two weeks after the initial foliar feeding. I sprinkle a light dusting either around individual, large plants or alongside rows with smaller plants (Figure 31 overleaf). For example, I'll sprinkle a circle around tomatoes or aubergines that runs just under the point where the foliage ends (the drip line). I'll run a band alongside a row of

Figure 31. You can side-dress an intensively planted garden with a circular pattern (*top left*) or fertilize rows with a straight-line approach (*left*). You can also fill with organic fertilizer a dibber hole made next to the plant directly in soil (*below left*) or punched through black plastic mulch (*bottom left*).

bean plants or onions. Remember, these bands or circles need only be a dusting and about 1 or 2 inches wide. I then gently water the plant to aid the entry of the fertilizer into the soil.

How do we do this feeding when a mulch covers the garden? If you have a loose organic mulch instead of plain soil, you can still make your circles or bands. Then use your watering can or a light spray from the hose to soak or wash the fertilizer through the mulch so it contacts the soil. If you are using black plastic or paper mulch, with your dibber poke two or three holes around each plant or one hole every 12 inches along the row. Make the holes about 2 inches deep, and fill them with fertilizer. Now gently water these areas to help wash the fertilizer into the soil.

Home-made Dispenser for a Special Boost
There are a few steps you might enjoy trying if you're looking for the super-productive, special plant, such as the marrow that will win a contest or the tomato plants for which you have little room and from which you expect the most. If so, try my hints for these special plants. If you are using transplants for tomatoes, peppers, auber-

gines or marrows, prepare a slightly deeper no-dig hole with the bulb planter. Now sprinkle in a couple of tablespoons of a mixed-nutrient organic fertilizer. Cover it over with about 1 inch of soil, or even better, with compost. Now treat your transplant as described in Chapter 2. Remember to use the organic rapid starter solution before putting the transplant in the hole.

Next, take an empty, rinsed, 1-gallon plastic orange squash bottle and carefully punch several holes from top to bottom on each side with a craft knife, screwdriver or other pointed object. Now cut out the bottom and leave the cap on to prevent quick downward drainage and to afford slow, sideward drainage. Dig a hole large enough to accept the bottle near your special plant or plants. If you have only one plant, place it within 12 to 18 inches of the plant. If you have a group of plants, such as three or four tomatoes or marrows, situate the hole in the middle of the group. Place your bottle, cut bottom up, into the hole so that the top edge is level with the soil line. Push soil around the sides to fill in any gaps. Now you have an in-soil liquid fertilizer dispenser!

About every three weeks, fill the dis-

Figure 32. Super plants, even though given a great start by the special no-dig hole, benefit from a plastic drinks bottle feeder for dispensing organic liquid fertilizers.

penser with your favourite liquid organic fertilizer (Figure 32). I prefer the diluted seaweed and Farmura mixture, but you can use manure, compost, tea or any other water-soluble fertilizer. The fertilizer solution will slowly seep out of the side holes of the bottle and diffuse into the soil and, hence, the root zone of your prize plant. Your reward will be the best-ever, most productive plants. If you're looking for size over productivity, remove most of the young marrows so as to channel nutrients into one or two.

Maintaining the Levels of Organic Matter

Now we'll take a look at maintaining levels of organic matter in your no-dig garden. If course, I am assuming your soil already has a reasonable amount of organic matter either from virtue of your being an organic gardener or from your starting a new garden in a sodded area. As you may recall, losses of organic matter are much more rapid in dug or tilled soil than in no-dig soils. Digging favours the bringing of organic matter to the surface where oxygen-loving surface microorganisms hungrily consume it. No-dig methods keep it protected down below, where the surface dwellers can't get at it. This feature makes maintenance quite easy, since we're not losing much organic matter.

Let's start first with the transplants. Your home-grown or commercial transplants are usually grown in potting compost quite rich in organic matter. If you purchase transplants, be sure they are in organic-rich compost and not in normal soil. Each time you put in a no-dig transplant, you will create an organic-rich island in your soil. By placing transplants in slightly different locations each year, you will gradually increase and spread the organic matter throughout your growing area. When your garden transplants die at the end of the season, do not pull them up, but simply cut the plants off at soil level. The roots left behind will help to increase the organic matter in the soil zone surrounding your original organic-rich no-dig hole. In a few years organic matter will spread throughout your garden soil. Of course you will recycle the removed tops of your finished plants into the compost heap.

A similar situation exists for plants raised directly from seeds outdoors. As you may recall, each furrow received a bottom filling of seedling helper, which you prepared from compost. You might also have used commercial worm castings, as indicated earlier. Being very rich in organic matter, these materials help raise your level of soil organic matter, just as with the transplants. By slightly shifting rows each year, you will spread organic matter. Again, leave the root systems of any finished plants raised directly from seed, except root crops, in the soil. Recycle the tops in the compost heap. Between transplants and seedlings, you'll have an organic-rich soil in no time!

Organic Oases

One other step for maintaining organic levels in your garden remains. Use the bulb planter to make the, by now, familiar organic oases. This step was actually part of the planting method we covered in Chapter 3 and was mentioned more recently in this chapter for accelerated introduction of organic matter. However, one very big difference exists now. This time we will be maintaining, not increasing, the level of organic matter in the soil. Place just one no-dig hole (not four) by each transplant, about 4 inches away. You will be making holes at 12-inch intervals about 4 inches to the right or left of each row. Fill each hole, not with straight organic matter as described for rapid build-up, but with the nutrient-fortified compost recommended as the organic oasis mixture in the section Special Helpers.

There you have it. The maintenance of organic matter is really so simple that it's part of the no-dig planting process. You get the easy planting with no-dig methods and the simultaneous maintenance of organic matter, whether you mulch or not. If you are using loose, organic mulch, just push it aside for the maintenance steps. Plastic or paper mulch poses no problem either, since the bulb planter cuts right through it.

Mulches remind me that we should get to the heart of the no-weed concept next. Let's consider the alternatives to weeding, especially those that don't tire our muscles or make our backs ache.

CHAPTER 5

MULCHING TO SAVE WEEDING AND WATERING

The decision whether or not to mulch is one that you must consider carefully. Although some disadvantages may arise with mulches, the no-weed return you get is quite inviting. The decision of whether or not to mulch really boils down to determining if the joy of not weeding outweighs the disadvantages of mulching. If less work is your primary motivating factor, mulches are the answer.

If you have been involved in gardening for a long time, you probably associate the late Ruth Stout with the popularization of the all-year-round mulching system. Certainly her approach – covering the garden with a deep layer of straw all year long – will give you a no-weed garden. But there are other ways to use mulches that can bring you no-weed status as well. There is even an alternative to mulches that will give you an *almost* weed-free garden. Let's consider your choices.

The Advantages and Disadvantages of Mulch

Firstly, let's examine the case for and against mulches in the garden courtroom. I'm sure none of you will dispute the smothering effect mulches have upon weeds. It's simply amazing how a few inches of organic mulch or a thin layer of plastic or paper mulch beat those weeds. Equally important in my mind is the ability of mulches to conserve soil moisture by acting as a barrier against the evaporation of water by sun and wind. The need for water is less, therefore, the need for work and time associated with watering activity is less as well.

Mulches also have a moderating effect upon soil temperatures. During the hot days of July and August, soil temperatures rise dramatically as the sun beats down on the garden. At night the temperature of the soil plunges. This seesaw of temperature extremes is not beneficial to your garden. Certainly, plants will continue to grow, but many will not do their best. A mulch acts as an insulating barrier, slowing both daytime heating and night-time cooling. Consequently, the soil temperature remains more nearly constant, thus favouring good plant growth.

If you are concerned about aesthetics or dislike rotten vegetables, mulches will please you with another advantage. A mulch in the flower garden prevents mud from splashing onto the flowers during rain or watering. Your flowers are always clean and beautiful. In the same way, mulches keep your vegetables clean and dry and prevent their contact with soil. Chances of ending up with a mouldy tomato or mildewed marrow are quite low.

An organic mulch or plastic/paper mulch offers several advantages as you can see. But the organic mulch offers yet another benefit. Decomposition of the organic mulch releases various nutrients, which rain or applied water slowly wash into the soil. The decaying organic matter at the soil surface also helps gradually to improve the soil structure and the entry or infiltration of water into the soil. Thus, you won't lose much soil to water runoff or wind.

Counteracting the Disadvantages of Mulching

If these advantages of mulching sound great, they are. Still, in all fairness, there are some possible disadvantages to mulching. However, keep in mind that you can work around any of these problems. Firstly, mulches retain soil moisture, a decided advantage during most of the garden season. But there is one time when too much soil moisture can be a problem. During germination too much moisture, especially where organic mulches are in place, can encourage the attack of seedlings by damping off disease. The solution here is really quite simple. You can delay the application of an organic mulch until the seedlings have become well established. At this point the seedlings will have outgrown their susceptibility to damping off. Delayed mulching with organic materials can also solve temperature problems that early mulching causes, as we'll see later. If you want to maintain a permanent organic mulch (à la Ruth Stout), then just push the mulch aside around newly planted seeds and young seedlings.

A second way to solve the excess moisture problem is to use black plastic mulch. While it conserves moisture, its nonorganic nature tends not to encourage damping off. As you will recall, in Chapter 3 we discussed methods for direct planting of seeds or transplants through plastic. The technique for planting seeds left a small, plastic-free zone on either side of the seedlings. Such a zone reduces moisture levels around the seedlings, thus preventing problems of excessive moisture with seeds or seedlings.

Another disadvantage to using mulches is that, while they moderate temperature extremes in the summer (or winter), they can slow soil warming in the spring. The problem is especially noticeable during cold, wet springs and with heavy clay soils. Both of these conditions result in cool soil temperatures. The mulch, since it's an insulator, tends to slow the rate at which the soil is warmed by the sun and rising air temperatures. Even the rapid warming that usually occurs in sandy soils can be slowed by a mulch cover.

So how do we resolve the problem of soil warmth? The old rule of 'don't apply a mulch until the tomatoes blossom' does have some basis in fact. When tomatoes blossom, soil temperatures have exceeded 55°F. Seeds of some warm-season crops, such as beans or marrows, require soil temperatures over 55°F in order to germinate properly. Other warm-season crops, like tomatoes or aubergines, won't set flowers at lower temperatures. You can be sure it's safe to mulch the garden when the tomatoes are in bloom. If the mulch causes the soil to warm more slowly, at this point, it will not be harmful. So, delaying the application of mulch will solve the soil-warming problem. If you have a permanent organic mulch on your garden, you can scrape it aside in areas where you will be planting early seeds or transplants to create localized warm spots where they will do the most good for your seedlings or transplants. To keep down weeds, you can apply your mulch early everywhere except in the immediate area you will be planting.

There's another way to solve the soil-warming problem besides delaying use of organic mulches. Organic mulches retard the warming of spring soil, but plastic mulches do not. In fact, plastic mulches, depending on their colour, actually increase soil temperatures to varying degrees. Black plastic mulches in particular absorb heat and help raise soil temperatures a few degrees.

Clear plastic mulch acts like a greenhouse and also raises soil temperatures several degrees or more. Using clear plastic as a mulch, you can pick sweetcorn two to three weeks earlier than normal. One problem you might have with clear plastics, though, is that they pass light. The greenhouse effect that warms the soil also encourages a fine crop of weeds. Still, there are ways to utilize clear plastic to get the benefits but not the weeds. We'll cover these techniques in Chapter 7.

Some people think the application of mulches is troublesome. I think that probably the main objection arises with mulches that are thin, such as plastic or paper. These mulches *can* be difficult to apply but need not be. Later on I'll show you an easy way to apply plastic mulches that will be secure against the blowing wind.

Mulches coupled with cool, wet spring weather can spell bad news for germinating seeds and tender young transplants. Still, solutions are possible. You can wait out the weather and apply your mulch when warmer, drier weather arrives. If you have an all-year-round organic mulch, push it away from seeds, seedlings and transplants until they have become well established.

If you are using an all-season black plastic mulch, don't worry about the coolness. The black plastic mulch helps to increase soil temperature by a few degrees. Instead you can worry about having too much rain, because the mulch slows evaporation. You may end up with a very soggy, wet soil that is low in air, a condition that favours rotting of seedlings and transplant

roots. To resolve this problem, you must take a few simple steps that will allow the plastic mulch to repel, not retain, water. Instead of immediately punching holes in the plastic to allow water to penetrate to plant roots, delay the punching of holes until the warmer, drier weather appears. This will make the plastic waterproof and will keep the soil drier.

You can take a second step to alleviate excess moisture at the planting sites. If you put in a transplant with the bulb planter, use part of the removed soil plug to create a small, sloping hill around the transplant. This slope helps to reduce drainage into the soil because it channels the water onto the plastic. Later, you can punch holes in the plastic to allow plenty of water to enter for the plants.

Follow the same procedure with seed rows that you cut through the plastic. After you slit the plastic and make your furrow with the ridger, leave the soil in place to hold down the edges of the plastic, as described in Chapter 3. Then build up the seedling row with extra soil or seedling helper to make it higher. Now you will have to recut your furrow, but cut it just deeply enough for the right seed depth. The position of the seeds should be about 1 or 2 inches above the nearby plastic surface. Essentially you will have a mini raised bed adapted to row size. You will get great drainage, thus alleviating the problem of excessive spring rains.

How to Lay Down Organic Mulches
Mulches are inexpensive and are probably one of the best garden investments you can make. I'm sure I need to say little about the familiar organic mulches, since many of you probably already use them. I'll just go over the basics and save most of my words to talk about the easy way to apply plastic

and paper mulches. Remember to apply organic mulches 2 to 4 inches deep.

Many choices exist for those who use organic mulches. Availability, cost, and personal preference will undoubtedly influence your choice. Bark mulches, for example, can be costly, do have a tendency to rob soil nitrogen from crops because of their high carbon-to-nitrogen ratio (see the section on compost in Chapter 4 for an explanation of ratio). Remember to apply nitrogen fertilizer before you put down your bark mulch. If you have composted the bark mulch, you won't need to use fertilizer, because the carbon-to-nitrogen ratio will change for the better during composting. Keep the bark mulch from direct contact with plants to avoid disease problems.

Another organic mulch, moss peat, is expensive and, unlike bark, it's hard to find a cheap supply under any conditions. I personally dislike moss peat as a mulch because it requires a lot of water and time to get wet. Another disadvantage to moss peat is that it dries out during droughts. Once it's dry, it becomes hard and difficult to wet and rain will run off it. It's best to keep moss peat as an organic amendment for growing mixtures and soils where you plan to plant acid-loving shrubs.

Some mulches, in particular sawdust and wood chips, are relatively common and inexpensive, but have some decided drawbacks. Unless you have composted them (and few people do), these woody materials have a very high carbon-to-nitrogen ratio. The high ratio means that these woody materials will steal soil nitrogen away from your plants as they decompose. Therefore, you have to put down some nitrogen fertilizer before you put on the mulch, if you want to avoid depleting your soil. This need for fertilizer translates into extra cost and work. I think sawdust and wood chips are more trouble than they're worth.

Now on to the last category, the organic mulches that I used to use; compost, grass clippings, leaves, straw or hay.

Compost makes an excellent mulch, especially if your soil is low in organic matter. It's one of the few mulches that also acts as a slow-release fertilizer. Water from your hose or from rain leaches out nutrients that microbial activity has converted to soluble forms. By the end of the growing season, the lower part of the compost mulch has become part of the upper soil profile. In a few years, you can have an organic-rich soil without any work.

The problem I faced was that my compost supply was never enough for all the uses I had in mind. You might say that I couldn't get enough of a good thing. I now reserve my compost for making the special fertilizer blends for seedlings and transplants, as I described in the previous chapter. Using it in this way also improves the organic conditions around the plants. The plus is that you need far less compost to take care of the area round or under plants than you need for a mulch covering a much larger area. Still, if you make lots of compost, you might consider using the excess as a mulch.

If you don't recycle your grass clippings to your lawn with a mulching mower, you can use the clippings as a garden mulch. Just don't apply your layer of grass clippings all at once. Do it gradually, because a thick layer of green clippings will heat up and form a dense mat as decay sets in. The mat will restrict the flow of air and water to the soil. Apply the clippings in thin layers and allow each layer to dry and turn brown before you add the next layer. One bonus in using grass clippings is that they contain nitrogen, which will eventually leach into your soil, thus slowly fertilizing your plants.

You can also use leaves as a mulch, as long as you're aware of a couple of problems that exist. Firstly, leaves are available mostly in the autumn. Such timing is great for winter mulches or the leaf compost heap but is bad for a summer mulch. To get around this problem, you can pile the leaves until next year, but if you're going to go to that trouble, why not prepare a leaf compost as I described in Chapter 4? The other problem is that leaves can mat into a soggy mess. To overcome the matting problem, you can mix the leaves with fluffy materials, such as hay or straw, or you can shred the leaves. Leaves do release some nutrients during decomposition as a mulch, but I prefer using them to make leaf compost.

Straw and hay all make reasonable mulches. You can sometimes buy spoiled hay at a modest price. The going rate for unspoiled hay argues against their use as mulches; however, if you find a bargain, these mulches are great for vegetables and the year-round mulching system popularized by Ruth Stout. As a flower-garden mulch though, hay is unattractive. Also, hay often carries large numbers of weed seeds. If you remove the mulch or turn it under, look out – you'll probably find that you have a luxurious crop of mixed weeds. Slugs seem to love this mulch, too.

Now I think you are ready for my mulching system that gives you a no-weed garden. As they once said in the movie *The Graduate,* 'The future is in plastics.'

The No-weed Mulching System

My solution to weeds is the use of a semipermanent to permanent mulch. In one sense my system may remind you of Ruth Stout's approach, but a big difference between my way and her way

concerns the choice of mulching materials. I recommend using black plastic rather than an organic mulch. If you object to black plastic as unnatural, I do have another option for you. A horticultural brown, heavy paper mulch is now available in rolls like black plastic (for suppliers of Hortopaper, see page 165). A second difference between Ruth Stout's method and my own is that my mulch can be either permanent or removable; Ruth Stout's mulch is permanent. A last point is the ease with which you can adapt black plastic to no-dig methods.

Tools and Materials

One tool is a must for the easy installation of black plastic mulch: the already familiar ridger. The second tool, the garden straightline, is optional. Can you make a straight line by eye? If not, you'll need the garden straightline. With these tools you can easily cover your garden with plastic or paper mulch in less than one morning or afternoon. Only a few hours of work will save several times as many hours of weeding and watering. You will be able to secure the plastic mulch tightly with my method. I know, since my mulches have survived heavy winds and even a tropical storm.

Make sure you have your mulch on hand before you begin. Black polythene can be bought in various sizes and thicknesses. Small quantities of this material are rather expensive to buy, so it is a good idea to buy a large roll and share it with someone else. The thickness you choose depends on exactly how you are going to use it: thin polythene is suitable for one season while you can reuse the thicker gauge.

How to Lay Down Plastic Mulches

Now let me tell you about my easy, quick, yet secure way to apply plastic

Figure 33. The first step in laying plastic mulch is to prepare one of the long side trenches with the ridger and straightline (*above left*). Next, make one of the shorter trenches at right angles. Complete the remaining trenches. Don't forget to put down the limestone, if you need it (*above right*).

mulch. First take your ridger and make one furrow roughly 3 inches deep to whatever length your plastic mulch requires. For the purpose of example, we'll assume we are working with a 4-foot-wide roll of plastic. I suggest you use the straightline helper described in Chapter 1 to assure that the furrow is straight (Figure 33). Next, make a second furrow at a right angle to either end of the first furrow. Don't make the

furrow 4 feet wide; instead make it about 40 inches wide, so that you can cover a 4-inch overhang on each side when you refill the furrow trench. Next, make the long furrow for the other side of the plastic mulch. Then complete the last short side. You now have a rectangular furrow outline ready to receive the plastic mulch.

Unroll a short bit of the roll of plastic and place about 4 inches in the short

Figure 34. Place the leading edge of the roll of black plastic in one of the short end trenches (*above left*). Use your foot or hoe to kick in the soil so that the trench is filled and the edge of the plastic is covered. Firmly press the soil with your foot to lock in the plastic. Unroll the plastic and continue to fill and press at the sides until all sides are done (*above right*).

furrow. Cover the plastic over with the soil on the outside ridge of the furrow (Figure 34). Now use your foot to press the soil down, thus locking in the short edge of the plastic mulch. Unroll the entire length of the plastic, and cut across the width at the other end. Don't forget to leave about 4 inches extra for burial. Work your way around the furrow line, pushing soil over the plastic edge with your hand. Using your other hand, pull gently to put a little tension on the plastic as you fill over the edges. If you leave the plastic too loose, blowing wind will make the plastic flap. Firm the soil around the edges of the plastic with your foot. You now have a securely installed sheet of black plastic. You can apply a paper mulch in the same manner (Figure 35).

One timesaving trick is to use your foot to mark off the 40-inch width of the bed. My shoe is roughly 11 inches long, so I know the correct width is just about equal to three and three-quarters times my shoe. To measure the width I just pace off with my shoes end-to-end and insert the straightline peg at the appropriate place.

Using this simple technique, you can mulch a good-sized garden in less than one morning or afternoon. Just make sure you don't do it on a windy day. The small amount of time you spend mulching is really a great investment when you consider the time and effort you will save throughout the season on weeding and watering. Yields will be a little earlier, because of the warming effect of the black plastic, and they'll be a little greater, too, because of less competition from weeds.

I'd like to offer a few helpful observations at this time. In some spots you will probably have to deal with the edge of the lawn. Here the ridger doesn't work as well. You throw the soil on the grass and have trouble recovering it. If you move the ridger inwards to avoid the problem, you leave an area for grass invasion. I do, however, have an answer to the problem. Sink a square-bladed

Figure 35. A paper mulch is shown on the left and black plastic on the right.

Figure 36. With grassy areas or for another installation method, use a square-edge spade to make a slit instead of a furrow trench (*top right*). Use your heel to close the slit after the plastic is pushed in with a flat, thin piece of wood. The completed mulch will smother the turf and leave rich organic matter in its place. A short-term installation method is to pin the plastic to the soil with U-shaped pins made from coat hangers (*bottom right*). Two U-shaped pins can be made by cutting the coat hanger in half and cutting off the hook.

spade or lawn edger about 4 inches into the soil. Pull the spade or edger towards yourself, making a cut that slants outwards (Figure 36). Continue cutting the slit to the correct length. Tuck the plastic edge into the slit. Now press the soil down and inwards on an angle with your foot from the slanted side of the slit. The pressure will close the slit, sealing the plastic firmly into the soil. Incidentally, you can use this technique of applying black plastic mulch in place of the furrow method, if you like it better. An alternative to making furrows or slits in the soil is to pin the black plastic to the soil with U-shaped pins made from wire coat hangers.

How close together you can place the black plastic with these techniques depends on what you want. With the ridger method, the shortest spacing between separate sheets is about 1 foot. Spacing that is any closer will not lock the sheets in place as securely. With the spade-slit method, you can butt sheets to within a few inches of each other. I like to leave about 12 to 15 inches between sheets. These uncovered areas make great pathways and help me to stay off the plastic, thus preventing soil compaction. Remember, the plastic sheets are roughly 4 feet across, a width that makes them highly adaptable to either band or bed planting. The uncovered areas between sheets afford you a nice, comfortable reach to the middle of the planting area. If these uncovered areas tend to become weedy, just mulch them with some hay or grass clippings or any organic mulch of your choice, Scrap wood boards can also be used to provide both weed control and a durable, narrow pathway.

I'll bet you have a lot of questions concerning the application of black plastic mulch. Let me try to answer them. First, you may be wondering when to apply the mulch. If you are applying plastic mulch for the first time, the earlier you apply it, the better. Remember, black plastic mulch has a slight heating effect, so you won't have to worry about slowing down soil warming if the mulch is laid early. The early application gets the jump on weeds and also fits more comfortably into your gardening schedule. It's difficult to plant and mulch at the same time. If you are late with your mulch and the weeds beat you to the garden, mow them down with a lawn mower if they are more than 2 or 3 inches high. Then just lay your mulch over the stubble. I usually apply my mulch sometime after I've planted my peas but before I plant onions and potatoes. Weeds have usually sprouted by then, but they are small and easy to cover. If you are replacing some black plastic mulch from a previous year, your main concern should be to replace it before the time you'll be ready to set your plants or seeds through it.

A reminder is in order here. If your soil requires pH adjustment with either limestone or sulphur, put the limestone or sulphur down before you apply your plastic mulch. If your soil is badly in need of nutrients, you can apply your organic fertilizers about one week after the pH adjustment and then lay your black plastic. Otherwise don't worry about fertilizing before mulching. You can apply fertilizer directly in the no-dig hole or furrow, or by using foliar spray, as I discussed in Chapter 4. You can also add organic matter to your soil after the mulch is down. This procedure, too, was covered in the preceding chapter.

What to Mulch with Black Plastic

Another concern you may have is what you can mulch with black plastic. My experience is that you can mulch just about anything. A few exceptions in my garden include peas, carrots, onions and sweetcorn. I do use black plastic mulch with the majority of my vegetables and flowers. It also works extremely well with strawberries. Paper mulch works equally well. Frankly, my experience with plastic mulch has been excellent. Don't hesitate to try out plastic mulches, even with crops the experts say don't work with mulches. For example, mulches and peppers supposedly do not mix well, but I planted my best pepper crop to date through black plastic. I think the early warming of the soil by the plastic got my peppers up and running well.

Keep another factor in mind. Although we'll cover it later in Chapter 7, it deserves a brief and certainly appropriate mention here. Black plastic has a moderate warming effect upon soil temperature. A cloche also warms the soil but it especially raises the air temperature around plants. When you combine a cloche over black plastic, you essentially create a time change in the protected area, that is, you advance your cloched area roughly two or three weeks into the future. You improve frost protection and provide an earlier harvest by using the cloche/black plastic combination rather than a cloche alone.

How Long to Use Black Plastic

Before I leave the subject of black plastic mulch, let's discuss one last point. How long do you leave the plastic mulch in your garden? That's a good question with several possible answers. One answer is to leave the mulch in place until it deteriorates. How long that turns out to be depends on the mulch's thickness and weather conditions. In my garden, the time works out to be about two years, after which I have to replace the plastic.

Another answer is to move the plastic annually at the end of the gardening season. If you opt for this approach, don't remove the plastic at the end of the gardening season. Instead, let it sit through the winter and remove it early the following spring as you replace it. This precaution prevents any ungerminated weed seeds from sprouting in the autumn or early spring.

The last option concerning when to remove the plastic involves using the black plastic for a few years and then not using it ever again. I discovered this option as a consequence of crop rotation. Each year I rotate my vegetables to keep diseases at bay. Since I grew a few vegetables without using plastic mulch, every few years I exposed small parts of my garden. These exposed sections remained weed free.

After some thought, I found the answer. It's in the combination of no-dig soil practices and the black plastic. Let me explain. You may recall from Chapter 1 that one advantage of using no-dig techniques is that you grow far fewer weeds as compared to a garden that's dug the conventional way. When soil is dug, deeply buried weed seeds are brought to the surface. These new soldiers replace the weeds that you fought so vigorously against the preceding year. With no-dig handling of the soil,

you have only those weed seeds near the surface with which to contend. If you wipe out those surface pests, you win the war, because there will be no replacements. At this point the black plastic mulch takes over.

When I first used the black plastic in my no-dig garden, I recalled that a large number of weeds had germinated early in the spring. The weed seedlings were quite small, though, and I just covered them over with the plastic mulch. The black plastic quickly killed the weeds and deeper weed seed reinforcements could not replace them because I was using no-dig practices. When I uncovered the soil (Figure 37), it was free of weeds and it stayed relatively weed-free during the growing season. The only weeds to appear after I removed the mulch were those that had a late spring germination time. These few weeds had not yet germinated when I applied the plastic, so they survived in the dormant stage. A few swipes with the Swiss reciprocating hoe wiped out the last survivors.

The conclusion is that you can go from a seriously weedy garden to a weed-free garden through the temporary use of black plastic mulch. The only other requirement is to use no-dig methods to keep the deeper weed seeds underground where they can't cause

Figure 37. Note the weed-free appearance of the soil after one year under black plastic. The nice thing is that the soil will stay relatively weed-free, even if you leave the mulch off now, so long as you use no-dig methods.

you any harm. Therefore, you may opt to stop using black plastic mulch after a year or two, if weed control was your only interest. Before you stop, though, you might want to reread the earlier part of this chapter. Other advantages of mulches, such as water conservation, might offer enough reasons for continuing the use of plastic or other mulches.

No-weed Gardening Without Mulch

I suppose a few of you readers are saying that you can get from a weedy to a no-weed garden without using a mulch as long as you use no-dig practices. Well, you are correct, but you will have to weed your garden for one growing season. The surface weed seeds will germinate in the early spring and because the mulch won't be there to smother them, you will have to wipe them out yourself. Show no mercy, as any survivors that go to seed will haunt you next year. Keep the nearby area weed free through mowing so that no wind-blown seeds get into your garden. If you are thorough, you will have no weeds the next year, because the no dig approach to gardening will prevent the exposure of deeply buried weed seeds the following year. If you use this approach, though, you will have more work than with a mulch.

If you want to garden without mulching, there are three key points that, if followed, will make your one-year weed battle easier. The key points are to use the most efficient weed remover, to adopt a ruthless weeding schedule (for weeds, not yourself) and to cultivate the soil to the right depth.

Efficient Weed Removal

The best weeder, as I explained in Chapter 1, is the Swiss reciprocating hoe. Its flow-through design, swivel action, and double-sided cutting edge make it easy to cut weeds just below the soil surface on both the push and pull strokes. You can, with proper scheduling, cut the need for tools to the bare minimum. The old adage 'The early bird gets the worm', could be paraphrased to say 'The early weeder wins the race'. Weeds are off and running early in the garden season. They may look small next to your peas or lettuce, but their root systems are large and are already stealing nutrients so that your crop yield will be less. Knock off those early weed seedlings on those cool spring days. The reciprocating hoe will make short work of them and save you a lot of work later.

A second trick for controlling weeds is to weed around seeds or transplants about four or five days after the initial sowing or planting. Although you may not see any weed seedlings, the weed seeds have germinated, because of the soil activity and watering associated with planting crops. Even no-dig transplanting holes and furrows disturb the soil a little. And, of course, soil disturbance is far worse with conventional digging. A quick swipe with your reciprocating hoe about 1 or 2 inches below the soil surface nips those weeds right in the bud, so to speak. Recently germinated weeds are very susceptible to the breakage and drying activity that cultivation with a hoe causes.

Weeding Schedule

Your next step to making your one-year weed battle easier is to settle into a regular weeding schedule. Spend 10 or 15 minutes once a week knocking off any weeds that have the audacity to invade your garden. If you plan on taking more than two weeks of summer holiday, hire a substitute weeder. Better yet, if you take extended summer holidays away from home, you should mulch your garden.

Don't ever let any weed go to seed. Some of those prolific weeds can set seed, if conditions are good, within six weeks of sprouting. Remember in Chapter 1 when we discussed the huge number of seeds an individual weed plant could set? If you miss a few, you could find your entire garden reseeded. This seed-setting profligacy accounts for the observation by Mark Kane, in the June 1982 issue of *Organic Gardening,* that removing 90 per cent of the weeds from a garden plot reduced the subsequent yield of weed seeds by only 10 per cent. The survivors had less competition and their already prolific seed production exploded by several factors.

This seed factor accounts for the next bit of advice. Weed your garden until frost, even if the crops have stopped bearing. Weeds won't stop setting seeds early, they go on until the freeze. If you stop weeding, you will have undone all your work for the next year. The surviving weeds will sow their seeds of destruction, which even no-dig methods won't stop, because these new seeds will be on the soil surface. If you weed late in the season, you'll also knock out any weeds that winter over as small plants. Remember, the weed war is grim. Show no quarter and leave no survivors.

Cultivation Depth

The third key point in making your weed battle easier involves the cultivation depth. You want to rid your garden of all those weeds, but you don't want to bring deeper seeds upwards where they can germinate. How deep is this zone of weed seed activation? My own experience says that you shouldn't cultivate deeper than 2 inches under any circumstances. I get good results when I cultivate anywhere from 1 to 2 inches deep with my Swiss reciprocating hoe. This depth of cultivation wipes out the weeds from near surface seeds but doesn't bring up the more deeply buried ones. Interestingly, gardener Peter Young experimented with depth of cultivation and weed control, and he arrived at the same conclusion, which he reported in the May 1983 issue of *Organic Gardening.*

If you keep these three key points in mind, you can wipe out your weeds in one season, but you must be diligent or you will have wasted all of your time and effort. The early weeding will knock out the majority of the weeds and the later weeding will be quick and easy.

As an aside, I'd also like to mention that bed, broad row, or band planting will also cut weed work. Wherever you practise intensive gardening, the closer spacing of crops produces shade underneath them and increased competition for soil nutrients. This combined with one-two punch knocks the wind right out of the weeds, making their start-up much harder.

The only downfall to the no-weed gardening approach without the use of mulch concerns perennial weeds. If weeds have overrun your garden, you won't be able to get away without using mulch. In a case like this, discretion is the better part of valour – go for the mulch and save yourself a lot of trouble.

CHAPTER 6
BEATING PESTS AND DISEASES

Organic methods of insect control are a good alternative to chemical methods, but some pests and diseases may elude control by organic approach. Because of my desire for safe vegetables and a clean environment for my family, I used organic methods for pest control. I took some produce losses and accepted them as the price I had to pay for safe pest control. However, I didn't like the losses and resolved to beat the pests that were causing me problems.

One day a few years ago, I came across the answer to safe pest control while reading a magazine article on the use of polypropylene fleece as a cloche (for supplier see page 165).

I found the use of the fleece as a cloche fascinating. Its light weight meant that it didn't need supports to hold it above the plants. You just draped it over the plants loosely and the growing plant adjusted the height. The porous nature of the fleece cloche allowed rain to penetrate it and also permitted air circulation, so I didn't have to provide ventilation, either. Bill and I decided to try this amazing cloche. We found extended harvests, improved yields and pest protection. In this chapter I'd like to take a closer look at this interesting material as it relates to pest protection.

Polypropylene Fleece Pest Protection
By now you are probably curious about the fleece, so examine it in the photographs in this chapter. Some of you might say that it looks familiar. Fabric shops sell a very similar product as interfacing for the tailoring of clothes. You can find bolts of interfacing in various widths and you could probably use it in the garden, except for the fact that interfacing is heavier than the fleece intended for garden use.

Fleece is white, porous and very light in weight. The width is ideal for making cloches over garden beds and wide rows and light can penetrate, so plants can grow under the material. In fact, I found that plants grew under the covering better than I had expected. It appeared to me that the reflection of light under the fleece allowed for its very efficient use, making the light received almost as effective as normal sun with uncovered crops. Although the pores in the fleece allow light, air and water to enter, they are too small for insect entry, so you have a carefee, safe form of plant protection with fleece.

How you install the fleece depends upon its intended use. Remember, you can use it for insect and disease protection, as a cloche, or both.

Installing a Fleece Cloche
Let's consider the use of the fleece as a cloche for insect and disease protection. For example, suppose you want to get aubergines off to a quick start but want to protect them from flea beetles (insects that eat hundreds of holes in plant

leaves and carry bacterial and viral diseases that eventually kill the plant). In a situation such as this, I suggest using black plastic mulch and a fleece cloche. Install your black plastic, using either the ridger or a square-edged spade to prepare the trench for the plastic. After you place the black plastic in the furrow or widened slit, don't cover the furrow or close the slit. Instead, slide about 4 inches of fleece right over the plastic, then close up the area with soil and foot pressure. You can also pin the plastic and fleece together to the soil with U-shaped pins made from coat hangers (Figure 38). This step gives you an almost 4-foot-wide, weed-free base covered by roughly 5 feet of fleece. The fleece will expand upwards as the growing plants take up the slack. When the plants become too tall to grow straight under the cloche or the temperatures inside the cloche become too warm for plant comfort, remove the fleece. Fold it up and store it, because you will be able to reuse it later.

Although my example involved transplants, you can also cover seeds with the fleece. Using the fleece over bare soil, you can successfully grow crops such as lettuce and peas with earlier-than-normal, direct seeding. While the seeds are germinating, the fleece protects them against insect damage.

You can also use the fleece over seeds to get what I call a thermal, protective seed blanket that lets you get earlier seed germination while protecting the seeds from birds. To install the blanket, prepare the furrow or slit as for black plastic, then put the fleece in the furrow or slit, cover it with soil and press the slit closed with your foot. Just leave a little slack, because you will only need to allow sufficient room for seedling growth for a few weeks.

You can, however, extend the width to almost 5 feet if you make your seed furrows deeper than normal. After you plant your seeds at the furrow's bottom, only partially fill the furrow with soil. For example, with sweetcorn, make a 6-inch-deep furrow and cover the seeds with the usual 1 inch of soil. This approach leaves 5 inches of furrow headroom before the sweetcorn plant

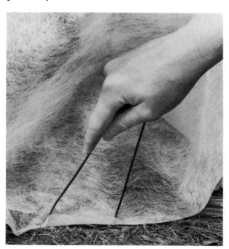 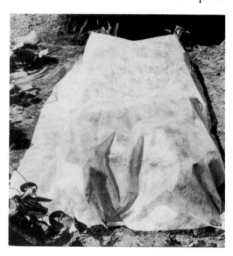

Figure 38. The fleece barrier and black plastic together can be pinned into the soil by wire coat hanger U-shaped pins (*above left*). This combined cloche and protector can give plants a head start, while keeping pests away (*above right*).

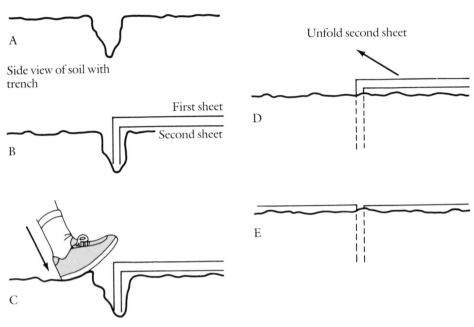

A

Side view of soil with trench

First sheet

Second sheet

B

C

Unfold second sheet

D

E

Figure 39. Larger areas can be blanketed by joining the edges of two sheets of fleece in a soil trench (A). Put the two edges in, fold one sheet over the other (B), foot-seal the trench (C), and unfold the second sheet (D, E).

encounters the taut fleece blanket overhead. You can gain even more headroom by anchoring the fleece with coat hanger U-shaped pins instead of trenches.

Suppose you want to blanket a larger area than the width of the fleece allows. Prepare the usual slits or furrows for one width of fleece but join two widths of the fleece at the same opening (Figure 39). Then prepare the furrow or slit to finish the installation of the second sheet. Can we adapt this protection using the fleece to our wood-sided mini-hills (see Chapter 3), where we want an early but protected start for marrows? Yes, we can. One approach is

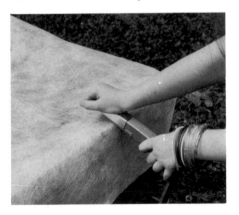

Figure 40. A fleece pest protector can be stapled or tacked easily onto the frame of a mini-hill.

just to tack or staple the fleece edges to the top of the wood frame (Figure 40), being sure to leave enough slack to allow some plant growth. You can also seal the edges of the fleece with soil at the outer edges between the wood and soil in the mini-hill.

Late-Season Plant Protection

Suppose you want to use the fleece for insect or disease protection with existing plants later in the season. For example, you might want to protect summer cabbage from caterpillars, strawberries from birds or carrots from carrot root fly. You can tackle these insect problems, or any other pest attack, with one simple step: cover the plants with the fleece before the pests appear. The HDRA publish two very useful booklets entitled *Vegetable Pest and Disease Control* and *Fruit Pest and Disease Control the Organic Way* available from them (for their address, see page 165).

At the first sign of the pest or, even better, just before, cover the plants with the fleece. You can cover plants in several ways, depending on whether the plants are growing in rows, bands or beds. First, inspect the plants to make sure no insects are present. If you find insects, get rid of them with the organic remedies recommended later in this chapter. These insects, if covered over, would lead a sheltered life with good meals. If you protect your plants against specific pests before or close to when they appear, you will find few or no pests when you make your plant inspection.

Next drape the fleece over the plants you want to cover, whether they are in rows, beds or bands. To secure the fleece, pin it into the soil with U-shaped wires. You can use any sturdy wire that you can bend into a U- or V-shape. Another possibility is to cut a coat hanger with a wire cutter. Make sure the wire pin is long enough to securely lock into the soil. A pin 5 to 6 inches long is usually fine. As you pin the fleece down (Figure 41), make sure you leave enough slack for the plant to grow during the protection period. You can place the pins at 2- to 3-foot intervals. The reason I suggest using pins to secure the fleece rather than using the trench method is because we are dealing with established plants and don't want to risk causing root damage by digging trenches.

Another way to protect large, individual plants, such as tomatoes, is to make a fleece bag. Drape the fleece over each plant, and gather the edges at the base of the plant. Secure the edges together with either string or a wire

Figure 41. Later in the season you can protect a group of existing plants from insects by pinning the fleece barrier over plants.

twist tie. Don't tie the string too tightly as you don't want to damage the stem. Essentially, you have made a fleece pest bag for each plant (Figure 42).

Using the various forms of the fleece protection that I discussed, you can protect seedlings, transplants or established plants from most insects and several diseases. Although the fleece barriers offer protection from any insect above the ground, they can't protect plants from a few soil dwellers like the cutworm because the insects lay their eggs too early for you to stop them. However, you can stop root maggots, because flying insects lay root maggot eggs during the garden season. You can also prevent insect-transmitted diseases such as cucumber wilt or various aphid- or leafhopper-carried viruses with a fleece barrier. Chapters 8 and 9 give specific recommendations for controling pests on crops.

When to Apply and Remove the Fleece Barriers

Are these barriers a temporary or all-season-long measure? The answer is mostly temporary, that is, only while the pest is active. Your experience will give you a rough idea of how long you should protect your crops with the fleece. If you notice that the pest has disappeared for a few days, you can remove the covers. Chapter 8 and 9 provide the covering time lengths for the individual crops, for the pests I know.

Long-term use of fleece barriers can interfere with pollination in some plants. Remember, these barriers keep all insects, including honeybees away from the plants. Any crop requiring pollination by honeybees, therefore, will not set fruit if the barrier is present at flowering time. The picture is not as bleak as it may appear, though. Firstly, we don't harvest all of our crops for fruit. Some crops are leaf crops, such as cabbage, lettuce and spinach. Some plants are root crops, such as beetroot, carrots, onions, radishes and turnips. Still other crops are flower crops, such as broccoli and cauliflower. The lack of pollen transported by honeybees to the plants' flowers therefore poses no threat to these crops.

Does the problem, then, occur with all fruit-bearing crops? Not really. Some fruit-bearing crops pollinate themselves and don't need insects to perform the job for them. Crops such as tomatoes and peppers set fruit with the help of the wind, which carries the needed pollen. As a matter of fact, it is possible to use the fleece for protection for peppers even during the time of flowering, because the wind will flow through the

Figure 42. Larger plants can be put into their own individual fleece bags.

fleece and move pollen around.

The problem actually occurs only with bee-pollinated plants. You can't completely cover such plants with a fleece barrier at flowering time, because you will interfere with bees travelling to the plant's flowers. If the fleece barriers are present, you must remove them. Although not being able to keep the barriers on the plants at flowering time seems to be a serious problem, it really is not.

Some pests cause trouble only before or after flowering time; for instance, flea beetles heavily attack aubergines right before flowering and adult aubergine maggots lay eggs on the young, developing fruit. If you cover the plant with the fleece before and after the initial burst of flowering, you will eliminate the pest problem. Unfortunately, you may also lose some of the later-setting fruit, but you can avoid this problem as well.

To get all the aubergines possible, you can pollinate the flowers yourself. Touch a flower with a soft, camel hair paint brush, then remove the brush and inspect it for a kind of yellow dust, or pollen grains. If pollen is present, twirl the brush around the flower, repeating the process with each flower on the plant.

Essentially, the fleece barrier and pollination can be compatible. Most plants pose no conflict either because their crops don't involve fruit, they don't need bees for pollination, or the pests that affect them aren't present during flowering time. You can easily resolve the problems with the few plants where pests, flowers and bees all coincide. I will point out these special problems and solutions in the sections on the individual vegetables in Chapter 8.

Home-made Insect Traps

Sometimes we can turn the insects' de-sire for food into a trap. Your garden can become a deadly trap for certain insects and yet not be a hazard to you, your family or beneficial insects. We can accomplish this simply by making the trap attractive to the pest insect.

Your vegetables and flowers, because of the colour of their foliage, attract certain insects. Their eyes key in on the reflected colours of the leaf, essentially yellow mixed with green. If you use this fact about insects to your advantage, you can make a sure-fire trap for them by simply adding a sticky substance to a material of the proper colour.

In years past, I made my own sticky, yellow traps by painting cardboard yellow and then applying a sticky substance to it. I eventually tired of painting, so I decided to buy yellow plastic corrugated cardboard instead (for suppliers see page 165). My labour went down, but the price of materials went up.

Finally, my no-dig partner, Bill, came up with an ingenious solution for recycling the yellow card for reuse. The secret to his recycling method involves using plastic freezer bags. Any size of clear plastic bag is acceptable, but I prefer to use the thin, inexpensive type that is about 11 by 14 inches in size. You can even use the plastic bags in which shirts come. Cut your yellow cardboard so that you can slide it inside the bag. Then coat the plastic bag with a sticky material, such as Trappit (for suppliers see page 165), petroleum jelly or double-sided tape. When your sticky substance becomes covered with bugs, simply slide off the plastic bag and discard it. Put on a new bag and coating and you're back in business, using the same piece of cardboard. If you prefer not to bother with the plastic bags and sticky coating, you can buy ready-made sticky cards.

Installing Home-made Insect Traps

There are several methods you can use

to install your insect traps in the garden. You can staple them onto stakes that you push into the ground, or you can hang them by strings. If you are using the former method, staple the yellow cardboard to the wood stake, then slide the plastic bag over the staked cardboard from the top. If you have a lot of trouble with wind, you can staple shut the open end of the bag. For the wood stakes I use thin wood strips. The thin wood allows me simply to staple the yellow cardboard right to the wood stake.

Another alternative for installing insect traps is to slide the yellow cardboard into the plastic bag with the open end of the bag on top, then staple string to the top of the bag. You can also staple the bag closed, but don't staple the bag to the cardboard because this will make recycling difficult. Tie the trap to a stake, such as a tomato plant stake, and you've got a suspended insect trap. Where vine crops are being grown on a fence or trellis, you can tie the traps to the netting, trellis, or fence that you are using as the garden's supports. You can also tie the traps to a string suspended between two poles, forming a sort of clothesline for insect traps.

When to Install Traps

At this point you may be wondering when to place your traps in your garden. The solution is quite simple. Watch your plants very closely and carefully for any signs of insects. As soon as you see any, install the traps. You will want to head off any and all pests before their numbers get too high, because high numbers of pests mean more traps will be needed and more damage will be done to your crops before you can get the pests under control. In particular, watch your tomato and marrow plants for whiteflies and your peas, cabbage and broccoli for aphids. These insects are the early arrivals — they most com-

monly appear on the early crops I just mentioned. Be especially sure that you check the undersides of the plant leaves for insects as well. After a period of time you will also want to watch the tips of roses and the undersides of marrow leaves for aphids. These sites seem to be the first attack zone of aphids if they haven't arrived with the earlier crops. Be sure you make your plant inspections frequently and early, because the sooner you get your insect traps in place, the sooner you will do away with your garden pests.

How Many Traps to Use

You may be wondering how far apart to place these sticky cards and how many you need for your garden. There is no simple answer, because the number of cards you need really depends on how bad the whitefly infestation is and how big your card is. With an 11-by-14 inch card, use one card for about every 10 square feet you want to protect from whiteflies and aphids. A larger or smaller card will increase or decrease, respectively, the protected area. Keep track of the card in terms of the number of whiteflies you find stuck to it. If the card becomes saturated with whiteflies in less than one week go to two cards per 10 square feet. Should one card go for a week or longer, great. If cards last two weeks or longer, cut down the number of sticky cards when you replace them.

The Quickie Method

Bill and I have one last suggestion. Should you wish, you can trap whiteflies quite rapidly, a point that might come in handy if you didn't notice the whiteflies until a large number were present. The secret to our technique lies in disturbance. Generally whiteflies fly off a plant infrequently, but if you disturb the plant, you get a cloud of 'flying dandruff'. Our idea is to cause whitefly flight from one side of the plant while having the sticky traps located on the other side.

To get rid of the whiteflies, Bill and I place two sharpened stakes at each end of a group of plants, whether rows, bands or bed. Next we run a taut cord between the two stakes, like a clothesline, and tie one sticky card every 3 feet along the line. Then one of us gets on the opposite side of the plants and directs a fine spray of water at the undersides of the leaves (Figure 43). To achieve a fine spray you can use a spray mister, an adjustable nozzle adjusted down to a fine spray, preferably on a curved hose extension. If you don't have the extension, don't worry – spraying the tops of leaves gets the whiteflies moving but just takes a little longer. In short order you capture the cloud of whiteflies on your sticky traps and you've solved your problem. We recommend using our technique twice a week.

Acceptable Sprays for Pest Protection
While the fleece barrier and sticky cards will solve most of your pest problems, you may wish to use an occasional insect spray. Perhaps you have only a few pests and don't wish to bother with either the fleece barrier or sticky card.

Maybe a pest has got completely out of hand and you want rapid control. What you need is a safe but reliable spray.

Soap Spray
One spray that Bill and I like is a soap spray. Soap sprays are gentle on beneficial insects, bees and birds. Based upon personal results in my garden, I like Savona Insecticidal Soap, which controls aphids, earwigs, fungus gnats, leafhoppers, mealybugs, scales, spider mites, thrips, and whitefly. This spray also has approval for use on vegetables and fruits, such as beans, broccoli, Brussels sprouts, cabbages, cucumbers, aubergines, peas, peppers, marrows and tomatoes. You can use it right up to the day of harvest. The soap spray is also useful on flowers, shrubs, ornamental trees and fruit or nut trees. You can even use it on house plants indoors and in the greenhouse.

Pyrethrum
Another favourite spray is pyrethrum. You can buy it in either its pure state or with piperonyl butoxide, which enhances its effect.

Pyrethrum controls a number of insects, such as aphids, thrips, flea beetles, leafhoppers, sawfly, weevils and capsids. Pyrethrum is safe, and you can use it up to the day of harvest.

Figure 43. Yellow cards 'hung on the line' trap whiteflies as they try to leave these marrow plants in a hurry when the water spray disturbs the leaves.

Derris

Derris is another natural organic insect-icide that I find valuable. You can use derris on a large number of edible plants and ornamentals up to one day before harvest. Derris eliminates aphids, cater-pillars, weevils, flea beetles, turnip fly, raspberry beetle and apple sawfly. You can also buy a combination product containing both pyrethrum and derris from the HDRA (for their address, see page 165).

While these organic insecticides are not harmful to the environment, you should still be respectful of them. Do only as the label says in terms of dilu-tion, spray schedules, harvest time, dis-posal and any other precautions. Don't breathe the spray and don't spray when it is windy, over 80°F (can harm plants) or going to rain in 24 hours or less. Always wash your hands well when you have finished spraying and rinsing your sprayer. If you spill any spray on your clothes, remove the clothes, wash the area of contact and wash the clothes.

The Bottom Line

Now let's look at the bottom line for pest control in your garden. Your first line of defence should be to use the fleece insect barier and the sticky, yel-low traps. Most times these methods will solve your pest problem. If you aren't able to control some pests or you suddenly discover a serious infestation of a pest, you can escalate the battle against insects by using the safest effec-tive spray, the soap spray. The last resort is to use either pyrethrum or derris or combine the two. Even going to level three, derris and pyrethrum is preferable to resorting to the use of chemical insecticides around your garden.

More Ways to Outwit Pests

The key to success is to take advantage of every worthwhile opportunity. This view is true in business, but it also holds true in the garden. If you take advan-tage of many of the materials and tech-niques I have mentioned in previous chapters, you will help to alleviate some pest and disease problems. Let's expand on this idea a bit further.

Polystyrene Cups for Insect Protection

Do the fat, curled, dismal-coloured grubs that attack your transplants, called cutworms, bother you? If so, take advantage of the way we suggested for growing transplants in modified polys-tyrene cups to alleviate your problem. Instead of removing the transplant and discarding the cup, use it as a cutworm collar. Simply break away the bottom of the cup with your hand, then sink the bottomless cup into the no-dig hole, allowing 1 to 2 inches of the cup to protrude above the soil level (Figure 44). By doing this, you will lock out the cutworm while still allowing the roots to grow through the slits in the sides and out of the bottom of the cup.

You can also use the polystyrene cup against pests by holding transplants over in the cups until they develop better. I have observed that the 12 fluid ounce cups have tremendous holding-over capacity. A few times I had some extra tomato and pepper plants left over. Rather than discard them I sup-plied them with water and fertilizer. To my surprise the plants grew large and actually yielded a few tomatoes and peppers while still in the cups. Some-times if you allow the transplants to mature a bit more, their resistance to some pests seems better. In other cases, you may miss an insect problem entirely by putting out the transplant a few weeks later than usual. Basically, the extra hold-over ability of the cups lets you either develop a more mature trans-plant or hold one longer than is possible

Figure 44. Cutworm collars are easy to make from our polystyrene cups, just remove the bottom of each cup.

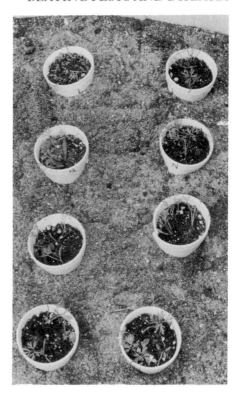

with conventional containers, probably due to the larger cup size and the special slit design that produces extra-good roots. Such a root system seems to hold up the transplant for those extra weeks.

I have also noticed that transplants are tougher and more resistant to insect attack if they are mature. You can produce a more mature, tougher transplant with the cups in one of two ways. For one, you can simply hold the transplant beyond normal planting time for two weeks. If you live in an area that has unsettled weather at your normal transplanting time, you might prefer this approach, because it gives you some leeway on weather. The other way to produce tougher transplants is to start your transplants two weeks earlier than normal in the cups. The extra advantage here is that an advanced transplant will give you an earlier harvest as compared

to the conventional transplant. Either way, don't worry – our cup system can handle the extra two weeks and still give you a great root system raring to go!

Our polystyrene cups can work to your advantage in another way beyond the cutworm situation mentioned earlier. Suppose you have the following situation. Perhaps your garden soil stays abnormally wet in the spring because there's a lot of clay, a high water table or an excessively rainy spring. Maybe you experience either poor germination or a high rate of seedling death from soil diseases or insects. With our cups you can bypass this problem time. Start all your seeds indoors, using our cups. When you place the transplants in the garden later, the garden soil should be drier and the transplants, being tougher than seeds or tiny seedlings, will pull through for you.

Cloches for Plant Protection

Cloches also give you advantages that are similar to those of the cup and can build additional protection into your garden. Suppose you put out transplants under cloches. Firstly, you get barrier protection against insects, especially with the fleece cloche (see next chapter).

Fighting Diseases

Diseases can sometimes be troublesome, but you can often keep them in check with some organic practices. For instance, certain diseases seem to be less of a problem when you feed your plants with seaweed extract. I have noticed few disease problems in my garden since I started using seaweed extract. Other gardeners and academic researchers have reported similar results, according to W. A. Stephenson, in *Seaweed in Agriculture and Horticulture* (see Chapter 4). This benefit appears to result from increased plant vigour caused by the use of seaweed nutrients. What can you lose, since you are guaranteed fertilizer value at the least and maybe insect and disease protection as an extra?

Some of the insect-fighting tactics I have described earlier also solve disease problems. I'm referring in particular to the use of the fleece either as a cloche or insect barrier. Certain insects carry diseases that they transmit to the plant when they feed. By keeping out insects with the fleece you also keep out certain diseases. Viral diseases carried by aphids can be avoided in this way.

Organic Matter, Resistant Plants, and Rotations for Disease Protection

Insofar as all garden diseases are concerned, your best defence is organic matter, resistant plants and rotations. The last two practices also offer considerable defence against insects. Firstly, let's look at organic matter. Considerable evidence suggests that organic matter reduces the incidence of several soil diseases, including root rots of beans, beetroot and peas; lettuce rot; and potato scab. In addition, organic matter increases the numbers of several soil microorganisms known to fight the pathogens that cause root rot, fusarium wilt and verticillium wilt. Organic matter also reduces nematodes in the soil. It would seem that organic matter works to your advantage in promoting soil and plant health, so make sure you keep up the organic matter levels in your soil with our no-dig methods discussed in Chapters 3 and 4.

Resistant plants are front-line soldiers in the battle against diseases and insects. Seed catalogues and seed racks are full of cultivars advertising their resistance to this or that disease. If you have a specific disease problem, use these tougher plants to your advantage. A list of such helpers is not possible here, but you can find disease resistant varieties of asparagus, beans, cabbage, cauliflower, celery, sweetcorn, cucumbers, aubergines, lettuce, onions, parsley, peas, peppers, potatoes, radishes, shallots, spinach, marrows and tomatoes. In addition, you can find resistance in a number of fruits and flowers. So why not stack the deck against diseases by making the right choice of plants when you have a problem?

Don't forget rotations! The problem with keeping plants in the same place is that disease-causing microorganisms build up huge populations if they have a food source (your plants) present year after year. By moving your crops around, you keep the disease-causing microorganism populations low because of starvation. While one crop may be food for a disease, another crop will be unacceptable, hence, the microorganisms will starve. Another help is that new plants may create a habitat for different organisms that are antagonistic to the original troublemakers. Rotations discourage a lot of soilborne diseases, such as verticillium and fusarium wilts, to name a few. So play musical chairs with your crops and keep those pests guessing!

CHAPTER 7
FASTER, LONGER, BIGGER HARVESTS

Less work is great. Getting more vegetables with less work is even better. Up to now in this book we have concerned ourselves with discussing ways to cut the amount of garden work. In this chapter, though, I'm going to change direction a bit by showing you how to get the most out of your no-dig no-weed garden. What we'll do is stretch the garden season at its beginning and end while getting more out of the middle, an idea any businessman would call increased productivity.

Cloches for Early Gardening

Mention early gardening to gardeners and you always get into a discussion on cloches. These protective devices are supposedly fantastic for getting early gardening starts, but I always used to wonder if the results that cloches produced were worth the trouble. I don't know about you, but I hate to spend my money and labour on something that fails to deliver all that it promises. In the past, cloches had disappointed me on numerous occasions. However, I finally found some cloches that I can now recommend with great enthusiasm.

Let's first look at the secret success that underlies the cloche, black plastic. Why do we need black plastic underneath the cloche? The answer to this question involves the fact that plants have two basic parts, each in a different environment: the shoot and the root. The plant's shoot is above the ground

and spends its time enveloped in the surrounding air. Shoot development heavily depends upon the temperature of this surrounding air. The root dwells in the soil, which heats up differently than does air. Root temperatures also have an effect on plant growth. Cloches trap the sun's heat and raise the air temperature around the plant, but they can't raise the soil temperature to as great an extent as air temperature. A straight cloche, therefore, produces uneven heating. By itself, it actually mixes the signals it gives to the plant's parts for growth. The cloche provides a warmer air temperature that advances the shoot two weeks into its growth pattern, but it does not provide the same warming benefits to the soil temperature to advance the root's growth pattern. Although the cloche does allow some growth movement and frost protection for the plant, it does not provide the full potential for these benefits that using it in combination with black plastic provides.

Now the need for black plastic becomes clear. The black plastic in place under the cloche allows the sun to heat both the air and the soil. The sun heats the air and the black plastic, which in turn conducts some heat into the soil, so the plant has warm roots and shoots. Although the black plastic affords much better plant growth, its benefits don't stop there. The warm soil that results from using the plastic radiates heat at night, offering more frost protection than is possible with using the cloche alone.

Exactly what can we expect from a cloche combined with black plastic? Clearly the dynamic duo of black plastic and cloches produces enough warmth to allow earlier planting. My experience indicates that you can plant your garden two weeks earlier than normal. I have even stretched three weeks of earlier planting out of a cloche/black plastic combination. Although in some years I had light but fatal frost damage occur within the three-week stretch, I've never had this problem when starting my plants only two weeks earlier.

The two-week head start figures apply for warm-season crops like tomatoes, peppers, beans, sweetcorn or aubergines. With cool-season crops such as peas, lettuce, broccoli, spinach and carrots, you can easily get a three-week and even four-week head start. Most gardeners think of needing a head start for warm-season crops. The earlier harvest of cool-season crops, however, is also possible with the use of cloches and black plastic. Don't neglect this possibility. The idea of enjoying peas or broccoli from your garden three weeks earlier than usual is quite attractive.

At this point I'd like to be even more specific about the benefits of using a cloche/black plastic combination. First let me tell you what I have observed with soil temperature. The use of black plastic with a cloche has produced a soil temperature 6 to 12 degrees higher than that of nearby, unprotected garden soil. The temperature variation depends on the time of day and whether the day is very cloudy or sunny. Air temperature increases have varied from 5 to 40 degrees. Again, air temperature variations relate to the same factors as do soil temperature variations.

By reading the above facts, I'm sure

you can see how April outside becomes May inside the toasty cloche. But what about frost protection specifics? Suppose you go for the early start and get tripped up by an unexpected late frost? My experience indicates that you can escape frost damage if temperatures don't go below 28°F. The odds of this occurring are quite low during the early part of the garden season, even if you plant two weeks before the average date of your last killing spring frost.

The combined black plastic and cloche also offer earlier crop yields; but surprisingly, the yields occur even sooner than the earlier-than-normal planting head start affords the plants. This happy turn of events stems from the accumulation of heat units. The cloche and black plastic trap more heat units than do unprotected garden areas. In fact, over a period of four to six weeks, the cloche system traps at least twice as many heat units as do the uncovered areas. The important thing to remember here is that heat units directly affect plant development, so the cloche system not only gives the plants a head start but also increases their growth relative to uncovered plants. The result is the earliest-ever harvest.

Types of Cloches

By now I'm sure you're eager to know what cloches I like. Based on my experience, Melbourne cloches and the fleece are the best cloches. The fleece cloche is made of the same material we discussed for insect protection in the previous chapter. The Melbourne cloches are clear polythene with precut ventilation slits. (Agriframes sell this type of cloche – for their address, see page 165).

First, let's look at the fleece cloche. The fleece cloche does not require supports or ventilation because the material is lightweight and porous. As a matter of fact, the weight is light enough that even onions can hold the cloche up as they grow. The natural ventilation provided by the fleece cloche removes the necessity for constantly opening and closing the cloche to ventilate the plants. The porous nature of the cloche prevents excessive heat build-up for periods up to six weeks. Addition properties of the fleece cloche include the ability to allow good rain and light penetration and the ability to serve as a very effective insect barrier.

The methods for the fleece cloche installation are the same as those described for insect protection in the previous chapter. You can either prepare a trench with the ridger or a slit with the square-edged spade and lock in both the black plastic and the fleece edges. Perhaps the easiest installation method is to pin both the black plastic and fleece together to the soil in one simple step, using the U-shaped pins made from coat hangers, as covered in the previous chapter. The 56 inch width of the cloche allows for easy installation over raised beds, mini-hills, and multiple rows or bands.

When installing the fleece cloche, remember to do one side of the cloche first, whether using a trench, slit or pins. Next, pin the other side of the black plastic to the soil as a temporary

measure. Using a few U-shaped pins to hold the black plastic steady, plant your seeds or transplants before you completely install the cloche. Plant seeds through the plastic with either the dibber or bulb planter and plant transplants with the bulb planter (see Chapter 3). Once you have completed the planting, you can complete the installation of the remaining cloche sides whichever way you prefer. Because the wind can move *through* the fleece cloches, U-shaped pins sufficiently keep them in place in windy areas and provide the easiest installation.

The slitted polythene cloche demands somewhat different treatment. The slits do allow for ventilation and rain entry, but I have noted that the slits also allow some insects to sneak in. The weight of this type of cloche also requires the use of wire hoops for support. Light entry through the slitted polythene seems as good as with the fleece.

At this point you might be wondering why I bother with the slitted plastic in view of the need for hoop support and some insect problems. In terms of crop earliness and higher yields, the slitted plastic has a slight edge over the fleece, possibly because the polythene's venting system retains more night heat. The slitted pieces in the plastic rise

Figure 45. To install a slitted polythene cloche over a black plastic mulch, start by pinning down one side of the plastic. The plastic is supported underneath by wire hoops. The finished polythene cloche is giving my crop a great head start.

upwards as the warm air under the cloche rises and pushes against them. This upward flex allows the hot air to escape. At night these pieces of plastic drop back into place once the hot air pressure disappears. During the cool night, then, these slitted pieces essentially close down the vents and keep the warmth inside the cloche. The fleece, on the other hand, loses heat in both the night and day because its pores are always open.

The installation of the slitted polythene cloche is about the same as for the fleece. You can use slits, trenches or U-shaped pins to secure the cloche, although the pins make the process easy. The hoops also offer extra hold-down power for the black plastic. Lay out the black plastic and pin it down with the wire hoops at 5-foot intervals. Next, plant either seeds or transplants through the plastic as already described. Finally, use the U-shaped pins to secure the plastic cloche and the plastic mulch directly to the soil, as in Figure 45. Figure 45 also shows a typical slitted cloche in my garden.

Cloche Crops

Warm-season crops that I have got off to good starts with these cloches include sweetcorn, cucumbers, aubergines, peppers and tomatoes. All produce well and early under cloches.

As previously mentioned, warm-season crops are not the only ones that can take advantage of the cloche. You can also get a head start and early harvests with cool-season crops grown under cloches. I have had excellent results with broccoli, lettuce and peas. The main point to remember with these and other cool-season crops is don't leave the cloche on too long because the later warmth can cut or even retard yields. Remove the cloches when temperatures remain near 50°F for a few nights. For cool-season crops, I prefer the fleece cloche, because it has less heat retention than does the slitted plastic.

Cloches for Late Gardening

Up to now we have talked about early starts or stretching the garden season at the beginning. You can also use cloches to stretch your garden season at the end. Let's see, we can add two weeks at the start for warm-season crops and three weeks for cool-loving crops. Can we do the same at the end? Yes! Essentially we can stretch the entire garden season by six weeks. In my area this means going from 195 to 237 days.

In the autumn, cloches address the same two needs they address in the spring: frost protection and extended warmth. At this end of the garden season, I use only the fleece cloche, because plants are usually too large for the slitted plastic cloche forms. Simply drape the fleece over the plant or plants, beds, rows or whatever you wish to protect, and pin it to the soil with coat hanger U-shaped pins.

Usually I find that my area gets hit with a frost around late autumn, then we enjoy two or three weeks of mild weather, which we refer to as 'Indian summer'. The weather that finishes warm-season plants follows the Indian summer lull. If I cover my tomatoes, peppers and aubergines with fleece I can ride out the first frost and coast into Indian summer. The fleece cloche protects the plants from the first frost but also provides the warmth that makes the tomatoes and other relatives ripen. The process of ripening is clearly much better under the cloche in comparison to nearby uncovered plants protected from frost only with newspaper.

The cloche of the fleece also lets you stretch cool-season crops past several frosts, a protection I find just great for those remaining broccoli, carrot, lettuce and turnip plants. When protected by the fleece, such crops seem to turn out so sweet after being hit by a few frosts.

With care you can reuse the fleece cloches a second time; but I don't recommend using them more than twice, because unnoticed deterioration sets into the cloche, reducing the amount of light that can pass through the fleece. This light loss reduces the heat units and also the plant growth and you lose the very advantage you hoped to gain with the cloche.

After their spring use, I lay the cloches out to dry in the sun, then I carefully fold the material and store it in the cellar. I recycle both the plastic and polyester a second time during the autumn for the late stretch. If you use cloches only in the spring, you can reuse them for the following spring. These cloches are relatively inexpensive, especially in view of what you get, so buy new ones after you have used the cloches twice.

Before leaving the subject of cloches, let me mention the 'poor man's cloche'. As its name implies, the cost is just right. You can get one of these cloches by rinsing out a 1-gallon orange squash bottle. Make sure you save the cap. Carefully cut out the bottom with scissors, a single-edged razor blade or, better yet, a craft knife. Now you have a portable cloche for individual plants. I suggest that you place a rock on top of the cloche to prevent the wind from blowing it over. Leave the cap on at night, on cloudy days or in cool weather. On hot days you can vent the cloche by removing the cap. Poor man's cloches are sufficient if you have only a few plants and wish a modest head start or light frost protection.

Efficient Gardening Techniques

By now you know that no-dig no-weed methods save you from a lot of work. In addition, you need less fertilizer, water and organic matter. Up to this point my theme has been getting the same for less, but now I'm going to switch gears to get the most from the least. What I'm talking about here is harvesting more crops without increasing the size of your garden or the amount of work, fertilizer, water or organic matter that you put into your garden. Anyone can reach this goal by taking advantage of four garden techniques: intensive planting, vertical gardening, interplanting and succession planting. The trick is to understand these practices so that you use them correctly and in a manner than benefits you.

Intensive Planting

Let's start with intensive planting. This approach increases plant density to the maximum so that you get the greatest possible harvest. The one caution here is that you can increase the planting density only so far before you run foul of the law of diminishing returns. After adding a certain number of plants to a given area, you introduce the elements of shade and competition. Some plants shade others, thus reducing photosynthesis and yields. Competition for nutrients and water increases beyond the carrying capacity of the soil. At that point you put the system into reverse: you get less from more.

As long as you are aware of the limitations, you can get more from your garden than you think. For example, the row concept of gardening is an inefficient use of space. The large spacing recommended between rows has little to do with the space needs of plants. The intent is to allow for mechanical cultivation between rows, that is, to leave you enough space for moving equipment between rows. But we don't have to worry about cultivation for a couple of reasons. Firstly, if you are using our no-weed concept and our suggested mulch, there are no weeds. No weeds between rows means no need for rows. Even if you are not using mulches, you will eventually have a no-weed garden by using our no-dig method. The other reason you don't have cultivation worries is that closely spaced plants will produce a soil cover that shades out weeds, thus reducing the few problems even further.

So why bother using rows or a lot of paths for getting around? All they do is cause soil compaction. We cut down on paths and eliminate rows, replacing them with blocks, beds or bands. Blocks are essentially squares, ideally sized about 4 feet on each side. Paths surround each block, thus giving you a chess board look. One very popular block approach divides the block into 1-foot squares.

Each crop's space needs determine the number of plants in a block. For example a 1-foot square is suitable for one plant of broccoli, cabbage, cauliflower, sweetcorn, aubergine or pepper. On the other hand, you can fit 16 beetroot or carrots in a square. A marrow would need nine squares of a block. If this block method is starting to sound familiar, it is. Some of you might recognize it from Mel Bartholomew's book *Cash From Square Foot Gardening* (Garden Way Publishing, U.S., 1986). If you want to use this block method, you will probably enjoy reading his book.

Let's move on to beds and bands, which differ from blocks in shape. The two planting patterns are rectangular rather than square. The distinction between the bed and band is in the width of the rectangle, with the bed being the wider of the two. The bed should be 4 feet wide and whatever length you choose. This width is just about right for an arm's reach to the centre of the bed. Anything wider can cause you inconvenience. The band, on the other hand, is narrower than 4 feet. By the way, if you use the suggested 4-foot-wide black plastic mulch, you have a ready-made bed (see Chapter 5). If you use less than the full width of the plastic, you can have a band complete with encircling pathway.

Prolific smaller crops might be more suitable to planting in a band and larger crops to a bed. For instance, I would plant beetroot, carrots, onions or radishes in a band, but sweetcorn, marrow or tomatoes in a bed. You can plant some crops in either a band or bed, depending on your food needs and preference.

Let's look at the possible spacing for some crops, starting with tomatoes. If you go by conventional spacing, tomatoes are garden hogs. Yet most of us don't think a garden is complete without tomatoes. I've seen suggested spacings between rows of 2 to 4 feet, but my own experience is that a spacing of 18 inches between staked tomato plants gives great yields. Incidentally, a major university recently publicized a finding that high-density plantings of staked tomatoes give the best yield at 18-inch spacings, a confirmation of my own ideas.

The discussion of spacing brings me to an interesting point. Is there more than one way to space and, if so, does it matter how you space? The answer to both questions is yes. If you use the conventional spacing approach, the usual pattern is to line up the plants side by side. The row concept dies hard, even with beds and bands. Instead you should stagger the plantings so that the plants are side by side only with every other row, as Figure 46 overleaf illustrates. Using this pattern, you actually squeeze a few extra plants in the area and get more uniform shading and use of nutrients and water. In plain English,

Less efficient · More efficient

Figure 46. Conventional single rows with equally spaced plants (*above left*) give you fewer plants in an area than does a staggered planting pattern with plants equidistant in all directions (*above right*).

you use space and soil more efficiently.

The 18-inch spacing rule also holds for the relatives of the tomato — aubergines and peppers. It also works for broccoli, cabbage, cauliflower and large cultivars of sweetcorn. Smaller cultivars of sweetcorn can get by with 12 inches of space between plants. This tight packing of sweetcorn makes it possible to grow sweetcorn in small gardens and assures pollination, thus all the ears form well.

Vertical Gardening

While intensive planting can give a mighty boost to the yields for any size of garden, there are three other practices that can make you an efficient but underworked gardener: vertical gardening, interplanting and succession planting. Let's talk about vertical gardening first. Vertical gardening is a natural for certain plants that, even at their closest allowed spacing, are space-hungry crops. If your garden is small, you might give up on growing the vining and climbing vegetables but don't. Us-

ing vertical gardening, you can tame these space-hungry crops to become little space users.

Suppose you had a dozen cucumber plants. If you planted these on the ground at intensive garden spacing, you would place one plant every 12 inches. Since the vines run about 6 to 8 feet in length, the mature plants would need roughly 100 square feet of space. Instead, if you put the cucumber plants in a vertical garden, you will lose only about 14 square feet of ground space. You cut down space needs to only 14 per cent of the original. No wonder vertical gardening has a popular following!

The only important vertical gardening need is upright support that is strong enough to bear the weight of the mature crop. Place your supports in an east-to-west line at the northern end of your garden so that the shadow cast by the support will not shade out your lower-growing crops. While less desirable, you can run the supports north to south on the western side of your garden. Here you lose only the late afternoon sun.

Over the years I have tried all kinds of crop supports. Figure 47 shows my current supports for my vertical garden. I originally chose chicken wire mesh because it was strong and I never had to worry about the weight of any climbing crop. The drawback to using chicken wire was the storage and reuse. Costs were high enough that I wanted to reuse the wire for at least three years, which led to the problem of whether I should install it permanently or temporarily. At first I put it up permanently, since the idea of taking it down and storing it wasn't attractive. I figured it would last three years if left up all year round, but of course it didn't. Rust appeared in no time and by the end of the second garden season, the rust weakened the wire to the point where I couldn't trust its strength the following year.

The next year I opted for temporary installation of the chicken wire but wasn't sure how to install it so that it would be strong enough for the crop but easy enough to take down. I solved the problem by using spring-latch cup hooks. These cup hooks have a metal strip under tension, which keeps cups from falling off them. You push the strips downwards with the cup handle or chicken wire and it snaps closed once the wire or handle is under it. To release it, you press the strip down with your finger and slide the wire out of it. I attached the screw-type cup hooks to wood posts. Although the wire went up easily and came down easily in the autumn, I didn't know where to store it. Also the wire never seemed to roll up neatly like the original roll, instead it appeared to enlarge by a factor of two or three. I had to cram it into the corner of my tool shed. I finally got tired of using chicken wire.

I have also tried nylon netting, which works well using the same cup hooks mentioned above. Nylon netting is relatively easy to store because you can fold it into a nice, neat package. The cost of nylon netting is moderate, and it lasts for several years.

To support the nylon net, I usually buy cheap grades of 8-foot-long 2 by 4s. I use a post hole digger to set the posts 2 feet deep. You can also pack the posts in concrete if you want very well-set posts. If you so desire, you can paint the wood with a wood preservative. Cuprinol manufactures a special wood preservative formulation that is compatible with soil and garden plants. Ask for Green Cuprinol.

Figure 47. Ready-made wire grow panels (shown here) and nylon net are both good supports for plants in vertical gardens.

For lightweight crops, such as cucumbers, peas and beans, I place the supports at 8-foot intervals. For heavy climbers, such as marrows, I place the supports at 6-foot intervals. In terms of support, I have found it helpful to weave a wire through the netting top and attach the wire to the wood support posts. This keeps the net from sagging in the middle. You will also need slings or support sacks for the marrows. Discarded tights make wonderful slings when you place them underneath the fruit and tie the tops at the crosspiece of the net. Remember, you can attach the net with cup hooks for easy removal or with wire brads for permanent installations.

The netting post support method places your netting 6 feet above ground. You may get some plant hangover at the top but nothing serious. The net usually comes in a 5-foot height and rarely in a 6-foot height. Start the net 1 foot above the soil. You may have to tie some plants, such as cucumbers, to the net bottom, but others, such as peas or beans, jump the 1-foot gap by themselves.

The main annoyance I found with nylon netting was its tendency to tangle, but tangles may soon become a thing of the past. This year I noticed that Burpee advertised an improved nylon netting that wouldn't tangle, so naturally I decided to try it. My initial impression was good. I haven't passed the acid test yet. As I recycle it for the next few years, I will be watching it closely for tangles. If this netting lives up to its promise, I may become a complete nylon net vertical gardener.

Another new support system that I have been using over the past few garden seasons is the grow panel. Grow panels provide good support strength, ease of assembly and disassembly and a sturdiness that promises a long life. I have been using my grow panels for three seasons and they still look great. They are 4 by 2 feet, with the heavy-duty wire forming 6-inch squares. You can tie the panels with twine or twist ties to two strong stakes and place them side by side to any desired length. Adjoining panels can share one stake. My cucumbers, beans and other climbers adapt admirably to them. If you can't find grow panels, you can use the wire reinforcement mesh used in concrete work as an adequate substitute. Builders' merchants usually carry the wire mesh. So far I've been happy with my grow panels because they are easy to store and install. As a matter of fact, I prefer using grow panels to nylon net for short vines, although nylon net wins for long vines.

To support grow panels, use sturdy wood stakes such as those you might use for tomatoes or dahlias. These stakes will offer sufficient support because the panels are only 2 feet wide. Since many of the panels are only 4 feet high, I start them 1 foot above the ground and tie them to the stakes with heavy twine or wire twist ties. The 5-foot height is fine for cucumbers and beans. If you don't want to start the panels 1 foot above the ground, you can fill in the last foot by stringing twine between the support stakes.

Before I leave the subject of vertical gardening, I'd like to mention one more item: the pea fence. This new product is 8 feet long and 3⅓ feet high. It folds into seven 14-inch sections. Usually this fence has long metal extensions on the bottom so you can stick it into the soil and it doesn't need any additional support. It's height limits it to use with the shorter pea plants, such as 'Oregon Sugar Pod' or 'Sugar Ann Snap Pea'.

Interplanting
Another gardening practice that can

produce a better garden is interplanting, a technique that puts two compatible crops in an area normally devoted to one. In this way you space more efficiently, but you also get a varied harvest over a longer time.

Generally, you pair the crops for one of two reasons. Firstly, you can place a crop that matures quickly with one that takes its time, so by the time you harvest the early crop, the later one is about ready to take over the available space. Another choice is to pair two crops not on the basis of harvest time but on the consideration of different growth habits.

Let's look at some examples of interplanting. My favourite is the marrow and lettuce combination, a combination that meets both requirements mentioned above. The first step is that the lettuce goes out as early transplants two to four weeks before the marrows,

because they are less tender, therefore, the lettuce reaches maturity before the marrows. Secondly, the plants differ in their growth habits (Figure 48). Marrows tend to rise as an inverted triangle from the base, giving you a compressed or squashed ice cream cone-shaped foliage mass. This shape leaves a lot of wasted understory space. But lettuce is low and compact, so it fits nicely in between young marrow plants.

I usually plant a double bed of marrows. I install two side-by-side sheets of the 4-foot-wide black plastic, leaving a 1-foot gap between the sheets. I then plant lettuce transplants into the soil row at 6-inch spacing for leaf lettuce, 9-inch for cos types, and 12-inch for crisp lettuce. Later on I put marrow transplants into the black plastic with the bulb planter. I place one row down the centre of each sheet at 3-foot intervals. I harvest the leaf lettuce first and

Figure 48. Marrows and lettuce make good interplanting partners. This photograph shows marrows planted to the left and right of the central row of lettuce. Early in the season there's plenty of room for both, as seen here. By the time the marrows need more space to grow, the lettuce is ready to harvest.

pick the Cos and crisp lettuce as the marrow leaves close overhead. The covering marrow leaves shade the lettuce below, thus letting it grow just a little longer into the hot days of summer. Now that's what I call interplanting at its best!

Other examples of good partners exist. You can mix onions with either carrots or leaf lettuce. Onions, being skinny and tall, leave the lower space for the leaf lettuce or carrots to spread out. You can also slip lettuce between cabbage or bean plants. Leaf lettuce matures quickly; after you pick the lettuce, the beans or cabbage fill in the space. For the same reason, you can tuck lettuce around broccoli or cauliflower.

Radishes also make a versatile planting partner. Since they mature ever so quickly, you can mix them with several plants that mature later; for example, you can mix radishes with lettuce, beetroot, tomatoes, peppers, aubergines or carrots. During sowing, you can mix the radishes with carrot seeds. Carrot seeds germinate very slowly and the fast-start radish seedlings provide an excellent visual marker for the row so you can weed early without worrying about the location of the carrots.

Early potatoes and marrows are a good example of plants with differing harvest times. Just plant the two side by side. After you harvest the early potatoes, the space-hogging marrows will quickly fill in the space. The same possibility exists with peas and marrows. You can also marry early tomatoes with winter cabbage. As the tomatoes slow down and you remove the tomato plants, the cabbage takes over. You can also mix dwarf beans with either tomatoes, peppers or aubergines. The beans come in quickly, and the others finish the race later. You can also mix spinach with these same plants, since spinach finishes more quickly.

Succession Planting

We have one more gardening practice to cover: succession planting. Here the use of space is efficient, but the main thrust is for continuous and longer harvests. You can accomplish succession planting in three ways. For some crops you can get a continuous harvest by the simultaneous planting of early, mid-season and late cultivars. You can also get the same effect by using only one cultivar but planting batches at two- or three-week intervals (Figure 49), for continuous harvests of the same crop. We can also get continuous, longer harvests with mixed crops by following the harvest of early-season crops with a succession crop placed either as seeds or transplants.

Let's look at some successions. You should sow some crops as early as possi-

Figure 49. A succession planting of broccoli is shown in the foreground. The youngest plants are on the left and the oldest on the right.

ble for two reasons. One is early harvest. Nothing beats early French beans as the season's first fresh vegetable. The second reason is that early harvests leave free space that you can fill with a succession crop. Early spring sowings are possible for broccoli, Brussels sprouts, cabbage, lettuce, onions, peas, swede and spinach. You can sow carrots, chard, Chinese leaf, kale, cress, chicory, garlic, mustard, parsnips, radishes, shallots and turnips a little later but much earlier than warm-season crops. All of these crops, the very hardy and hardy vegetables, are potential candidates for a succession plan. All you need to know is the number of growing days left in the season after you harvest the early crops. This number helps to determine which crops can mature in the remainder of your garden season. For example, radishes finish producing in 25 to 30 days, leaving a lot of free time and empty space. You can follow the radishes with French beans and follow the beans with swede. Even if the swede gets tagged by a frost or two, don't worry, the swede is hardy and the frost just sweetens it. That's what I call a triple-play succession.

Not all successions can be triples, though. Some are only doubles, but even doubles help you win the continuous, longer harvest game. For instance, you can follow radishes with carrots, celery, French beans, lettuce or onions planted as sets. You can harvest early potatoes and still get in a planting of sweetcorn. How about sneaking in some beetroot, late cabbages, or carrots after your peas? Perhaps you still have time after your sweetcorn finishes to get in an autumn crop of spinach, swede or turnips. You only have a little time left? Maybe you can fit in something quick like leaf lettuce or radishes.

Successions are quite numerous. You make the choice, but keep some points

in mind. When you replace some vegetable, try not to pick a successor that's closely related. The second crop, if closely related, could be susceptible to the same insects and diseases as the first one. Also, keep track of your remaining days. If you have 40 days to the killing frost, don't plant French beans, which need 50 or more days to grow and are frost-tender. You could try a crop that needs 50 days but can tolerate a few light frosts; for example, chard, cress, kale, lettuce or mustard could fit the situation. You must also watch out for temperature preferences for coolness or heat. Lettuce, peas, radishes or spinach do not make good midsummer fillers but would work out late in the summer.

At this time I'd like to remind you of the transplant nursery in Chapter 2 (Figure 13) and tell you how this nursery provides me with plants for succession planting. I keep my leftover transplants in it and use it to hold our outdoor production of transplants in the modified polystyrene cups. For example, I start various vegetables from seed directly outdoors in the cups. These transplants are started at various times throughout the season. My choice of crops is not guesswork but deliberate planning for successor crops. When space becomes available, I simply grab several cups and the bulb planter. In just a few minutes I can plant a complete succession crop via the no-dig method.

As a gardener interested in the most for the least, you certainly have numerous choices. I'm not saying you should practice all the methods we just covered. In some cases you must choose one or the other. For example, do you interplant marrows with early peas or succeed the peas with French beans? As for myself, I put major emphasis on intensive planting and vertical gardening. I do use interplanting and successions, but I use them carefully and selectively with certain crops. My aim is to provide enough vegetables for fresh use and some for cellar and freezer storage. It's nice to have several lots of excess vegetables, but make sure your surplus is not for show but for consumption. Use the previous techniques with vegetables your family appreciates.

In the next chapter, you will find helpful hints for individual vegetables. Perhaps the hints will help you to choose among intensive gardening, vertical gardening, interplanting and succession planting.

CHAPTER 8
THE NO-DIG VEGETABLE PATCH

This chapter will supply you with all the information you will need to grow vegetables. I will list the plants alphabetically, breaking down the information for each plant into the following categories: choices, culture, pests and harvest. Wherever possible, I will tie the facts to the techniques and information covered in the preceding chapters.

I would like to mention that I intend the figures I give for the days to harvest for each crop to be only rough guides. The range I give results from planting both early and late cultivars at their earliest possible time as seeds. Later plantings, such as those used in succession planting, often mature more quickly because of the increasingly warmer weather in which they grow. If you use transplants, remember to count the time required to grow them as part of the time to harvest. Keep the suggested harvest days in mind, but rely more upon visual inspection if the crop is new to you.

Aubergines

Choices
Most aubergines look like a large egg with a smooth, shiny, deep purple skin. Cultivars of this type include 'Black Enorma' and 'Bonica'. One aubergine cultivar, the 'Oriental Eggplant', looks like a small egg complete with a colour change from white to yellow. Although aubergines are a long, warm-season crop and sometimes fare poorly in more northern areas, breeders have developed cultivars for shorter season areas. These varieties include 'Dusky Hybrid'. Those of you who enjoy gourmet baby vegetables would like a variety called 'Little Fingers'.

Culture
Gardeners generally start aubergines as transplants because of the long season requirement. The earliest date for setting out aubergines is about ten days after that for tomatoes or three weeks after the last killing spring frost. Night time temperatures should be at least 50°F or even better, 55°F. Daytime temperatures should be over 60°F. Aubergines are a touch more sensitive than tomatoes.

I sow aubergine seeds about ½ inch deep in the 12 fluid ounce modified polystyrene cups. The seeds germinate in about 10 to 15 days at 70°F or faster on top of the refrigerator. Plants should be thinned to one aubergine for each cup. Start your transplants six to eight weeks before their outdoor planting time. I place my aubergines in an intensive planting pattern using a spacing distance of 18 inches.

Aubergines generally tie up space for most of the garden season. Aubergines can follow an early-season crop like lettuce, peas or radishes. You can interplant aubergines with established spring lettuce, because the aubergines will fill in the space after you have picked the lettuce.

Black plastic mulch is a natural for aubergines because they prefer warm, moist soils. Just use the bulb planter to place your transplants through the black plastic. Aubergines are also big feeders so I suggest that you add organic matter and fertilizer in the no-dig hole for big feeders.

Pests

The main pests of the aubergine are aphids and glasshouse red spider mite.

Harvest

Aubergines require about 60 to 70 days from transplanting to the first harvest. You can pick aubergines at any time, but you will get the best ones if you pick them before their seeds are hard. With conventional aubergines, pick them when they have a 4-inch diameter and while their skin is shiny. With any aubergine variety, dull colour is usually indicative of mature seeds. Pick aubergines by cutting their stems, which are quite tough, with either a sharp knife or a small pruner.

Beans

Choices

A large choice of beans confronts the gardener in most general seed catalogues and garden centres.

Beans come in three basic types. One type is the French bean, having edible pods that are usually yellow or green, although purple is also available. The pods are thin and cylindrical. Runner beans, on the other hand, are wide and flat. It is best to eat French beans while they are young and before they become full sized, otherwise, the pods become

Figure 50. This photo shows my no-dig no-weed vegetable garden at the height of the season.

inedible. The second type of bean is the butter bean and broad bean. These beans are best when they have grown to their full size but are not fully mature. The pods of butter and broad beans are inedible. Gardeners grow the third type of bean, the haricot and flageolet bean, for its fully mature, dry beans removed from the pods.

You can find all three kinds of beans in either dwarf or climbing forms. I happen to prefer climbing beans in my vertical garden, but many of my friends like the dwarf forms. Climbing beans take longer to bear than dwarf types, but their harvest period is longer. Of course, you can extend the harvest of dwarf beans by employing succession planting.

Suggesting the best kinds of beans to grow is like picking out a car – essentially it is a matter of personal choice. My own choices of beans to grow after several years of experimenting are the following pole varieties: 'Blue Lake', 'Enorma' and 'Romano'. The first type I mentioned is an old standby, the second is a long, smooth bean that produces a very large crop, and the third is a flat, green bean sometimes called the Italian pole bean. All three types are fine for fresh use or for freezing.

Culture

French, broad and haricot beans are tender so never plant them into the soil below 50°F or they will rot. Butter beans require even warmer soil, about 70°F. I usually wait to plant French bean seeds and transplants until the soil has warmed up to 55°F as shown by a soil thermometer. Since French bean seeds are large, direct no-dig sowing is possible with the dibber, ridger, or bulb planter, 1 or 2 inches deep.

If you want a head start or have cold, wet springs, I suggest you grow bean transplants in our polystyrene cups. In cooler areas butter bean transplants are a must to allow for proper plant maturation. I usually plant three groups of two seeds each next to the cup rim (12 fluid ounce size) at 12, 4 and 8 o'clock positions. After seed germination, I thin the number of plants down to three plants for pole and bush types. Germination takes roughly 7 to 10 days at 70°F. Bean seeds do not require any special treatment or light during germination. Start bean seeds three to four weeks prior to the time of transplanting or sow them in cups outdoors at normal planting time under the outdoor shelter (see Chapter 2, Figure 5), if you don't care for early beans but have cold and wet soil.

Cups having three climbing bean transplants work out very well in an intensively planted vertical garden. Just place the transplants at 12-inch intervals in a row planted alongside some form of vertical support. Dwarf beans, three to a cup, can have an intensive spacing of 6 inches between cups in the row and 12 inches between rows. This spacing gives you a completely filled-in bed or band. For continuous yields, plant French dwarf beans at two-week intervals. You can also use French dwarf beans as successive plantings after harvesting early crops such as beetroot, broccoli, early potatoes, lettuce, peas, radishes or spinach. For succession purposes you can continue bean plantings up to two months prior to your first killing autumn frost. You can interplant dwarf beans with lettuce, onions, peppers or tomatoes.

Pests

Bean pests include bean aphids and spider mites. You can control all of these pests by using soap spray, derris or pyrethrum.

Rust seems to be the only disease I occasionally see, when the leaves become speckled or covered with a rusty colour. You can avoid this disease or others by not picking beans or handling the plants when they are wet. If you have a serious rust problem, choose varieties having rust resistance. Mosaic and anthracnose can also occur, but resistant varieties are available.

Harvest

Pick French dwarf beans when the beans are about one-quarter to one-third their full size. Their pods are almost full sized at this point, have soft tips, and produce a nice snap when broken. Continue picking the beans to encourage further bean production. For a real treat, prepare French beans Chinese style, that is, stir-frying quickly. If you plan on freezing French beans, select a cultivar described as good for freezing and don't overblanch them.

Pick butter beans when the pods are green and full-sized with beans nearly full-sized. Remove haricot or flageolet beans from dry, brown pods. After the pods become dry and brown, cut the entire plant at the soil line. Leave the roots in the soil to build up organic matter. Hang the plants stem end up in a garage or other dry place for further drying. When the pods become brittle, you can remove the beans.

Beetroot

Choices

The main decision to make concerning beetroot is whether you want an early or midseason beetroot for fresh use ('Avonearly', 'Boltardy') or a beetroot for winter storage ('Detroit', 'Little Ball', 'Monodot'). You can also choose various shapes, such as globular ('Cheltenham', 'Greentop') or cylindrical ('Cylindra', 'Forono') and you can also choose between two colours, red or golden ('Burpee's Golden'). If you are looking for a baby gourmet variety or a really sweet beetroot, try 'Little Ball' and 'Sweetheart' respectively.

Beetroot, while grown as a root crop, also offer the bonus of producing leaf greens. Just remember not to pick all the leaves on a plant prior to harvesting the beetroot, because you'll get a poor crop of beetroot if you do. Should you like beetroot greens, you might want to consider 'Green Top Bunching'. An even better choice if you like beetroot greens is to grow a beetroot relative, Swiss chard, which is grown only for its greens.

Culture

Beetroot is mostly a cool-season crop. Swiss chard can take more heat than other greens and it is the best choice of greens for summer harvests.

You can sow beetroot seeds directly outdoors as soon as you can work your soil. The ridger works best for planting this seed, but you can also use the dibber. For quick germination (10 to 14 days), soak beetroot seeds in luke-warm water for 12 to 24 hours. You can mix radish seeds with the beetroot seeds as a marker and earlier crop. Keep in mind that beetroot 'seeds' are actually fruits that contain several seeds. You must thin to one beetroot per 3-inch square for intensive gardening, no matter how carefully you space the seeds. Sow beetroot and Swiss chard seeds ½ to 1 inch deep. Intensive plantings of Swiss chard are one plant per 12-inch square.

To get a head start, you can also sow beetroot three weeks earlier in our 12 fluid ounce polystyrene cups. Plant three seeds to a cup at the outer cup edges in equally spaced positions. Thin each spot to leave only the strongest seedling. You can place each transplant triplet such that all bulb-digger holes are equally distant from each other at 6 inches, a spacing that is fine for intensive gardening.

For succession planting, sow beetroot directly into the garden or in our cups at three-week intervals. Remember, the last crop should mature before the hot weather starts. You can follow beetroot by planting succession crops such as French beans, late sweetcorn or late marrows. You can also interplant beetroot with leaf crops such as cabbage, lettuce or spinach.

Pests

The main pest to bother beetroot is leaf miner. The fleece barrier can eliminate this problem, as can a combined pyrethrum/derris spray. Leaf spot and scab may occur in young beetroot, but good soils and rotations seem to ward off these problems.

Harvest

To produce an excellent beetroot harvest, you must keep weeds under control. Planting beetroot transplants through black plastic gives excellent yields.

With the exception of the winter storers, which need roughly 80 days, beetroot is usually ready to harvest in 50 to 60 days. The best beetroot is picked in the cooler part of the season and has a 1½-inch diameter, although you can pick beetroot up to 3 inches in diameter. Swiss chard needs about 70 days to harvest. If you pick *only* the outer leaves when they are up to only 12 inches tall, you'll get tender leaves and have a longer period for harvest.

You can store late beetroot by packing it in moist sand and placing it in a cool, dark cellar. You can store Swiss chard by freezing it.

Cabbage and Relatives

Choices

I've included a number of related crops here under one heading because they have several similarities. These crops include broccoli, Brussels sprouts, cabbage, cauliflower, Chinese kale, kohlrabi, and mustard. We collectively call all of these plants brassicas.

With broccoli, the main crop comes from the large, terminal cluster of green buds. Later in the growing season, you can harvest the small sprouts at lower positions. Some broccoli varieties produce more and larger lower buds. My favourites for extended harvests are 'Mercedes' and 'Calabrese Corvet'. 'Green Comet' is a good variety producing early crops.

The best tasting and sweetest Brussels sprouts are those you harvest in the autumn after a touch of frost. Sprouts mature from the bottom up, so you do get a somewhat extended harvest. 'Peer Gynt' is a well-known reliable Brussels sprout, but there are many other varieties to choose from.

Cabbages offer many choices, varying in their head shape and colour, their harvest time (early, midseason, late and winter cabbages are available) and the smoothness or crinkledness of the leaves within the head. I'll make only a few cabbage suggestions, since choices are numerous and good. The earliest producing cabbages are 'Greyhound' and 'Hispi'. For red or purple cabbage, try 'Red Drumhead' or 'Ruby Ball'. If you like crinkled leaves, go for 'Savoy King' or 'Wivoy'. For winter storage, try 'Lariat', 'Late Danish' or 'Wisconsin All-Season'.

We grow cauliflowers for their large, edible head, which is essentially a thick flower cluster. Most cauliflowers are white, although a purple form is available. Some kinds of cauliflower require tying of the leaves for blanching the head, while others are self-blanching because of their curved outer leaves. The purple varieties of cauliflower require no blanching and retain their colour when used fresh in salads but turn green upon cooking. To grow the purple varieties, try 'Royal Purple' or 'Purple Cape'. Good examples of white cauliflowers are 'Dok Elgon', 'Snow Crown' and 'All the Year Round'.

Chinese cabbage is more like lettuce than cabbage and this vegetable is becoming increasingly popular. Varieties include 'Tip Top'. 'Saucepan' and 'Green Rocket'.

Gardeners grow kohlrabi for the swollen bulbous stem portion that grows near ground level. Essentially kohlrabi looks like a small turnip sitting above ground. Kohlrabi's raw taste is somewhat similar to that of a water chestnut, while its cooked taste seems to mingle the flavours of cabbage and turnip. Some older kohlrabi choices are 'Purple Vienna' and 'White Vienna'; while a newer variety is 'Fekara'. Kohlrabi colours vary from white to purple.

Culture

As a rule all the brassica crops, if planted as transplants, will germinate in 10 to 14 days at 70°F. Cauliflower tends to come a little quicker at 10 days and kohlrabi later at 14 days and the other brassica crops tend towards the middle of the range. Sow the seeds ½ inch deep. You can easily grow all the brassica crops as transplants in our polystyrene cups with one plant to an 8 or 12 fluid ounce cup.

For intensive plantings of brassica crops, use an 18-inch square. If you plant in rows, set the plants 18 inches apart within the rows and have 18 inches between rows. Brussels sprouts work out better with 24-inch spacing. Some specific facts for each brassica crop follow.

Broccoli is best set out in the garden as transplants, starting them five to seven weeks ahead of transplanting them. Because broccoli is very hardy, you can place the transplants outside two or three weeks prior to your last spring frost. For a continuous crop, you can use an early and late cultivar, sow transplants at two-week intervals or select a cultivar noted for continued production of lower buds after the main harvest. Don't forget to start transplants for an autumn crop of broccoli, as well. Set out autumn transplants about two-and-a-half months before your killing autumn frost. Depending upon your garden season, you can follow spring broccoli with beetroot, carrots or French beans or an autumn crop of lettuce, spinach or radishes. You can interplant broccoli with lettuce or spinach.

Brussels sprouts taste best when you grow them as an autumn crop. You can set transplants out four months before the first killing autumn frost. Start the transplants six to eight weeks ahead or sow seeds directly outdoors at this same time. Brussels sprouts can follow any early crop that allows enough time for the sprouts to mature, such as radishes, lettuce, peas or spinach.

Cabbage is hardy, even hardier than broccoli. You can set transplants out three to five weeks before your last spring killing frost. I suggest that you use transplants and put them out early, because heat and cabbage don't mix well. Start cabbage transplants four to six weeks before you wish to plant them in your garden. Autumn cabbage transplants can go out about three months prior to the first killing frost. For continuous harvests you can mix early, midseason, late or winter cultivars of cabbage. You can follow early cabbage with French beans, marrows or late sweetcorn, late cabbage can follow beetroot, early potatoes, lettuce, peas, radishes or spinach. You can also interplant cabbage with lettuce, radishes, carrots, beetroot or spinach.

Cauliflower is more tender and fussier than the other brassica crops. You can put transplants out no sooner than two weeks before the last killing frost in the spring. Start the cauliflower transplants five to seven weeks before you plant them in the garden. Don't delay planting your transplants in the garden beyond your last spring frost, because cauliflowers do poorly in hot or dry weather. For an autumn crop, directly sow the seeds in the garden about three months before the autumn frost. The interplanting and succession of cauliflower is similar to that of broccoli.

You can either sow seeds directly or as transplants about three months prior to the first killing frost in the autumn. You should set out the transplants when they are five to six weeks of age. Chinese cabbage can follow any non-brassica crop that allows enough free space for the cabbage to grow.

Kale can have either curly or uncurly leaves and does best in cooler weather but can take more heat than cabbage. You can sow the seeds directly into the garden as soon as you can work the soil, or you can set out five- to six-week-old transplants two to four weeks before the last killing frost in the spring.

You can plant five- to seven-week-old kohlrabi transplants up to three weeks before the last killing spring frost or you can directly sow kohlrabi seeds when your garden soil is workable. Sowings at two-week intervals will give a continuous crop.

You can handle mustard transplants and direct spring sowings in the same manner that you handle kale. You can plant seeds at three- or four-week intervals for successive crops. An autumn sowing of mustard is possible about eight weeks before the killing frost.

Pests

Brassica crops experience similar pests and diseases. Use crop rotations to eliminate pest and disease problems and be sure that brassica crops do not succeed each other in the same place. The brassica crop pests that are of most concern include the cabbage aphid, looper, root maggot, worms and harlequin bug. Bacterial pesticides containing *Bacillus thuringiensis*, such as Bactospeine WP (available from the HDRA and Chase Organics – for their addresses, see page 165) will control cabbage loopers and worms. Soap sprays work well for aphids and harlequin bugs. With pyrethrum and derris, you can control all of the pests with the exception of the root maggot. To control the root maggot, you must stop the adult fly from laying eggs by using the fleece barrier over the plants. The flies appear about one month after the last killing spring frost in my area. Paper disks placed tightly around the plant stem will also control root maggot. The main disease problem of brassica crops is club root which you can control by using crop rotation and resistant cultivars.

Harvest

Pick broccoli before the buds start to open and show yellow. Cut the head with a sharp knife, taking a few inches of the main stem. Lower sprouts will develop and give you additional harvests over several weeks.

With Brussels sprouts, cut off the miniature heads close to the stem with a sharp knife. Harvest the lower parts first, when the sprouts are 1 inch to 1¼ inches in diameter. Ripening of Brussels sprouts gradually proceeds from the bottom up to the top of the plant, so your harvest will continue for several weeks. If you want to rush the harvest, remove the upper leaves and terminal leaf cluster to speed ripening.

Pick cabbage when the heads have

formed well, are firm and are glossy green. Heads should weigh 2 pounds or more and be a whitish colour inside. Judge the readiness of Chinese cabbage heads by days to maturity and size.

With cauliflower, you have to do some extra work, unless you have a self-blanching variety. Once the upper leaves of the cauliflower curl away and start to expose the head, pull them together and tie them with string. If the weather is warm, the head will be ready to pick in three to five days; in cool weather it can take up to two weeks. Make sure you pick the head when the curds are white and tight. If the curds are discoloured, loose and look like rice, the head is too old.

Harvest kale and mustard leaves for salads or greens before they become tough and woody. If you harvest the outer leaves of the plants and don't disturb the growing points, the plants will keep on producing leaves for a longer harvest.

Pick kohlrabi when it is 2 to 2½ inches in diameter, before it becomes tough and stringy. Toughness sets in when kohlrabi is 3 inches in diameter.

Broccoli, Brussels sprouts, cabbage, cauliflower and Chinese cabbage all mature in 60 to 100 days. Kale and kohlrabi need 55 to 70 days and mustard is ready to pick in 35 to 45 days.

Carrots

Choices

Carrots vary considerably in shape from long and pointed to blunt and cylindrical to short and round. Too many cultivars exist to name them all, but I would like to mention a few. Short carrots, such as 'Suko' or 'Kundulus' are better to grow if your soil tends to be shallow or heavy. If you like little baby carrots try 'Early French Fame'. If you like juicy carrots, then try 'Mokum'.

Culture

Carrots have only one fussy requirement, but it is very critical. The slightest obstruction, such as a stone, can deform the roots of a carrot. Heavy soils also stunt root formation. To grow carrots you need a sandy deep loam that is free of pebbles. If you don't have sandy, deep loam, use a raised bed as discussed in Chapter 3, to grow carrots.

You can sow carrot seeds with the ridger as soon as you can work the soil, roughly three weeks before your last killing frost. Cover the seeds with ½ inch of soil. Germination is slow, taking 14 to 21 days. You can put some radishes in the row, because they will germinate quickly and mark the rows. Be sure to rid your garden of weeds as soon as you see them otherwise, they will have a large head start by the time your carrots come up.

For a really quick carrot crop, start your carrots in our polystyrene cups, planting seeds at the outer cup edge and thinning to three transplants per cup, equally spaced along the rim. Start the carrot transplants about six to eight weeks before you expect the last killing frost in the spring.

For intensive spacing, thin the seedlings to stand 2 or 3 inches apart in all directions. If you use the transplants in the polystyrene cups, place the cups equally distant at 3 inches.

You can sow succession crops of carrots at three-week intervals up to 75 days before autumn frosts, but keep in mind that the best growth of carrots occurs at 60° to 70°F. Avoid planting so that carrots finish up during hot weather. Interplantings of carrots with lettuce work well, as do carrots and radishes or onions. You can follow early crops such as peas or radishes with a planting of carrots.

Pests

Carrot flies lay eggs that become maggots which tunnel through the carrots. These dark green flies appear about a month after the last spring frost, so you can ward off these pests by covering the carrots early with a fleece blanket. Sage plantings nearby also seem to repel the carrot fly. Later plantings that miss the carrot fly are another possibility for thwarting this pest. Carrot-willow aphid is another troublesome pest you might come across. It can inject the crop with a disease called carrot motley dwarf disease.

Harvest

You can pick carrots that are from finger size up to 2 inches in diameter. A rough guide to harvesting is that carrots mature in 65 to 75 days from seed. The flavour of the carrot is best closer to maturity when its pale orange colour becomes bright orange. If at any time the tops of the carrots expose themselves, cover them with soil to prevent them from turning green. Carrots intended for storage should be a late crop picked near maturity. Storage is best under cool, moist conditions, such as in sand or sawdust in an unheated cellar. You can also leave carrots in the ground and cover them with several inches of hay or straw. You can dig your carrots up to the time the ground freezes.

Courgettes

Choices

Courgettes grow on large, sprawling vines on bushy plants. We use immature courgettes in the summer and don't store them for winter. The skin of courgettes is fragile and yellow, green or whitish green in colour, while the flesh is usually a white to cream colour. Courgettes are generally cylindrical, club-like or flattened and acorn-like in shape.

Many cultivars of courgettes exist so it's difficult to choose favourites. New introductions also occur frequently, making the decision even harder. As such, we can't cover all cultivars in this book. Bill and I have favourites, which we realize may not be yours. We try new kinds every year, always comparing them to our 'old reliables'. Our following thoughts on courgettes we have known may help you to make your decision on what varieties to grow.

My favourite courgette is 'Richgreen Hybrid Zucchini', although other good varieties include 'Buccaneer', 'Burpee Hybrid Zucchini', 'Cocozelle', 'Green Magic' and 'Grey Zucchini'. Yellow forms of zucchini are also available, such as 'Gold Rush'.

Culture

Plant courgette seeds 1 inch deep. It doesn't pay to put the seeds out until two or three weeks after the last killing spring frost, because courgettes are warm-season plants. Seeds germinate in seven to ten days at 70°F. You can use the ridger, dibber or bulb planter for outdoor sowing of seeds.

You should grow courgettes as transplants if you want to have them early for food. Also, early plants often resist some insect pests much better. Start the courgettes in the 12 fluid ounce modified polystyrene cups about four weeks before you wish to set them in the garden. You can set them out two weeks after the last spring frost. If you use a polypropylene or slitted polythene cloche, you can put the transplants in the garden a week or two earlier. The cloche combined with black plastic will give you a three-week edge.

Make sure you put down black plastic at the same time you start your transplants. In this way, you will warm the soil to prepare it for the transplants, especially if you put a cloche over the plastic. Intensive plantings of courgettes consist of placing single plants down the middle of 4-foot-wide sheets at 3-foot intervals. Put the plants in the soil with the bulb planter, making sure that you put some organic matter and fertilizer in each hole, as suggested for big feeders in Chapter 4. You can also plant courgettes in mini-hills (see Chapter 3).

Pests
Aphids may carry cucumber mosaic virus. Control aphids with soap sprays or derris.

Diseases that bother cucumbers can also attack courgettes, with the most troublesome being powdery mildew. Rotations and early plantings avoid most of these diseases.

Harvest
Pick courgettes when they are 5 to 8 inches long. Your fingernail should easily pierce the skin of courgettes if they are ripe. Make sure you keep picking the courgettes to assure continued later yields.

Cucumbers

Choices
When it comes to cucumbers, many more choices exist than you may think. Conventional salad cucumbers are long and narrow, while pickling types are somewhat shorter and wider. Seedless cucumbers also exist and are milder, much longer and more slender than conventional cucumbers. Most seedless cucumbers are greenhouse varieties, but a few cultivars are also available for outdoor planting. You can even find a cucumber that is yellow and looks a bit like a lemon – the 'Crystal Apple'!

Some cucumbers have all female flowers instead of both male and female flowers. These all-female types (gynoecious) produce more cucumbers than conventional types do.

A few of the many conventional hybrid cucumbers for salads include 'Conqueror' and 'Telegraph'. If you want early conventional cucumbers, try 'Early Triumph' or 'Early Pride'. If cucumbers make you burp, try some of the burpless ones such as 'Burpless Tasty Green'. If you have limited space but you don't want a vertical garden, try the dwarf forms such as 'Patio-Pik F_1', and 'Bush Crop'. For pickling cucumbers try 'Bestal' and 'Gherkin Couda'. If you like the idea of gynoecious cucumbers with heavy yields, try 'Sweet Success' (also burpless). For a taste treat, try some of the seedless cucumbers such as 'Telegraph Improved'. Japanese cucumbers that are similar to these include 'Suyo Long' (has ridges), 'Chinese Long Green' (smooth) and 'Kyoto' (smooth). Plant these seedless cucumbers away from regular cucumbers to prevent pollination and seed formation.

Culture
Cucumbers are a warm-season crop, so plant them directly outdoors no earlier than one or two weeks after the last killing frost. Moisture is also critical to cucumber growth and cucumbers have a visual way of showing that they are not receiving enough moisture. As such, cucumbers and moisture-conserving black plastic mulches make a great partnership. Plant cucumber seeds about ½ inch deep with the ridger or dibber.

To get very early cucumbers, start the seeds indoors four to six weeks before outdoor planting times. At 70°F cucumbers germinate in seven to ten days. I use our polystyrene cups (12 fluid ounce) and thin to one cucumber plant per cup. Remember, cucumbers are finicky about transplanting, so start them in our specially modified cups. Cucumbers are a natural for vertical gardens. I place seeds or transplants at

12-inch intervals for intensive plantings. Initially you may have to tie the cucumbers to your vertical supports to encourage them to climb.

If you want a longer harvest, grow early and late cucumbers. You can also put in a second sowing four to five weeks after the first, which could also follow an early vertical crop, such as peas.

Pests

Plants may be attacked by glasshouse red spider mite. If they are, spray with derris.

Some diseases that attack cucumbers include powdery mildew, anthracnose, verticillium wilt, stem rot and viruses. If these diseases trouble your cucumbers, look for resistant varieties of cucumbers, rotate your crops, and be sure to clean up all debris in the area. These diseases can be carried over in debris from infected plants.

Harvest

Pick cucumbers when they become dark green but are not overly large. As cucumbers get bigger and show yellow or white, seeds have formed and the cucumbers become bitter. European and Japanese types being seedless, can get much bigger than conventional cucumbers. Days to harvest are 55 to 70, depending upon the cultivar.

Herbs

I would like to say a few quick words about herbs. While I don't grow all of them, I do grow a few favourites like parsley, basil and dill. Many herbs dislike transplanting, so I recommend using our modified polystyrene cups, which produce great herb transplants from seed that go ever so nicely into the garden with the bulb planter. The ones I've tried grow well with the use of black plastic. Sow the seeds indoors at 70°F about four to six weeks prior to your first frost-free date. Use the 12 fluid ounce cups, thinning to one plant per cup. After you harden the transplants, put them into your garden about one week after your frost-free date. Many herb seeds have special requirements for germination, such as refrigeration prior to sowing or light during germination. Other herb seeds have short lives and you can't save them.

I know of about three dozen herbs. Detailed information as such is beyond the scope of this book. If you intend to grow herbs, I suggest you consult other sources of information. Many books exist, but I find two to be most helpful, *Planning the Organic Herb Garden* by Sue Stickland (Thorsons, 1986) and *The Herb Book* by Arabella Boxer and Philippa Back (Octopus, 1980).

Lettuce

Choices

Head qualities determine lettuce choice. One of the most popular types of lettuce has a firm, hard head and is grouped with the crisp lettuces, often called the iceberg type. Crisp lettuce is the hardest to grow for home gardeners and has the least heat resistance, but a large number of people still wish to grow it. Of all the crisp lettuces, I would recommend 'Lakeland' and 'Webb's Wonderful'.

A second lettuce group, the cabbage lettuce, has heads that are loose and soft. The taste of cabbage lettuce is much better than that of the crisp lettuces and its heat tolerance is slightly better. Some of the cabbage lettuce cultivars include 'Buttercrunch', 'All the Year Round' and 'Avondefiance'.

A third group consists of lettuces that have a rosette of loose leaves, essentially no head, and we call them loose-leaf or leaf lettuce. Leaf lettuce has a good taste and moderate heat resistance. Leaf lettuce also has colour variations. A bronze-green/crimson variety is 'Red Salad Bowl' while a typical green leaf lettuce is 'Salad Bowl'. For the lovers of baby or gourmet vegetables, there is 'Tom Thumb'.

The last group consists of lettuces with tall, slender, upright, loose heads and we term them Cos lettuce. Cos cultivars include 'Little Gem'. 'Lobjoits Green Cos' and 'Winter Density'.

Culture

Lettuce is a cool-season crop. Heat causes lettuce to bolt (flower), whereupon the taste becomes bitter. You can plant lettuce seed outdoors as early as you can work the soil. Transplants or seeds can go outdoors one to three weeks before the last killing spring frost. Seeds should be fresh, not saved, because they are short-lived. The germination of lettuce seeds requires light. You can directly seed with the ridger, using ¼-inch-deep scratches. I usually start lettuce transplants four to six weeks ahead of outdoor planting time in 8 fluid ounce cups. Press the seeds lightly into the growing mixture, thinning to one plant to a cup. Twelve fluid ounce cups can carry two or three lettuce transplants. At 70°F the seeds germinate in seven to ten days. Succession planting at two-week intervals will extend the harvest, but make sure you stop the plantings so that the last lettuce matures at average temperatures no higher than 65°F. You can resume your lettuce plantings in late summer.

Lettuce, especially the heading types, requires considerable moisture to grow. Lack of moisture causes a failure to head. As such, black plastic and lettuce are great partners. I usually place leaf lettuces with the bulb planter at 6-inch intervals for intensive plantings through black plastic and I give the heading types 12-inch squares in which to grow.

In the spring you can follow lettuce with dwarf French beans or beetroot. In the autumn you can follow the French beans with more lettuce. You can interplant lettuce with marrows, dwarf French beans, cabbage, broccoli, carrots or onions.

To get a few weeks more time out of lettuce in the warmer weather, shade it by stretching the fleece material or cheesecloth across some poles, like a roof. Another approach to extending the growing season of lettuce is to interplant the lettuce with something that shades the lettuce at its maturity, such as marrows, climbing beans or tomatoes.

Pests

Aphids, lettuce root aphids, cutworms and slugs can be troublesome to lettuce plants. Use soap sprays to knock out the aphids, leave part of the polystyrene cup rim in place to foil cutworms, and hand-collect slugs at dusk with a torch. You can also sprinkle wood ashes or limestone around the plants to rid them of slugs, because slugs don't like to cross this dry barrier.

Some diseases that bother lettuce are grey mould and viruses. If you have trouble with grey mould, remove and burn the infected parts and make sure you keep your vegetable garden clear of debris as this can harbour the spores responsible for the mould. If your vegetables fall prey to viruses, destroy them. Ensure that you keep your garden clear of dead leaves and so on and when buying new seeds or plants, choose disease-resistant cultivars where possible. Controlling aphids will help prevent the problem arising as they can spread viral diseases.

Onions and Relatives

Choices

Choices abound in the onion group. You can have yellow, red or white domestic onions. If you pick onions when they are immature, that is, pencil-thin to marble-size onions, we refer to them as spring onions. Somewhat similar to spring onions, Japanese onions have more pronounced leaves and a bulb that is thinner and softer but more thickened at the neck than that of spring onions. Unlike spring onions, Japanese onions do not develop into large onions if you let them grow longer. There are also mini-onions, sometimes referred to as pearl onions. Pearl onions are popular creamed or in a mixed pea and onion dish. There is even an onion variety that forms bulblets on top (the tree or Egyptian onion).

Chives, garlic, leeks and shallots are also members of the onion family. We grow chives for their small leaves that have a delicate onion flavour. One form of chive grown infrequently has a garlic-like flavour. We grow garlic for its flavourful bulb, which splits into cloves. Leeks have a slight, soft, flattened bulb with a sheath of leaves. The flavour of leeks is milder and sweeter than that of onions. Shallots have a multiple bulb that we use when young. Shallots have a delicate flavour and find use in gourmet cooking as do leeks.

Onions are available in a variety of shapes, sizes and colours. 'Ailsa Craig' produces a large globe-shaped bulb with a mild flavour and is often grown for exhibition. 'Sweet Sandwich' becomes very mild after it has been stored for a few weeks and is suitable for eating raw. If you would like to grow a red onion, I would suggest you try 'Carmen'.

You can pull any one of these onions young as spring onions. Cultivars that essentially remain spring onions throughout their development are the Japanese spring onions, such as 'Ishikuro' and 'White Lisbon'. A good pearl onion is 'Aviv' (Surrons), while the tree onion usually sold as Egyptian tree onions is probably 'Perennial Tree'.

There are few other names for garlic. Usually it is classified as either the early white, or Mexican, type or the late pink, or Italian, type. There are no other names for chives either, with the exception of the garlic version called garlic chives. A number of leeks are available, such as 'Musselburgh', 'Lyon' and 'Gennevilliers Splendid'. Suppliers sell shallots as 'Dutch Yellow' or 'Giant Long Keeping Red'.

Culture

You can grow domestic onions (yellow, red or white) from seeds, sets or plants. Sets are convenient, plants produce more quickly, and seeds are cheaper but take longer to mature than sets or plants. You can produce your own transplants easily with seeds or get results with direct seeding. One plus with seed is that you have a much larger choice of cultivars. You can plant all forms outside two to four weeks before the last killing spring frost, using the ridger for seeds, sets and plants or the dibber for sets or plants.

When planting onions, be sure you use fresh seeds as onion seed ages rather quickly. Start your seeds eight to ten weeks ahead of your putting-out date. I use the 12 fluid ounce polystyrene cups for my transplants and cover the seeds with ½ inch of growing medium. Seeds come up in 10 to 14 days at 70°F. You can thin the plants to about three equally spaced transplants per cup. When you plant the transplants in your garden, put in the whole group with the bulb planter or each transplant separately with a dibber. If you don't want this

Figure 51. These onions need to have soil mounded around their bases to cover the exposed bulbs.

bother, just buy and plant sets, covering the sets with 1 inch of soil. Set transplants to the depth at which they were growing. You can also plant seeds directly outdoors in a ½-inch ridger scratch. Use a 3-inch spacing between every plant for intensive plantings of onions. You can follow onions with French beans or interplant them with lettuce.

You must raise leeks as transplants because they take a long time to mature. Use the same standards for cups, seed depth and germination time as you used for onions. Place each leek transplant in a dibber hole so that only 2 inches of leaf protrudes. If you do this you won't have to mound soil at the plant base to blanch the lower part of the leek later. Leeks are a touch hardier than onions.

You can easily raise chives as transplants, but be sure to use fresh seeds. Lightly press the seeds into the growing medium. Use a 12 fluid ounce cup and thin to four transplants per cup. Seeds germinate at the same rate as onions. Put the transplants into the garden with the bulb planter, placing four holes close together and putting in four groups. This pattern will fill in nicely

and give you a good clump. These plants are perennials, so planting chives is a once-and-done job. Just divide the clump every two or three years.

Gardeners usually plant shallots as a clove from the multiple bulb and you can use either the dibber or bulb planter. Set the cloves deeply enough so that the soil barely covers them. You can also plant garlic cloves with the bulb planter, covering the cloves with about 1 inch of soil.

Pests

One insect which is a real pest to onions and their relatives is the onion fly. If this pest arrives on the scene, put up your fleece barrier. Diseases that affect the onion family include smut, downy mildew, neck rot and viral diseases. I never have these disease problems, most likely because I rotate my onions on a three-year schedule. Remember also to keep the space free of garlic, chives, leeks and shallots during this time, because the same diseases can attack these onion relatives.

Harvest

Domestic onions require 110 to 130

days from seed to harvest, while foreign onions need 125 to 185 days. Shallots usually need 90 to 110 days to mature, garlic needs 150 to 180 days and leeks need 180 days. You can pick immature onions as spring onions and immature shallots as green onions. Onions, shallots and garlic are mature when their tops fall over and dry. At this point, you can lift the bulbs, air-dry them on a rack inside a garage and store them in a cool, dry place. You can pick chives at any point, but take only part of the leaves or a fraction of the total leaves if you take the whole leaf, so the plant can keep on growing. You can rinse, chop and freeze chives in a plastic bag for later use. Pick leeks when they are 1 to 1½ inches in diameter, and pick clustering onions any time during the season.

Peas

Choices

As my first crop to go into the soil, peas mark the start of a new garden season. You have some choice with peas. The standard garden pea comes either smooth or wrinkled, with the wrinkled ones having the sweeter (and better) taste. Next we have the old edible-podded peas, mangetout. More recently another edible-podded pea appeared, snap peas. The difference between this new cultivar and the older one is that the edible pod lasts much longer and is sweeter, and you consume the pod with larger peas than with the mangetout.

Standard garden peas include 'Lincoln', 'Alderman' and 'Hurst Green Shaft'. For early peas, try 'Little Marvel', 'Feltham First' and 'Meteor'. If you're into freezing peas, try 'Multi Star'. You say you love pea soup? Then go for 'Century'.

'Oregon Sugar Pod' is a fine example of a mangetout cultivar. The first new snap pea, 'Sugar Snap' is tall, requires support, and harvests later than newer introductions, but I think that taste-wise, it's the best. 'Sugar Rae' is short but not early. Short and early choices include 'Sugar Anne' and 'Sugar Bon'. Besides good taste, 'Sugar Snap' shows a touch more heat tolerance and frost resistance than do garden peas.

Culture

Peas are an early, cool-season crop and are a legume crop, like beans, which pulls free nitrogen fertilizer from the air if you inoculate the seeds with the required bacteria (see Beans).

You can seed peas directly into your garden as soon as you can work the soil. In most cases this time period works out to be anywhere from one to five weeks before your last killing frost in the spring. You can use the ridger, dibber or bulb planter to plant pea seeds, covering the seeds with 1 to 2 inches of soil.

I suggest the following intensive planting system. Firstly, provide some support for the peas, whether it be pea sticks, nylon net or a pea fence (see Chapter 7). Next, plant a double row, one on each side of the support and 9 inches away from the support, which gives you roughly 18 inches between the rows. Seeds germinate in 7 to 14 days depending on soil temperature.

If you lose a lot of seeds to rot prior to germination or just want the earliest peas possible, try the following planting system. Soak pea seeds overnight at room temperature, then plant several seeds 1 inch deep in each 12 fluid ounce modified polystyrene cup. The seeds should come up in seven days or less. Perform the steps just mentioned four to six weeks before normal outdoor seeding time. At the same time, lay down a strip of black plastic where your peas will go in the garden, then put up your vertical supports. The black plastic will warm the soil just enough to get your transplants off to a good start. Thin each cup to three nicely spaced transplants. Put the transplants through the plastic with the bulb planter, using the double row concept and leaving 3 inches between each cup hole in the row. About one month later, cut and remove the plastic to prevent over-warming of the pea roots. This entire process will give you the earliest ever peas.

For a more continual pea harvest, you can plant early and late cultivars or sow the same peas at ten-day intervals. Make sure your last sowing occurs before daytime temperatures frequently start to reach 60°F. You can follow peas with another climbing crop, such as climbing beans or cucumbers or with crops such as sweetcorn, beetroot, carrots, French dwarf beans, late cabbage, or marrows.

Pests

The pea weevil is sometimes trouble-some to pea plants. If you sow your peas after mid-June and before mid-July, you should not be bothered by pea moths. If you are going to be visited by pea thrips, you will see them on the plants from June onwards. Aphids can be despatched with soap sprays, derris or pyrethrum. Rotations and garden sanitation ward off weevil problems. Pea thrips, pea moths and aphids can also be troublesome. Disease problems of peas include powdery and downy mildew, foot rot and fusarium wilt; but crop rotation appears to control these diseases.

Harvest

For the best pea quality, carefully pick them in the morning. Damaged vines yield less for later pickings. With garden peas, look for well-developed green peas, making sure that you pick them before the peas start to harden, other-wise, they become starchy and lose their sweetness. You can also pick dried peas for pea soup. You should refrigerate peas upon picking and use them quickly if you wish the peas to be sweet.

Pick mangetout when their pods are flat and the peas are just forming. If you miss this stage, treat mangetout in the same manner as garden peas. Pick mangetout peas with green pods and nicely developed but not hard peas. The sweetness of snap peas is much more stable than with the other kinds of peas. Most snap peas have a string, which you remove prior to raw or cooked con-sumption. Freezing of snap peas is possible, but the results are not as good as with garden peas.

Peppers

Choices

We can divide peppers in two basic groups: sweet and hot or chilli. Sweet peppers are mild and go from green to red or yellow when ripe. You can use sweet peppers raw in salads or you can stuff or fry them. Hot peppers vary from zesty hot to steamy knockouts. Although usually long and tapered, hot peppers also come in round or sausage shapes.

Standard sweet peppers of the green to red types include 'Bell Boy', and 'Comape'. If you want huge peppers, try 'Big Bertha'. Yellow versions include 'Top Banana' and 'Yellow Lantern'.

If you would like to grow hot pep-pers I suggest trying 'Hot Gold Spike' and 'Red Chili'.

Culture

Peppers require warmth and time for results. Yields are often fickle for several reasons. Blossoms fail to set fruit below 55°F or if the humidity is low. Low soil moisture or prolonged high tempera-tures also reduce fruiting. The first fruits, unless picked off, reduce subsequent yields.

It's preferable to start peppers as transplants six to eight weeks ahead of setting-out time. Peppers can go out about one week to ten days after the last killing spring frost. I place seeds ½ inch deep in the modified polystyrene cups. At 70°F seeds come up in roughly two weeks, but placing transplants on the top of a refrigerator (75°F) can cut this time to ten days. Thin the pepper plants to one plant per 12 fluid ounce cup.

For the earliest and biggest yields of peppers, put down black plastic about three weeks before you put out the transplants. The plastic warms up the soil, giving your peppers a quick send-off. Later, the plastic helps retain soil moisture, which encourages fruiting. Plant the peppers at an intensive 12-inch spacing with the bulb planter. You can add organic matter to the hole if you wish; but don't add any more fertilizer other than the organic rapid starter solution, because adding too much nitrogen to the soil causes peppers to leaf excessively with few fruits.

After your peppers are in the ground, cover them with a fleece cloche. The cloche warms up the air, giving you earlier fruit set. Remember, fruit set ceases below 55°F. When the first one or two pepper flowers just start to fruit, pinch them off, and you will improve later total yields.

Pests

The main pest that attacks peppers is the glasshouse red spider mite.

Diseases of the pepper plant include bacterial spot, blight, anthracnose, tobacco mosaic virus, cucumber mosaic virus and curly top virus. Aphids and leafhoppers spread the diseases, so keep after these pests if they appear. Smokers can also transfer tobacco mosaic virus so if you smoke, wash your hands well

before touching peppers. Rotations help to keep disease problems down as well, but make sure you keep the areas free of pepper relatives: aubergines, potatoes and tomatoes.

Harvest

Peppers start producing in 55 to 75 days from transplants, depending upon the cultivar. You can pick peppers green or when they turn yellow or red. Cut the fruit and leave a piece of attached stem, because you can very easily damage pepper plants and cause yields to go down if you pull the peppers off the stem. In addition, just before frost you may find that you have a huge crop of green peppers in various stages of development, as I usually do. I pick them all when frost threatens. After washing them, I core the pepper and cut it into strips, placing the strips (without blanching first) into freezer bags to freeze them. As recipes call for peppers, as in pizza, I take what I need from the bag. While softer than freshly cut peppers, frozen peppers taste great after a little cooking. My wife and I enjoy the pepper strips all winter long, especially uncooked in salads.

Potatoes

Choices

Potatoes come with either white or red skins. We grow some potatoes specifically for baking and others for boiling. We grow early potatoes for fresh, short-term use and late potatoes for storage.

The most popular early potato, 'White Cobbler', has good baking qualities but poor storage qualities. 'Red Pontiac', a red-skinned potato, is an early-to-midseason, all-purpose potato that stores reasonably well. 'Kennebec' boils well and 'Russet Burbank' is a good baker. Both of these cultivars are late, brown-skinned, and have good storage qualities.

Culture

Potatoes are a cool-season crop with moderate frost tolerance. The potatoes or tubers form best when days are on the short side and temperatures are around 60° to 65°F.

We don't plant potatoes from seed but rather from seed potatoes, because potatoes do not grow uniformly true from seed. That is, young plants grown from seed will not produce plants (or potatoes) exactly like the parents. Although there is a potato called 'Explorer' that comes true from seed, I was quite unhappy with its size and yield when I grew it. The best seed potatoes are little tubers that weigh between 1 and 2 ounces and have at least one eye, such as 'Spud Buds' from Park Seed. You can also buy cut pieces of potato that have dried and contain one eye as seed potatoes or make your own, but be sure you get medium-sized, certified seed potatoes to avoid disease problems.

You will easily grow the best potatoes you have ever had if you lay black plastic mulch down two weeks before your last killing frost in the spring. Using your bulb planter, place 4-inch-deep holes at spacings of 12 inches in all directions. After the organic rapid starter solution soaks into the soil, put a piece of seed potato in each hole and cover it. You will get sprouts in two to three weeks. You need not worry about weeds or mounding with soil – just remove the plastic at harvest time and dig.

You can plant late potatoes a few weeks or more after you have planted early potatoes and in the same manner. Plant late potatoes so that they will mature around the time you expect the killing autumn frost for best results.

Pests

Trouble can come to your potatoes in the form of aphids, but soap sprays can control these. If you are having trouble with scab, make sure that you do not use limestone before potatoes during crop rotation. Applying limestone once potatoes have been lifted separates limestone as far as possible from your next crop of potatoes.

Diseases that affect potatoes are scab, blight and viruses. Viral diseases are carried by aphids, so aphid control is important. The microorganism that causes scab fares poorly in a soil of high pH. Addition of organic matter to the soil when growing potatoes will help to lower the pH. Rotations and sanitation in the garden help to prevent diseases, and some degree of resistance is available with some cultures.

Harvest

Harvest new potatoes when the potato top flowers. New potatoes boil and cream well, but you must use them quickly. Harvest mature potatoes when the tops wither or about two weeks after the tops have frost-blackened. Carefully dig the potatoes with a fork. Don't wash them, but allow them to air dry for a day or two in a cool place, such as a garage. Store the potatoes in a cool, dark place. Potatoes mature in 90 to 120 days, depending on the cultivar. A final note: discard any potatoes showing green because this discoloration means there is a toxin present.

Radishes

Choices

Pungent radishes come in either globular, elongated globular or long, narrow shapes and they can be red, white, red and white (bicolour) or black. Based upon days to maturity, heat resistance and planting time, radishes can be grouped as early (spring) radishes, mid-season (summer) radishes and late (autumn or winter) radishes.

Examples of red spring radishes are 'Cherry Belle', 'Saxa Short Top' and 'Prinz Rotin'. 'Sparkler' is a bicolour spring radish, 'Pax', 'White Globe' and 'White Icicle' are white varieties. Late radishes (for autumn and winter harvest) are 'Black Spanish Round', 'Mino Early' and 'China Rose'.

Culture

You can sow radishes as soon as you can work your soil but not earlier than a month before your last killing frost in the spring. Use the ridger to plant them and cover the seeds with ½ inch of soil. While radish transplants are possible in the polystyrene cups, I see no advantage to using this approach. Seeds germinate rapidly, usually in four to six days. You can sow spring radishes at seven- to ten-day intervals for successive harvests, stopping at midspring and resuming in the autumn because spring radishes do poorly in warm weather. Thin the radishes to roughly 2 or 3 inches in all directions.

To stretch the radish season, use successive plantings of midseason radishes, which tolerate more heat than the early ones. Start planting midseason radishes about a month after you have planted the spring radishes, and discontinue plantings in the late spring. For autumn and storage radishes, sow late radishes in the late summer to early autumn, leaving about 5 to 6 inches between the autumn radishes.

You can also interplant spring radishes as seeds with beetroot or carrots. The radish seeds germinate quickly and mark the rows long before the slow beetroot or carrots appear. After you harvest the radishes, the beetroot or carrots fill in the space. You can interplant radishes with early crops such as lettuce or spinach, as well. Dwarf French beans make good fillers between spring and autumn radishes.

Pests

The only radish pests of note are flea beetles and root maggots. Use pyrethrum or derris to control the beetles. The root maggot is the same one that attacks cabbages, so don't utilize the same space for both crops. You can stop the root maggot with the fleece barrier. Some people even use the radish as a trap crop to keep root maggots away from cabbage.

Harvest

Spring radishes mature in 20 to 30 days, and you can pull them when they are the size of a large marble or bigger. Don't let them go much beyond maturity, as warm weather causes splitting, pithiness and extreme pungency. Summer radishes are ready in 35 to 45 days, and late radishes need 50 to 70 days. Store late radishes in moist sand in a cool cellar.

Spinach

Choices

Some spinach is described as being bolt resistant. Bolting refers to the formation of flower stalks and seeds by the spinach, an event that warm weather brings. Spinach is not worth harvesting after it bolts because the flavour turns bitter. Bolt-resistant spinach can take a bit more heat than ordinary cultivars, adding a week or two of extra harvest time.

Spinach varieties include 'King of Denmark', 'Long Standing Round' and 'Norvak'. The differences among these varieties involve bolt resistance, disease resistance, and degree of uprightness, a characteristic involving the leaf angle. The more upright forms of spinach experience less soil splash from rain and thus require less washing prior to cooking. New Zealand spinach has an advantage over other types of spinach in that it grows in the warmer months.

Culture

You can plant spinach seed as soon as you can work the soil, usually one to five weeks before your last killing spring frost. Use the ridger to plant the seeds, and cover them with ½ inch of soil. Seedlings appear in eight to ten days. Transplants are possible with polystyrene cups but offer no advantage except a few weeks extra on harvest time. Thin the seedlings to stand 3 inches apart in all directions for intensive plantings. For a continuous harvest, continue sowings at seven- to ten-day intervals until about six weeks before daytime temperatures will exceed 75°F. You can resume plantings in late summer, stopping about five weeks before your killing autumn frost. You can follow early plantings of spinach with sweetcorn, French beans, marrows or tomatoes and you can interplant spinach with onions or carrots.

Fill the summer void with a sowing of New Zealand spinach about two weeks after the last spring frost. You can make successive plantings at two-week intervals, but stop about ten weeks prior to the killing autumn frost. Ordinary spinach can take a few light frosts, but New Zealand spinach can't. Soak the seeds for one to two hours in water, starting out at 120°F, to improve germination. Using the ridger, sow seeds about 1 inch deep. The seeds will germinate in 12 to 20 days. Thin the plants to stand about 4 inches apart in all directions for intensive plantings.

Pests

Aphids and leaf miners are sometimes troublesome to spinach. Soap spray rids your spinach of aphids, but the only remedy for leaf miners is to put up the fleece barrier to prevent the adults from laying eggs. If you already have leaf miners, put your fleece barrier up about two weeks before the last killing spring frost and keep it in place for six to eight weeks, roughly when egg laying takes place. Also, make sure you keep the garden free of lamb's-quarters, because this weed hosts the leaf miner.

Harvest

Harvest spinach and New Zealand spinach by picking individual leaves. Don't take more than a fraction of the plant's leaves and you will be able to stretch the harvest. If you have successive spinach plantings, you can harvest the entire plant. Spinach is ready to harvest in 40 to 50 days, New Zealand spinach in 70 days.

Swedes and Turnips

Choices

Swedes and turnips are part of the cabbage group, but unlike the crops treated under cabbage, we grow swedes and turnips for their roots. As such, I prefer to treat them separately. These two root crops do differ from one another. Swedes are larger, hardier, require a longer growing season and have more neck at the leaf crown than do turnips. Swedes have a more pungent taste as opposed to the sweeter, milder taste of turnips. While the swede greens are edible, they are quite strong in flavour and are smooth and waxy. The more preferable turnip greens are rough and hairy. Most turnips have white flesh and most swedes have a yellow interior, but exceptions do exist.

Swede choices include 'Western Perfection' and 'Magnificent'. Many choices of turnips exist, such as 'Purple Top Milan', 'Gilfeather', 'Tokyo Cross', 'Snowball', 'White Milan' and 'Golden Ball'.

Culture

It is best to grow Swedes as an autumn crop, because of their cool-season requirement and longer growing season. Treat turnips as either a spring or autumn crop.

Plant both swedes and turnips about ¼ to ½ inch deep with the ridger, using either transplants or direct sowing. You can obtain earlier turnips with transplants, but it is impractical to try to obtain earlier swedes with transplants because you should harvest them near frost to get the best taste. However, swede transplants started at normal seeding time offer improved germination over direct seeding in the summer.

You can start turnip transplants four to six weeks ahead of their garden planting time and swede transplants at the outdoor seeding time. For swedes, sow the seeds three to three-and-a-half months before the expected autumn frost. You can plant spring crop turnips, either as transplants or as direct seedings, three to five weeks before the last killing spring frost. Autumn turnip crops go in two to three months before the autumn frost. I use 12 fluid ounce polystyrene cups for each transplant. Seeds germinate in seven to ten days at 70°F.

Intensive plantings of swedes and turnips need 8- and 4-inch spacing, respectively. As an autumn crop, both can follow peas or French beans, early sweetcorn or early potatoes. You can also interplant spring turnips with lettuce or spinach.

Pests

The pests and diseases that attack turnips and swedes are the same as those that attack cabbage. The most serious pest is the root maggot, but the fleece barrier can keep it in check. You must use crop rotations, remembering to keep the space free of any plants listed under Cabbage.

Harvest

The best time to harvest swedes is just after a light frost. You can store them in a dustbin in moist sand or peat in a cool but frost-free place (a garage is ideal) for 2 to 3 months.

Harvest turnips when they are 2 to 3 inches in diameter because mature turnips become tough and woody. Turnips fare poorly in storage. You can harvest greens at any time but they are best at a young age in terms of taste and tenderness.

Tomatoes

Choices

Tomatoes come in essentially two shapes: round and oblong. Round tomatoes vary from small, cherry-size ones to 1-pound or 2-pound giants. Their colours vary from red through pink and orange to yellow. Oblong tomatoes are plum tomatoes and pear tomatoes. Most are red, except for the yellow pear form. The plum tomatoes have a higher solids-to-liquid ratio and we mainly grow them for making tomato sauce. With their lower liquid content, they simmer to a thick sauce in less time.

If you want to grow tomatoes with outstanding flavour, try 'Gardener's Delight' or 'Harbinger'. 'Tigerella' produces an unusual-looking fruit that is red with yellow stripes! Dwarf tomatoes require less attention than the standard varieties I've just mentioned. 'Red Alert' and 'Pixie' are good flavoured dwarf tomatoes that are well worth trying.

If you want to make ketchup, 'Super Roma VF' is a disease resistant variety that makes very good ketchup.

If you want to try growing yellow tomatoes, look for 'Yellow Perfection' and 'Golden Sunrise' – they're certainly good if you're looking for something different.

Culture

Tomatoes are a long warm-season crop best grown from transplants. I suggest using the 12 fluid ounce modified polystyrene cups to grow your transplants, planting seed about six to eight weeks before your outdoor planting time. Plant three seeds in each cup, covering them with ½ inch of soil. At 70°F seeds germinate in eight to ten days, however, if you keep them on top of a refrigerator at 75°F, the seeds will germinate in five to seven days. Thin to the strongest plant for each cup. Use the bulb planter to put the transplants in the soil, making sure you dig the hole deeper than the plant to accommodate some fertilizer and organic matter. For normal plantings, put the transplants out in the garden about two weeks after the last killing spring frost.

If you want the earliest possible tomatoes, pick an early cultivar, be it large or small. Plan on putting your transplants out in the garden either on the date of your last killing frost or a few days later. Start your transplants about six to eight weeks before that date. About four weeks before your hardened transplants will go out in the garden, put black plastic over the garden soil, covering it with either a fleece or Melbourne cloche. The combined unit will raise the soil temperature considerably, so your tomatoes will go into warm soil. Also, tomatoes fail to set fruit below 55°F, so this extra soil warmth is especially important.

When you put your tomatoes out in the garden, undo one side of the cloche. Make a hole in the ground 2 to 3 inches deeper than the soil ball from the cup. Place a few handfuls of combined organic fertilizer, compost and soil into the hole, then add your rapid starter solu-

tion. After the solution drains into the soil, insert your transplant root ball, adding soil as needed. Finally, replace the side of the cloche. When you see blossoms on your tomato plants, either shake the plants for pollination or leave the cover off for an hour at noon. When hot weather consistently arrives, remove the cloche cover. Sit back and enjoy those early tomatoes!

Intensive plantings at 18-inch intervals are possible for determinate and staked, indeterminate tomatoes. If you stake your tomatoes, insert the stakes with your transplants to avoid root disturbance. Place large, unstaked tomatoes at 4-foot intervals. The use of black plastic is essential with unstaked tomatoes to eliminate the number of rotted tomatoes resulting from soil contact.

Some pruning is usually necessary with staked tomatoes. I suggest that you use a 6-foot-tall stake, tying the main stem to the stake and allowing the first sucker to become a second stem, which you tie to the stake. Trim off any other suckers. At weekly intervals, check the plant growth and continue to add ties.

You can, if you prefer, grow tomatoes in special wire cages instead of using stakes. You can buy ready-made square or circular cages. They often have wire prongs that let you anchor them into the soil without stakes. You can also make your own cages and a special wire is available for the purpose, with openings large enough to let you insert your hand to pick tomatoes. I make my own circular cages, 18 inches in diameter, and anchor them by tying each one to a short stake.

For a succession of tomatoes, plant either early and late choices or early, midseason and late cultivars. You can interplant tomatoes with various established brassica crops such as broccoli, cabbage or cauliflower.

A few words about the long storage tomatoes are in order. Start 'Long Keeper' tomatoes as transplants one month to six weeks after you start regular tomatoes, because you will plant it and pick it later than ordinary tomatoes. You can store 'Long Keepers' in the cellar. Mine have lasted until the end of January! The taste, while not as good as fresh summer tomatoes, is definitely superior to store-bought tomatoes.

Pests

Tomato pests include aphids, cutworms, eelworms, tomato moth, tomato whitefly and glasshouse red spider mite. You can rid your plants of aphids with soap sprays and of whiteflies with yellow sticky cards or soap sprays. Whitefly also give in to pyrethrum and derris. Use the polystyrene cup collar to ward off cutworms.

Some troublesome tomato plant diseases are potato blight, root knot, botrytis, stem rot and viruses. Use of a three-year rotation will keep diseases in check. Make sure you control aphids and so on with soap sprays or pyrethrum/derris because they can be carriers of viral diseases.

A nondisease disorder is blossom end rot. Blossom end rot comes from a combination of acid soil, low calcium, and inadequate water. A soil test with the addition of limestone, and mulching with black plastic will solve the blossom end rot problem.

CHAPTER 9
THE NO-DIG FLOWER GARDEN

I do enjoy my vegetable garden and hope to have one every year for as long as I can. And I'm sure that no-dig and no-weed methods will certainly make more years of gardening pleasure possible. However, to paraphrase a famous quotation, Man cannaot live by bread, or vegetables, alone. Each year I look forward to another side of gardening which offers its harvest in beauty and pleasure. Vegetables may be the 'bread' of gardening life, but flowers are the beauty.

Each year I plant those stalwarts of the flower garden, annuals. Their continuous parade of colour satisfies my need for attractive displays in my front and back gardens. Annuals also keep our table vase full of colour. If you think about annuals, I'm sure you'll find many more uses to add to the list. Let's take a closer look at annuals.

We consider any plant that produces stems and leaves with flowers and seeds and then dies in one growing season an annual. Annuals can be flowers or vegetables, but we will only concern ourselves with annual flowers in this chapter.

When considering annuals, most people think of about a dozen popular flowering plants: ageratum, alyssum, begonias, celosia, coleus, geraniums, impatiens, marigolds, petunias, salvia, verbena and zinnias. But did you know that there are actually over 150 annuals? Most of us get into the top-dozen rut

simply because garden centres push these plants during their spring bedding plant sales and all our neighbours have these plants. The point I'm trying to make is, dare to be different! Make a point of trying at least one new annual each year. You'll never run out of choices among the various seed catalogues.

Why do so many gardeners plant annuals? I think a very basic answer to this question is that annuals are easy to grow. Just about anyone can have good luck with growing annuals like marigolds or zinnias and, by using the no-dig approach, no one can say they have an excuse for not growing annuals in terms of work. Annuals also supply the greatest reward for the least amount of money. An inexpensive package of annual seeds can easily produce two dozen or more quickly growing plants and in no time reward you with colourful flowers. If you think of just about any colour or shade you'd like to see in your garden, some annual will fit the bill. There are even many annuals with two colours in their flowers, such as with some petunias and zinnias. Often, flowers such as marigolds and zinnias will last all season.

But colour is not the only characteristic that gives variety to flowers. Some annuals, like allyssum, are low to the ground, while others, like snapdragons, zoom upwards. Flowers can be tiny verbena or big sunflowers. Some flow-

Figure 52. This sequence of photographs shows a no-dig, no-weed flower garden from the time of transplanting through the growing season. The flower garden is located on my front lawn.

ers are simple in form, as with single petunias, while others are complex, like salvia. Yet other flowers, like impatiens, grow and bloom in shade, while zinnias fill your hot, dry corners with colour.

What can you do with annuals? Certainly, annuals are flowers of many uses. Anywhere you want a touch of colour, plant annuals. Put an island of flowers in your lawn or along a border, such as your property line, driveway, or walkway. If you have limited space, plant them in a window box. How about planting flowers in a container for touches of colour that you can move in a flash? You can use the colourful blossoms of annuals to hide the yellowing foliage of early spring bulbs. Need a touch of colour while your perennials are getting larger or to compensate when they are not in flower? Just add annuals and water. Need something to jazz up the space around a tree trunk or in a shaded corner? Then plant some shade-tolerant annuals.

Do annuals work with the no-dig methods? Certainly! Figure 52 is a time sequence showing my no-dig raised flower bed on my front lawn. This garden, along with a flower island in my back garden, resulted from transplants I produced in our modified polystyrene cups and planted with the bulb planter. you can use the bulb planter to put transplants anywhere that you want a touch of colour (Figure 53). If you want rows of annuals raised directly from seeds for cutting purposes, use the ridger. If you just want to plant a few seeds here and there, use the dibber.

It is very easy to raise annuals as transplants for planting with the bulb planter, as, essentially, you grow annual transplants in the same manner as you grow vegetable transplants (see Chapter 2). You can raise annuals directly in the modified polystyrene cups or start them first in trays. You can leave them in trays after thinning or transplant them into the cups.

Descriptions of some of my favourite annuals, along with cultural information and suggested uses, follow. You should be able to find annuals to fit all your needs. Please note that I omitted the depth at which to plant seeds, because the seed packages supply this information. As a rule of thumb, you can cover any seed to two or three times its thickness, except for seeds that need light for germination, which you just lightly press into the soil. I will indicate any special requirements, like light for growing the seeds.

Figure 53. The no-dig planting method allows you to make holes wherever you want to pop in a few annual flowers for extra colour, without disturbing other plants. This photograph shows annual begonias planted in my perennial bed near the chrysanthemums.

Acroclinium

The flowers are semidouble or double and the daisy-like plant is about 15 inches tall. The flowers come in pink, rose and white and appear from midsummer to early autumn. This annual makes a colourful bed or border planting and is suitable for cutting and dried arrangements.

Sow the seeds directly in the garden after frosts have passed or start transplants six to eight weeks ahead of outdoor planting time. Germination takes about 14 to 20 days. Use individual transplant containers, because this plant can be difficult to transplant. Space the plants at 6- to 9-inch intervals in full sun. If you wish to dry the flowers, pick them before they fully open.

Ageratum

Ageratum is popular for its blue flowers, a colour that's somewhat uncommon in annuals. Other ageratum colours are available, but to my eye they are not as attractive as the blue. The flower heads are dainty little fluff balls under 1 inch in diameter. Flowers appear throughout the summer and autumn until frost. Dwarf compact plants have a height of 5 to 6 inches, which makes them great for edging borders or for placement in rock gardens. There are also taller forms available, which are suitable for use as cut flowers.

Ageratum seeds require light to germinate and you can sow them outdoors after all frost danger has passed. For earlier blooms, start ageratum transplants eight to ten weeks ahead of the time you will place them out in the garden. The seeds germinate in five to eight days. Pick any dead flowers to promote continuous blooming. In the autumn, you can pot up some plants for indoor colour. Cultural needs include full sun to light shade and plenty of water, with 6- 8-inch plant spacing.

Alyssum

Another name for alyssum is sweet alyssum, because of its fragrant flowers. In very warm areas, this plant becomes a perennial. Its flowers are numerous and tiny, giving the impression of mounds of flowers. Alyssum colours include white, violet and rose. Most cultivars tend to be 3 or 4 inches tall, although a few kinds can reach 9 inches in height. Alyssum blooms quickly from seed (45 to 70 days) and is ideal for edging purposes or for rock gardens. Mix alyssum with low-growing spring bulbs for colour and for screening of yellowing foliage after the bulbs have finished blooming.

You can directly sow alyssum seeds when your last killing spring frost passes. For very early bloom, start alyssum transplants six weeks earlier. The seeds germinate in 8 to 15 days. Space alyssum plants at 5 to 8 inches when you plant them. If the plants become shaggy, quickly shear them and follow with water and fertilizer to bring back heavy flowering. It is best to plant alyssum in full sun.

Amaranthus

Some gardeners call this flower amaranth for short. Two of its cultivars are better know as love-lies-bleeding and Joseph's coat. Noted for its brightly coloured foliage, amaranthus comes mostly in hues of scarlet, with some gold or bronze shades. It grows to a height of 3 feet and finds use as scattered colour accents or massed groups in flower beds.

You can plant amaranthus seeds outdoors after all frost danger is past or you can start transplants six weeks ahead of the time you would plant amaranthus outside. Amaranthus seeds need about ten days to germinate. Space the plants at 12 to 18 inches apart, and use them in your hot, dry areas where the soil is only ordinary to poor.

Arctotis

This daisy-like flower, often called African daisy, displays hues of white, orange, apricot, yellow, pink, red and terracotta. The stem grows 10 to 18 inches tall, but I prefer the dwarf forms at 10 inches. Arctotis flowers are good for cutting and for displaying in flower beds. Blooms appear during the summer and autumn.

I suggest growing transplants about six to eight weeks ahead of outdoor planting time. Plant the transplants in your garden when frost is no longer a possibility, spacing them at 12-inch intervals. The seeds germinate in about 25 days. Arctotis plants need full sun and can tolerate heat and dryness. Use them freely for cut flowers to promote further blooming.

Asters

We often call these flowers Michaelmas daisies. Aster flowers are full bodied and available in many shades of blue, crimson, lavender, peach, pink, purple, rose, white and wine. Plant heights vary from dwarfs of 6 inches to giants of 3 feet. The lower aster forms are good to use for edging and massing in flower beds, while the taller ones are excellent for long-lasting cut flowers and colour groups in the flower bed. Asters also make good container plantings. The one drawback to asters is that after you have cut the first midsummer blossoms, few additional flowers will appear, so I suggest you make succession sowings for continuous cut flowers.

Aster wilt can be a serious problem to your asters, so make sure you get varieties that offer wilt resistance. The best approach to producing asters is to grow transplants about six to eight weeks ahead of outdoor planting time, putting the transplants out in your garden after all frost danger has passed. Aster seeds germinate in 8 to 14 days. Space tall varieties at 12 to 15 inches and dwarfs at 6 inches. Asters need full sun to grow and be sure you rotate asters each year.

Balsam

This relative of the impatiens has small, rose-like blossoms available in cerise, mauve, pink, purple, red and white. The usual height for balsam is 30 inches, but 10-inch dwarf forms are also available. While unsuitable as a cut flower, this plant is beautiful for colour masses in the flower bed. Use the dwarf varieties for edging and containers. Flowering starts in early summer and continues until frost.

You can plant balsam seeds directly in your garden after all frost danger has passed. For earlier blooming, start balsam transplants six to eight weeks ahead of outdoor planting time. Balsam seeds germinate in 8 to 14 days. Space the larger forms at 12-inch intervals and the dwarf forms at 6- to 8-inch intervals. Balsam plants grow best with full morning sun, followed by afternoon shade, and they need plenty of water.

Begonias

These plants are popular garden annuals. Their leaves vary from waxy green to bronze in colour and their small, simple flowers come in pink, red, rose and white and are prolific and continuous from summer until autumn. Double rose-like flowers and variegated foliage are also available. Begonia heights vary from 6 to 12 inches. Begonias are great for edging, colour masses in flower beds, colour accents, window boxes and container plantings.

Begonia seeds are very tiny and require light for germination, a slow process requiring two weeks to occur. The initial growth of begonias is also slow, so it is best to start begonias as transplants 10 to 12 weeks ahead of outdoor planting time. Put the plants outside after all frost danger has passed. When planting begonias, space them 8 to 12 inches apart from each other in light shade. They make great companions for impatiens. You can lift begonias out of the soil in the autumn and use them as houseplants. Also, begonia cuttings root easily in sand, soil and water.

Blue Lace Flowers

Blue lace flowers or, to give them their Latin name, *Didiscus caerulens*, grow to heights of 30 inches and have long-lasting virtue as cut flowers.

You can sow blue lace flowers outdoors at the same time you sow carrots or you can start tranplants six to eight weeks ahead of outdoor planting time. I suggest that you use individual containers for your blue lace flower transplants, because transplanting these flowers is no easy task. Blue lace flower seeds need darkness and are slow to germinate, usually requiring two weeks or more. Space the plants 10 inches apart from each other. Full sun and cool weather allow best growth, while hot weather usually terminates the flowering period.

Brachycome

Also known as the swan river daisy, this 9-inch plant bears daisy-like, fragrant flowers in shades of blue, rose, violet and white. The summer-flowering plants are useful for edging, bed colour masses, rock gardens and cut flowers for small bouquets. The bloom period of the brachycome is relatively long.

You can directly sow brachycome seeds outside after all frost danger has passed or start them four to six weeks ahead of outdoor planting time as transplants. Since the plant requires a long season, transplants are better to use than direct seeding. Germination usually occurs in two weeks. When planting, space the plants 6 inches apart. Cutting the plant encourages more flowers to appear. The brachycome plant tolerates dryness.

Browallia

Most gardeners grow browallia for its heavenly blue flowers – an unusual colour among annuals. Cultivars are also available with lavender and white flowers. The browallia flower is small and simple with five petals. The plant grows to a height of 10 to 15 inches and is best used for colour masses in flower beds, window boxes and containers. Flowers appear during the summer.

I suggest that you grow browallia transplants, starting them indoors eight to ten weeks ahead of outdoor planting time. Browallia seeds require light and germinate in about two weeks. You should not place these plants outside until all frost danger has passed. Space browallia plants at 8 to 10 inches, assuring they will have good sun with some afternoon shading. The browallia also makes a good potted greenhouse plant.

Calendula

Some call these annuals pot marigolds. Their petals are used to flavour soups and add colour as a substitute for saffron. Calendula flowers are chrysanthemum-like and come in colours of apricot, cream, gold, orange or white. You can expect flowers from early summer until frost. The plants grow from 1 to 2 feet tall. Calendulas are good cut flowers if you pick them when they are near to or in bud. For colour, plant them in masses in your flower border.

Calendulas are cool-season plants so you can sow calendula seeds outdoors after the danger of heavy spring frosts has passed. For the maximum number of blooms, start calendula transplants six to eight weeks ahead of outdoor planting time. The seeds require darkness and germinate in 10 to 14 days. You can space plants at 8- to 12-inch intervals in full sun, being sure to provide a good water supply. Pick the dead flowers to assure further blooming.

Californian Poppies

Californian poppy blossoms are silky, single or double petalled and have a saucer-like shape. They can be bronze, gold, orange, rose, scarlet, yellow or white in colour. The plants grow 1 to 2 feet tall and have interesting, lacy silver-grey foliage. Blooms appear most of the summer. Californian poppies (*Escholzia californica*) make beautiful colour masses or accents in flower beds. For cut flower use, pick them while they are in bud.

Poppies transplant poorly but bloom quickly from seed. Although poppy transplants are feasible in individual containers, they offer little advantage over direct seeding. Sow seeds as soon as you can work the soil and germination will occur in 10 to 12 days. Thin the plants to an 8-inch spacing and provide them with full sun and dry, sandy soil. Remove dead poppy flowers to encourage continued blooming.

Candytuft

This flower appears in masses of lilac, pink, purple, rose or white in late spring or early summer. The plant reaches a height of 12 to 15 inches and you can use candytuft for rock gardens, edging, in flower borders or as a cut flower. It has a pleasant fragrance and looks especially nice among the foliage of the smaller spring bulbs.

You can either sow the seeds outside as soon as you can work the soil or start transplants six to eight weeks ahead of outdoor planting time. Seed germination occurs in 10 to 15 days. Candytuft requires cool weather, full sun and 6-to 8-inch spacing. Pick dead flowers to encourage the growth of new flowers.

Cape Marigold

We also call these flowers African daisies, but don't confuse them with arctotis, because their genus is *Dimorphotheca*. The flowers are daisy-like with dark centres and come in buff, cream, orange, salmon and yellow. Good uses for Cape marigolds include edging, massing and cut flowers. Keep in mind that, like all daisies, the flowers close at night. Flowers bloom throughout the summer and autumn.

Although you can plant seeds outdoors after frost danger has passed, you would be wise to grow transplants, starting them about five weeks ahead of outdoor planting time. Seeds germinate in 10 to 15 days. Make sure you have fresh seed, because it doesn't last very long. Space the plants at 8- to 10-inch intervals in full sun. Cape marigolds can tolerate hot, dry areas.

Carnations

You can get perennial carnations to bloom in one season. Carnations possess a well-known spicy fragrance and delicately fringed petals. The ones we grow at home are similar to the florist's carnations but smaller. Carnations grow 12 to 18 inches tall and come in pink, purple, red, scarlet, white and yellow. Carnations are great for cutting purposes and for adding colour plus fragrance to the flower border.

To get flowers in one year, start transplants eight to ten weeks in advance of outdoor planting. Carnation seeds germinate in five to ten days. Put plants out when frost dangers have passed, using 10-inch spacing and planting them in a sunny location.

Celosia

The common name for celosia is cockscomb and two forms are available. One form is plumed or feathery, while the other is velvety, crested and more like a cock's comb in appearance. Celosia heights vary from 1 to 3 feet. The crested form is usually red or gold, while the plumed form comes in red, orange, apricot, yellow, rose, pink or bronze. This plant makes a colourful display in flower groups in borders or islands. It is good as a cut flower and quite valuable for dried flower arrangements. Celosia flowers appear throughout the summer.

You can sow celosia seeds directly after frosts have passed, or you can start transplants four to six weeks ahead of outdoor planting. The seeds germinate in 10 to 15 days. Plant smaller cultivars at 12-inch spacings and larger forms at 18- to 24-inch spacings. Celosia requires full sun and a good water supply.

Cleome

Some people call this flower the spider flower, because of the appearance of its seed pods. The delicate, orchid-like flowers come in lavender, pink, rose and white and appear throughout the summer. The plant is somewhat large at 3 to 6 feet in height. You can use cleome for backgrounds or unusual accents. For cut flowers, pick cleome in the bud stage.

Do your outdoor sowing after all danger of frost has passed or start transplants four to six weeks earlier. Space the plants 2 feet apart in a sunny location. The cleome plant can tolerate heat, drought, and even some shade.

Cobaea

Another name for cobaea is cathedral bell or cup and saucer plant. Although this plant is perennial, its rampant growth makes it a good candidate for annual use. Cobaea flowers are either blue or white 'cups' resting on a green

'saucer' and the vine can grow as much as 20 feet in one season. You can best use cobaea for temporary screening or a rapid cover for a trellis or wall. It's flowers last throughout the summer.

Sow cobaea seeds outdoors when all frost danger has passed or start transplants six weeks in advance of outdoor planting. Put the seeds into the medium vertically, as they germinate poorly with the broad side down. Seed germination takes place in 15 to 20 days. Plant cobaea at 2-foot intervals in full sun, although some shade is acceptable. The cobaea needs moderate amounts of water.

Coleus

We treat this tender perennial, noted for its colourful foliage, as an annual. The variegated leaves come in many colour combinations, such as pink, white and green or red and light green. Coleus leaf shapes also vary somewhat, with edges from notched to frilled. Plant heights usually vary from 1 to 2 feet, although some plants can be smaller or larger. You can use coleus for coloured accents or masses in the garden and in window boxes or other containers.

I suggest you use coleus transplants, starting them about eight weeks ahead of outdoor planting time. Coleus seeds need light and germinate in 10 to 15 days. Bottom warmth can be quite helpful, too. Do not put transplants outside until all danger of frost has passed. Depending on their height, space the transplants at 10 to 18 inches. You will get the best colour from the coleus if you plant it in a sunny area, but it can tolerate shade. Pinch back the plant, if you want it to get bushy. Also pinch off the unattractive lavender flower spikes that grow on the plant. You can remove the coleus from the soil in the autumn for an indoor potted plant or you can root coleus cuttings in sand or water.

Coreopsis

Coreopsis annuals are sometimes listed under Calliopsis. This daisy-like plant has single, semidouble or double flowers in brown, crimson, orange or yellow. Dark centres and banding occur in some varieties. Both low and high forms, reaching heights of 12 and 36 inches, are available. You can use coreopsis as colour masses, edging (the low form) or for cut flowers. The flowers appear all summer long.

You can sow the seeds outdoors when frosts no longer threaten or start transplants six to eight weeks ahead of outdoor planting. Coreopsis seeds germinate in five to ten days. Place coreopsis plants at 8- to 12-inch spacings in full sun. The plants can tolerate heat and dryness.

Cornflowers

Although most people are familiar with the blue variety, there are also pink, purple, red, rose, white and wine varieties available. The ruffled and tufted flowers bloom on plants that vary in height from 12 to 36 inches. The taller forms are best for backgrounds to lower plants, because the lower leaves of cornflowers often look ratty. The dwarf forms are nice for edging. Cornflowers are good for cutting and even for putting in a buttonhole.

You can sow cornflower seeds directly as soon as you are able to work your soil as these are hardy annuals. You can also start transplants four to five weeks early. Cornflower seeds require darkness and germinate in one to two weeks. Thin dwarf varieties to 6 inches and tall varieties to 12 inches. Keep the flowers picked to encourage continuous blooming, which at best doesn't last long. To lengthen blooming time, you will need to make succession plantings.

Plant cornflowers either in full sun or light shade.

Cosmos

These daisy-like single and semidouble blossoms come in lovely warm shades of crimson, lavender, pink, purple, rose and white. The plant heights vary from 30 to 48 inches. Flowers appear from midsummer to frost and are good for cutting, but the best use for cosmos is in border backgrounds, especially against fences or walls. Taller cosmos varieties may need staking.

After all danger of frost has passed, you can sow seeds outdoors, but I suggest that you start transplants six to eight weeks ahead of outdoor planting time for earlier flowering. Seeds come up in five to ten days. Plant cosmos at 18-inch intervals and continue picking the flowers to promote further flowering. Cosmos requires a sunny location and can tolerate poor soil.

Dahlias

You can grow bedding or dwarf dahlias from seed as annuals. Flowers can be single, semidouble or double in shades of apricot, lavender, pink, purple, red, white or yellow. Bicolours, such as red and white combinations, also occur. Flower shapes, as with the large perennial dahlias, also vary and include anemone, cactus, pompom and decorative forms. Dahlias can grow from 12 to 36 inches in height. You can use them for colour masses all summer in the border or as cut flowers, if you pick them before they fully open and dip the cut stems briefly in boiling water.

It is best to start dwarf dahlias as transplants four to six weeks ahead of outdoor planting. Their seeds germinate in five to ten days. You can plant your dahlia transplants outside in full sun after all danger of frost has passed, spacing them 18 inches apart. You can dig the tubers in the autumn after the tops have blackened from frost. It is best to store tubers with some dry moss peat in a plastic bag in a cellar but, because bedding dahlias grow so easily from seed, I don't bother saving the tubers.

Dianthus

Commonly called pinks, dianthus flowers are fragrant and available in lilac, pink, rose, white and bicolour varieties. They have either single or double frilled petals. Dianthus heights vary from 6 to 18 inches and the flowers bloom in the early summer. Pinks are good for colour masses, edging and for cut flowers.

After the danger of frost has passed, sow seeds directly into your garden or start transplants six to eight weeks ahead for earlier and longer flowering. Germination occurs in five to ten days. Set the plants 6 to 9 inches apart and, after flowering, give the plants a light shearing to initiate more blossoms.

Four O'Clocks

In warmer areas, these flowers from grandmother's early garden days become perennials and, of course, open in mid to late afternoon, or all day when the sky is cloudy. The trumpet-like flowers come in lavender, pink, red, salmon, white and yellow. Appearing late in the season on 18- to 36-inch plants, these fragrant flowers are good for border colour late in the summer.

Plant the seeds outdoors when all frost danger has passed, or start transplants four to six weeks earlier for faster blooming. Plant spacings of 12 to 18 inches are acceptable. Four o'clocks require full sun and can tolerate heat and poor soils.

Gaillardia

Also called blanket flower, this aster-like flower comes in shades of gold, orange, red and yellow on 18- to 24-inch-tall plants. The gaillardia lasts all summer and makes a good cut flower. You can best use gaillardias in colourful masses for the border or bed. A dwarf form for edging purposes is also available, as are bicolours in the larger cultivars.

After frost danger has passed, you can sow the seeds directly in your garden. You can also start transplants four to six weeks ahead for earlier flowers. Germination requires 15 to 20 days. Be sure to use 1-foot spacing when planting gaillardias and keep picking the flowers to promote further blooming.

Gazania

The gazania comes in cream, gold, orange, pink and yellow colours, although dark centres and bicolours also occur. Gazania heights vary from 8 to 12 inches and the flowers appear all summer, closing at night like other daisies. The best use for the gazania is for colourful masses in borders or beds.

Sow gazania seeds outdoors when the danger of frost has passed. To get earlier blooms, start transplants five to seven weeks ahead of outdoor planting time. Germination takes 8 to 14 days to occur and requires darkness. Space the gazania plants 6 to 10 inches from each other in full sun. The plant performs just fine in hot, dry conditions. You can lift this plant from the garden in the autumn and use it indoors as a potted plant.

Globe Amaranth

The globe amaranth has clover-like flower heads in lavender, orange, pink, reddish purple, rose and white and grows on plants 18 to 24 inches tall. Blooming occurs from midsummer to late autumn. The globe amaranth dries well for arrangements when fully developed, makes a good cut flower, and interesting massed plantings in borders.

You can sow seeds directly after frost dangers have passed, but you will get quicker results by using transplants. Start transplants six to eight weeks ahead of outdoor planting. The seeds germinate slowly in 15 to 20 days. Soaking the seeds overnight in luke-warm water helps to quicken germination. Space globe amaranths 10 to 15 inches from each other and plant them in full sun. The globe amaranth can tolerate heat and dryness.

Gloriosa Daisies

Improved versions of the black-eyed Susan (the latin name is *Rudbeckia hirta Tetra 'Gloriosa'*), these plants have single, semidouble, and double dark-centred daisies in shades of gold, mahogany and yellow. These hybrids bloom easily from seed the first year, so you can treat these plants as annuals even though they are perennials. Gloriosa daisies grow 24 to 36 inches tall and you can use them as colourful masses and cut flowers.

Start gloriosa daisy seeds six weeks ahead of outdoor planting, if you wish to use them as annuals. Seeds germinate in five to ten days. Space the plants at 12 to 24 inches in your garden after the frost has passed. The plants grow best in full sun and will tolerate heat, drought and poor soil.

Gypsophila

Another name for gypsophila is baby's breath. The dainty masses of flowers come in pink, red and white and the plant grows 12 to 24 inches tall. Blooming starts in early summer and doesn't last very long. To lengthen the time of flowering, you must use succession plantings. This plant adds an attractive touch to borders.

Baby's breath is hardy and you can sow it as soon as you can work the soil. You can also start transplants six to eight weeks ahead of outdoor planting. Gypsophila seeds need 10 to 15 days to germinate. Plant spacings of 8 to 12 inches are adequate, and full sun provides the best results with baby's breath.

Heliotrope

This plant has small clusters of violet flowers and a delightful fragrance and grows to 12 to 20 inches in height. The vanilla-scented flowers appear throughout the summer. The heliotrope plant makes an attractive addition to the border or window box.

The best approach to growing it is to start transplants 10 to 12 weeks early. Seeds need three to four weeks for germination. After all frost danger has passed, put the transplants outside at spacings of 12 inches between plants. Full sun affords the best results. You can pot heliotrope in the autumn or take cuttings for a winter potted plant.

Hollyhocks

Make sure you get the annual, not perennial, form of hollyhock. This 3- to 5-foot tall plant produces many single, semidouble or double flowers along its spike throughout the summer. Flower colours include cerise, pink, rose, scarlet, white and yellow. Tall hollyhocks may require staking, but they make a nice background in borders or against fences.

The best method for attaining sure blooms is to start transplants eight to ten weeks ahead of outdoor planting. Hollyhock seeds need light and germinate in 10 to 14 days. Put the transplants outside once the frost has passed, spacing small forms at 18 inches apart and larger ones at 24 inches. The hollyhock needs full sun.

Impatiens

Commonly called busy lizzies, these succulent plants have simple flowers in shades of fuchsia, orange, pink, salmon, scarlet and white. Their heights vary from dwarfs at 6 inches to large forms at 30 inches. Impatiens bloom throughout the summer and add colour to edgings, borders and containers.

You can sow seeds directly after all danger of frost has passed, but it is preferable to use transplants. Start seeds 10 to 12 weeks ahead of outdoor planting time and be sure to provide the seeds with light. The seeds will germinate in 15 to 20 days. When transferring the transplants to the garden, space small varieties of impatiens at 12 inches and larger ones at 18 inches. These plants do well in shaded areas and make good companion plants to begonias. If you grow impatiens in the sun, you must keep them evenly moist.

Kochia

Also known as summer cypress, this bushy plant looks like a small evergreen and possesses foliage that turns a reddish colour in the autumn. It grows 24 to 36 inches tall, and you can use it as a temporary hedge, background or an unusual accent.

You can sow kochia seeds directly after all frost has gone or you can start transplants four to six weeks ahead of outdoor planting. The seeds need light to germinate, a 10- to 15-day process. Space kochias 18 to 24 inches apart and provide full sunlight and adequate moisture. You can give kochias a light shearing to improve the plant's shape.

Larkspur

Larkspur is the common name for the delphinium. It is also called rocket larkspur. The larkspur is noted for its blue flower spikes up to 4 feet tall. Shades of pink, purple, red and white are also available. The larkspur blooming period is from late spring to early summer. You can use larkspur for cut flowers and border backdrops, such as in front of fences. Make sure foreground plants conceal the often unattractive lower foliage of larkspur.

Sow the seeds of this hardy annual as soon as the soil is workable. Better yet, start transplants six to eight weeks early. Seeds require darkness and germinate in 8 to 15 days. Get fresh seed, as larkspur seed does not stay fresh for long. A spacing of 12 inches between plants is acceptable. You may have to stake the plants and you definitely must keep picking the flowers to encourage continued blooming. The larkspur plants need full sun but not heat, because they are cool-season plants.

Lobelia

This low, compact or trailing plant grows 4 to 6 inches high and is covered with dainty, simple flowers throughout much of the summer. Flower colours include blue, rose, violet and white. You can use lobelia for edging borders and rock gardens and the trailing forms are nice in containers and window boxes.

Lobelia grows slowly, so I recommend using transplants started 10 to 12 weeks ahead of outdoor planting, putting them outside after all frost danger has gone. Seed germination takes 15 to 20 days. Space the lobelia plants at 6 inch intervals and, if blooming slows, give them a light shearing. Lobelia does well in full sun to light shade. You can root cuttings for use as potted plants at the end of the season.

Lupin

Annual lupins are lower growing and not as showy as perennial lupins, but they are nevertheless worth growing. Pea-like flowers in blue, orange, pink, purple, red white or yellow appear on 18-inch-tall spikes. Lupins provide colour in beds, borders and backgrounds. They bloom in late spring and early summer.

You can directly sow seeds as soon as the soil is workable, but it is wiser to start transplants in individual containers, which provide room for the taproot to grow. Soak the seeds overnight to quicken germination, which takes 15 to 20 days. Start the plants six to eight weeks ahead of outdoor planting. When transplanting, space the lupins 12 to 18 inches apart, depending on their height. Tall forms may need staking. Full sun to light shade is best for plant growth. If your summers get hot early, you may need to use an organic mulch to keep roots cool, because lupins are cool-season plants. Regularly remove any dead flowers.

Marigolds

Marigolds are clearly a favourite annual. Marigold colours include several variations of mahogany red, orange and yellow. A white marigold is also available. The plant heights vary from 6-inch dwarfs to 36-inch giants. Most of the flowers are of the double form but a few singles and semidoubles are available. Marigolds, depending upon the choice of cultivar, are useful in beds, borders and containers, or for edging and cutting purposes. The flowers bloom throughout the summer until frost.

You can sow marigold seeds directly after frost. However, you will find that transplants are really easy to grow and they bloom much earlier than directly sown seeds. Start transplants four to six weeks ahead of outdoor planting and allow five to seven days for germination to occur. Space marigolds at 6- to 18-inch intervals, depending on their height and be sure they receive full sun. Dead-heading is not essential, but improves the growth of the plant and the size of the flowers.

Morning Glories

These vines with their funnel-like flowers grow from 3 to 20 feet, depending upon the cultivar. While the blue variety is popular, morning glories also come in crimson, lavender, pink, violet and white. The flowers wilt in full, hot sun but bloom beautifully in the morning (hence, morning glory) and on cloudy days. Use morning glories in a trellis, lattice or net.

Soak morning glory seeds in warm water for 24 hours, because their hard coat will prolong germination. After soaking, the seeds germinate in five to seven days. You can sow the seeds directly after all danger of frost has passed or start transplants four to six weeks ahead of outdoor planting. Use 12-inch spacing when planting outside and be sure the plants receive full sun and moderate watering. Morning glories tolerate dry soil.

Nasturtiums

These old-time flowers vary from the 12-inch bushy kind to an 8-foot climber needing support. The colours include orange, rose, red and yellow and the flowers can be single or double, with some being fragrant. The blooms appear throughout the summer. The bush forms are useful in beds and borders, while the climber is good as a background screen or in hanging baskets. Some people use peppery-flavoured nasturtium leaves in salads.

The seeds need darkness to germinate in 7 to 12 days and you can sow them in your garden after the danger of frost has passed. You can also grow nasturtiums from transplants in individual containers started four to six weeks ahead of outdoor planting. Space plants 8 to 12 inches apart in the garden, and be sure they receive full sun to light shade. Don't overfertilize nasturtiums or you'll have lots of leaves and few flowers.

Nicotiana

Another name for nicotiana is tobacco plant. Nicotiana has star-like trumpet flowers that are especially fragrant in the evening. The flowers can be lavender, pink, red or white in colour. The flowers continue to bloom throughout the summer, until frost and they make colourful accents for borders.

Direct sowing of seeds is possible after all danger of frost has passed, but transplants are better, especially to achieve early flowers. Start transplants six to eight weeks ahead of outdoor planting time and be sure to provide light for seed germination, which takes 10 to 20 days. Space the plants at 10-inch intervals in your garden. If flowering stops, cut off the spent flower stalks to allow for additional blooms.

Nierembergia

The cup-like, small, violet-blue flowers bloom on 6- to 12-inch plants although another variety of nierembergia grows 24 to 36 inches tall and has white flowers. Nierembergia flowers appear in late summer. The low forms are good for edging, rock gardens and borders, while the larger ones are good for borders.

For use as an annual, start nierembergia as transplants 10 to 12 weeks early. The seeds need 15 to 20 days to germinate. Put the plants outside after all frost dangers have gone, spacing them at 6- to 12-inch intervals. Light shade to full sun is acceptable for growing nierembergia.

Nigella

Love-in-a-mist is another name for this plant whose flowers can be pink, purple, red or white and resemble cornflowers. The plant grows 12 to 24 inches tall and you can use it for colourful massing in a bed or border. You can also use it as a cut flower or dry its unusual seed pods for use in dried flower arrangements. Nigella flowers appear from midsummer through to the autumn.

Nigella is a hardy annual whose seeds you can sow as early in spring as you can work the soil. The seeds germinate in 10 to 15 days. You can also use transplants, starting them four to six weeks ahead of outdoor planting and using individual containers, because the nigella doesn't transplant well. Place the plants at 8-inch intervals and in full sun.

Ornamental Grasses

For an unusual accent, why not try a clump of ornamental grasses? Many are tall, upright, graceful plumes, some are dainty and others nod gracefully in the breeze. Many ornamental grasses are available, especially from Thompson and Morgan (for their address, see page 166). The heights of ornamental grasses vary considerably, with some cultivars approaching 4 to 5 feet. You can use ornamental grasses in dried arrangements.

Lightly press the seeds into the ground as soon as frost dangers have passed or start transplants four to six weeks ahead of outdoor planting time. Plant ornamental grasses in scattered clumps for best effect, and be sure they receive full sun.

Pelargoniums

Often called geraniums, pelargoniums are well known for their colourful flower clusters of pink, red, salmon and white, growing to heights varying from 15 to 24 inches. Besides providing colour in the flower bed, these plants also look beautiful in containers and window boxes. The flowers bloom all summer long and you can cut pelargonium flower heads and float them on shallow water for an unusual flower arrangement.

Although you can buy plants, you can grow your own more economically. Make sure you get seeds of hybrid series specially developed for raising from seed, such as the Sprinter hybrids. Start the seeds 10 to 12 weeks before the last heavy spring frost, as pelargoniums grow slowly. Pelargonium seeds need bottom heat (top of refrigerator) and germinate in 20 days. Plant your transplants in the garden after the frost danger has passed, placing the plants 12 to 16 inches apart. Pick off spent flower clusters to allow continuous blooming. Pelargoniums need full sun and moderate dryness to grow.

Petunias

These attractive annuals are another favourite, with their simple funnel, exquisite double or ruffled flowers. Their fragrance is slight, but their colours include just about every hue, with a number of bicolours also available. Petunia heights vary from 10 to 18 inches. Petunias bloom throughout the summer and make colourful additions to beds, borders, window boxes, hanging baskets and other containers.

Petunia seeds are extremely fine. It is best to sow them indoors and grow transplants, starting about ten weeks ahead of outdoor planting and providing light and some bottom warmth (top of refrigerator) for germination. At 70°F, petunia seeds germinate in 12 to 14 days, while at 75°F, they germinate in ten. Place plants outside after all danger of frost has passed, spacing the smaller petunias at 8 inches and larger ones at 12 inches. After the first flush of bloom, cut back the tips and spent flowers to allow for more blooms. Allowing petunias to go to seed stops blossoms, so continue to pick spent blooms throughout the season. Full sun and moderate moisture provide the best growing conditions for petunias.

Phacelia

This plant comes from California originally and has lovely, blue, bell-like flowers. It reaches a height of 9 inches and blooms throughout the summer. Use the phacelia as a colourful mass in the rock garden or as edging for borders and beds.

After frost, you can sow phacelia seeds directly in the garden. If you choose to grow transplants, start them six weeks before outdoor planting time and use individual containers for these somewhat fussy plants. Germination occurs sporadically in 12 to 25 days. Space phacelias at 6-inch intervals and pinch their tips when young to encourage fullness. Full sun and warm to hot summers are best for growing this plant.

Phlox

Make sure you get the annual forms of phlox, which have colourful clusters of simple flowers in lavender, pink, red and white. Phlox heights vary from 7-inch dwarfs to 15 inches and flowering occurs throughout the summer. Use the dwarf forms in edgings and rock gardens and use the tall ones for massing in beds or borders or for cut flowers. The flower clusters may show sporadic wilting of individual flowers, so pick the wilted ones off the cluster for best appearance.

You can sow the seeds outdoors as soon as the soil is workable, because phlox are hardy annuals. You can also start the seeds as transplants in individual containers six to eight weeks earlier, putting them outside when frost dangers have passed. Save some of the weaker transplants, as they often develop the best colours. Phlox seeds require darkness, cool conditions (55° to 65°F), and 10 to 15 days for germination. Use a spacing of 10 to 12 inches for phlox, be sure the plants will receive full sun, and remove faded flowers to encourage further blooming.

Polygonum

Polygonum is often known as knot-weed. The dense heads of pink flowers bloom on plants only 3 or 4 inches tall. You can use polygonum for edging and in rock gardens. The flowers appear during the summer.

To grow polygonum as an annual and get flowers in one season, you must start transplants six to eight weeks ahead of planting outdoors. Germination occurs slowly, in 20 to 25 days. Put the transplants outside only after the danger of frost has gone. Polygonum can spread quickly and become invasive in areas where the winter temperature does not fall below 0°F. The plants can tolerate full sun to light shade.

Portulaca

Another name for portulaca is sun plant. The ruffled, cup-shaped flowers can be single or double. Colours are numerous and include warm shades of cream, gold, pink, red, rose, salmon, white or yellow. The portulaca plant is only 4 to 6 inches high but forms a spreading mound up to 2 feet across. The flowers close in cloudy weather and at night. Portulaca works nicely as edging or in a rock garden. The flowers appear from midsummer on.

You can sow the seeds directly in your garden after all danger of frost is past or start transplants about six weeks ahead of outdoor planting. Portulaca seed germinates in about 10 to 15 days and requires light. Space the plants at 12- to 14-inch intervals in full sun. Portulaca can tolerate heat and dryness quite well.

Salpiglossis

Salpiglossis has velvety flowers resembling deep petunias, with splashes of contrasting colour on their petals. The colours include blue, purple, red, rose and yellow, and the plant grows about 30 inches tall. Salpiglossis flowers appear from midsummer to frost. They make colourful backgrounds in beds or borders and work well as cut flowers.

Seeds can be sown outside when frost dangers have passed, but for early flowers, start transplants eight weeks earlier. The seeds require darkness and are so fine that you must press them into the growing mixture and cover them with cardboard or newspaper. Germination requires 15 to 20 days. Place plants in the garden at 8- to 12-inch intervals in full sun. They also may require staking. Salpiglossis does not grow well where summers are hot.

Salvia

This attractive plant has spikes of flowers that appear from early summer until the first frost. Salvia colours include the well-known red, as well as lavender, pink, purple, rose and white. Another closely related species of salvia has blue flowers. Ten-inch dwarf cultivars and 3-foot giants are available. Salvia makes a bright addition to the border or bed, and you can dry the blue form.

Because salvia takes a long time to reach flowering, it is best to start it as a transplant. Start red salvia six to eight weeks ahead of outdoor planting, and be sure to provide light. Salvia seeds have short lives, so be sure you use fresh ones. Start blue salvia 12 weeks early. Germination for both forms takes 12 to 15 days. Plants can go outside after the danger of frost has passed. Give the blue forms a spacing of 12 inches and the red forms 15 inches. Be sure your salvia gets full sun and plenty of water.

Scabiosa

Other names for this annual are pin-cushion flower and scabious. The pincushion-like flowers are fragrant and available in blue, pink, purple, red, rose or white. Plant heights vary from 18 to 36 inches. The flowers are attractive in borders and beds and are good for cutting. They bloom throughout the summer.

You can sow scabiosa seeds directly after the danger of frost has gone, but for earlier flowering, start transplants four to six weeks ahead of outdoor planting time. Seed germination takes 10 to 15 days. Space the plants 6 to 12 inches apart, depending upon their final expected height, and in full sun. Remove spent flowers to encourage the blooming of more flowers. Scabiosa does not grow well in extreme heat.

Shell-flowers

Another name for shell-flowers is bells of Ireland. The flowers are apple green and bell-like, appearing all along the tall stem. The flowers bloom late in the summer on plants 24 to 36 inches tall. The actual flower is tiny, white and fragrant and grows in the base of the green shells or bells. You can use these flowers freshly cut, but they are best known for use in dried flower arrangements.

Sow shell-flower seeds outside as soon as you can work the soil, because they are hardy annuals, or start transplants about eight weeks earlier in individual containers, a necessity due to the shell-flower's taproots. Seeds need light and coolness (55°F) for germination, which is slow at 25 to 35 days. Space the plants at 12-inch intervals in full sun or light shade and provide moderate watering. For drying purposes, cut the flowers when they are at their peak.

Snapdragons

These colourful annuals are a tradition in many flower gardens. The flowers are thought to resemble the jaws of a dragon and generations of children have learned how to open the jaws by pressing the bottom of the flower. Snapdragons come in every colour except blue and double flowers are also available. Snapdragons can range from 7 to 36 inches in height. The flowers appear from summer until the frosts come. Use the smaller forms for edging and larger forms for backgrounds. You can also use snapdragons for colourful massing in beds or borders and as cut flowers.

While you can sow seeds in place, it would be wise to use transplants because snapdragons are actually perennials that we use as annuals. Start your transplants six to eight weeks ahead of outdoor planting. Germination requires 10 to 14 days and light. Plants can go outside after all danger of frost has passed at spacings of 6 inches for small forms and up to 12 inches for the larger ones. Some tip pinching will encourage young plants to branch and produce more flowers. Snapdragons require full sun.

Snow on the Mountain

This annual, usually sold under its Latin name *Euphorbia marginata*, has white-edged green foliage and flower bracts. One hardly notices the actual flower. The plant grows from 24 to 30 inches tall and, when cut, the stems produce a milky sap that can irritate eyes and skin. The best use for the plant is for accents or to separate more colourful flower groups. Because the lower parts of euphorbia tend to become bare, you might want to use some low annuals in front of it for concealment.

You can sow the seeds directly in your garden after the danger of frost has passed or start transplants six to eight weeks earlier. Germination is in six to eight weeks. Provide 12-inch spacing of plants. This plant can take full sun to light shade, heat and drought. If you use it in a cut flower arrangement, seal the cut stem end by dipping it in boiling water. Wash off any milky sap that gets on your hands.

Statice

We sometimes call statice by another name, sea lavender. Its delicate airy flower clusters come in blue, lavender, purple, rose and yellow and appear in late summer on 30-inch plants. Statice dries well and is very popular for use in dried arrangements. Other uses include bed, border, and rock garden displays and cut flowers.

You can start statice directly outside when frosts have passed, but transplants are better to use because statice blooms late. Start transplants eight to ten weeks early. Germination requires 15 to 20 days. Space the plants at 18-inch intervals and be sure they have full sun and good drainage. Keep statice drier than your other plants.

Stock

Stock flowers are fragrant during the summer and autumn and appear as blue, pink, purple, red, rose, white or yellow rosettes. The single or double flowers bloom on plants 12 to 30 inches tall. Stocks make good cut flowers and colourful masses in the bed or border.

Because summer heat can prevent flowering, it is best to start stock as transplants six to eight weeks ahead of putting them outside. The seeds require light and germinate in seven to ten days. After frost dangers have gone, put the plants in the soil at 12-inch intervals. Stock requires sun and plenty of moisture and does poorly in extreme heat.

Straw flowers

These annuals have full paper-like or straw-like flowers in orange, pink, purple, red, salmon, white and yellow and reach heights of 12 to 30 inches. Straw flower blossoms appear from midsummer until the frosts and are excellent for dried arrangements, cut flowers and bed or border use.

You can directly sow the seeds after frosts have passed or as transplants four to six weeks before outdoor planting time. Germination requires light and occurs in seven to ten days. You can space the plants at 9- to 12-inch intervals in your garden. Full sun and heat make for great straw flowers. Be sure you pick straw flowers just before or at their peak for drying, for the flowers open further as they dry.

Sunflowers

Although we know these annuals best for their large, daisy-like flowers, which form big, central seed heads, there are also some cultivars of dwarf size, 15 to 36 inches, some with double flowers and some with brown, bronze, gold or even red flowers. The most familiar form reaches up to 12 feet in height with flowers over 1 foot in diameter. We use sunflowers for screening, bird food and fun for children, who love to watch the little seed slowly grow into a gigantic plant that's taller than they are.

Sunflowers grow so rapidly that transplants are unnecessary. Sow the seeds after all danger of frost has passed. Germination is in 10 to 14 days. Depending upon the cultivar, space the plants from 24 to 48 inches apart. You may need to do some staking. Sunflowers need full sun but can succeed even in poor soil.

Sweet Peas

Sweet peas have fragrant, pea-like flowers in colours of blue, pink, purple, red, rose and white. The plants vary in size from 9-inch bushy dwarfs to 7-foot vines. Blooming occurs from late spring through to early summer. You can use the dwarf forms in beds or containers and the vining types for screening or background purposes.

Sow the seeds outdoors as soon as you can work the soil or start transplants four to six weeks ahead of outdoor planting time. Soak the seeds in water for 24 hours or put a nick in the seed coat with a file to improve germination. Germination can take 10 to 14 days. Space the plants 6 to 9 inches apart and provide support for the climbing forms. Full sun and cool weather afford the best growth. If your summer heats up early, use some of the more heat-resistant varieties. An organic mulch can keep the roots cool and improve warm-weather performance.

Thunbergia

Commonly known as black-eyed Susan, the simple, five-petalled flowers with their dark centres faintly suggest an image of dark eyes. The vine reaches a height of 5 feet and produces orange, yellow and white flowers in the summer. Incidentally, not all thunbergias have the dark centre. The thunbergia is useful for screening purposes or for cascades in a window or porch box.

You can sow the seeds outdoors after frosts have passed, or start transplants six to eight weeks ahead of outdoor planting time. Germination takes 10 to 15 days. Space the plants at 6- to 12-inch intervals in full sun to light shade. Thunbergia does poorly in extreme heat.

Torenia

Another name for torenia is wishbone flower, due to the wishbone appearance of the stamens inside the flower. The flowers look like miniature gloxinias with violet-blue lips and a yellow throat. The plant grows from 8 to 14 inches tall and produces flowers during the summer through to the frosts. The torenia is useful for edging, containers and as a bedding plant.

It is best to start transplants 10 to 12 weeks ahead of outdoor planting time. Germination requires 15 to 20 days. Space the plants 6 to 8 inches apart in full sun in cool climates only and in light to partial shade in warm climates. Dryness results in poor plant performance.

Verbena

This sprawling and trailing plant generally reaches 15 inches, although it sometimes spreads as much as 24 inches. Clusters of tiny flowers having contrasting centres (usually white) cover the plant and come in blue, maroon, pink, purple, rose, scarlet and white. The plant is a good edging for borders, looks nice in rock gardens or window boxes and is reasonable as a cut flower. Blooming occurs through the summer and early autumn.

For best results, start verbena transplants 12 to 14 weeks before outdoor planting time. The seeds need darkness for germination, which takes 20 to 25 days. Plant the transplants outside in full sun after the danger of frost has passed, using a spacing of 12 inches between each plant. Shear off spent flowers to afford continuous blooming. Verbena will tolerate heat.

Vinca

Periwinkle is another name for this perennial, which we often grow as an annual. The trailing plant varies from 6 to 18 inches tall and has simple pink, rose, white or purple-blue flowers that appear in the summer. Some forms have a darker or contrasting centre eye. The plant is useful for groundcover, edging, bedding and containers.

Start the seeds as transplants eight to ten weeks ahead of outdoor planting to assure blossoms, since vinca is a perennial. Germination takes 10 to 15 days.

Space vinca transplants 6 to 12 inches apart in a sunny to lightly shaded location. Vinca can tolerate heat and dryness.

Zinnias

In my book, zinnias rate as highly as marigolds do in terms of substantial returns for little work. Zinnias are available in all colours, with the exception of blue. You can also buy bicolour forms. Zinnia heights vary from 10 to 30 inches. The flowers are single or double and come in many forms, such as daisy-like, semidouble and pompon. Zinnias are great cut flowers and excellent addition to the bed or border. You can also use them as plantings for containers and edges. The flowers appear from summer until the frosts begin and contrast nicely with marigolds.

You can sow zinnias after the danger of frost has gone or you can prepare transplants four to six weeks ahead of outdoor planting in individual containers. Germination takes five to seven days. Space the small cultivars at 6-inch intervals and large ones at 12-inch intervals. Zinnias thrive in full sun and can take the heat or dryness. Avoid crowding them and overhead watering if powdery mildew is a problem in your area.

SUPPLIERS

HDRA (Henry Doubleday Research Association) Sales Limited
National Centre for Organic Gardening
Ryton-on-Dunsmore
Coventry CV8 3LG

Suppliers of seeds, Farmura, worm casts, Savona insecticidal soap, derris, pyrethrum insecticide and organic fertilizers

Agriframes Limited
Charlwoods Road
East Grinstead
West Sussex
RH19 2HG

Supplier of Melbourne cloches

Biological Control Systems Limited
Treforest Industrial Estate
Mid Glamorgan CF37 5SU

Suppliers of Trappit, a clear, sticky substance for using in insect traps

Chase Organics (GB) Limited
Coombelands House
Coombelands Lane
Addlestone
Weybridge KT15 1HY

Suppliers of seeds, seaweed meal, SM3 liquid seaweed, Agryl P17 (polypropylene fleece), derris, pyrethrum, worm casts, seed and potting composts and organic fertilizers, Hortopaper, bone meal and Melbourne cloches

Corruplast Limited
Moreland Trading Estate
Bristol Road
Gloucester GL1 5RZ

Suppliers of Correx, a plastic corrugated board for making insect traps. Remember to ask for yellow.

Cumulus Organics and Conservation Limited
Timber Yard
Two Mile Lane
Highnam
Gloucester GL2 8DW

Suppliers of soil test kits, hoof and horn, blood, fish and bone, Farmura, liquid seaweed, worm casts, dolomitic limestone, seaweed meal, derris, perlite, vermiculite, leather meal and Swiss reciprocating hoes

Samuel Dobie & Son Limited
P O Box 90
Paignton
Devon TQ3 1XY

Suppliers of knee pads and seeds

Elm Farm Research Centre
Hamstead Marshall
Berkshire RG15 OHR

Offers a soil analysis service

Jemp Engineering Limited
Canal Estate
Station Road
Langley
Buckinghamshire SL3 6EG

Supplier of propagators, electrically heated bases for seed trays and soil warming cables

S. E. Marshall & Company Limited
Regal Road
Wisbech
Cambridgeshire PE13 2RF

Suppliers of seeds

Maxicrop Garden Products Limited
Bridge House
High Street
Tonbridge
Kent TN9 1DR

Supplier of liquid seaweed

Suffolk Herbs
Sawyers Farm
Little Cornard
Sudbury
Suffolk
CO10 ONY

Supplier of Swiss reciprocating hoes, seeds and other sundries

Super Natural Organic Garden Products
Bore Place Farm
Chiddingstone
Edenbridge
Kent TN8 7AR

Supplier of liquid plant food, which can be used instead of fish emulsion

Sutton Seeds Limited
Hele Road
Torquay
Devon TQ2 7QJ

Suppliers of seeds

Thompson & Morgan (Ipswich)
    Limited
London Road
Ipswich
IP2 OBA

Suppliers of seeds

Transatlantic Plastics
23 Brighton Road
Surbiton
Surrey
KT6 5LR

Suppliers of black polythene and
cloches

Turning Worms
Unit 42
Glan Yr Afon Industrial Estate
Llanbadarn
Aberystwyth
Dyfed SY23 3JQ

Supplier of seed and potting composts

WOLF-Tools for Garden and Lawn
    Limited
Ross-on-Wye
Herefordshire HR9 5NE

Suppliers of the ridger and other tools

WEIGHTS AND MEASURES CONVERSION TABLE

Length

Inches

¹⁄₁₆ inch	2mm
⅛ inch	3mm
¼ inch	6mm
½ inch	13mm
⅜ inch	1cm
¾ inch	2cm
1 inch	2.5cm
1¼ inches	3cm
1½ inches	3.8cm
2 inches	5cm
2½ inches	6cm
3 inches	8cm
4 inches	10cm
5 inches	12cm
5½ inches	14cm
6 inches	15cm
6½ inces	16.5cm
7 inches	17cm
7½ inches	19cm
8 inches	20cm
9 inches	23cm
10 inches	25cm
11 inches	28cm
12 inches	30cm
14 inches	35.5cm
15 inches	38cm
16 inches	40cm
18 inches	46cm
20 inches	50cm
24 inches	61cm
30 inches	76cm
36 inches	91cm
40 inches	1m
48 inches	1.2m
56 inches	1.4m

Feet

1 foot	0.3m
1½ feet	0.46m
2 feet	0.6m
3 feet	0.9m
3½ feet	1m
4 feet	1.2m
5 feet	1.5m
6 feet	1.8m
7 feet	2.1m
8 feet	2.4m
10 feet	3m
20 feet	6m

Weight

Pounds and Ounces

1 ounce	28g
2 ounces	56g
1 pound	0.4kg
2 pounds	0.9kg
3 pounds	1.3kg
5 pounds	2.3kg
8 pounds	3.6kg
10 pounds	4.5kg
25 pounds	11kg
50 pounds	22.7kg

Capacity Measures

Fluid Ounces

8 fluid ounces	240ml
12 fluid ounces	340 ml (⅔ pint)

Pints

⅓ pint	200ml
2 pints	1.1l
3 pints	1.7l

5 pints	2.8l	**Temperature**	
8 pints	4.5l	***Fahrenheit***	
		0°F	−17°C
Gallons		5°F	−15°C
½ gallon	2.3l	6°F	−14°C
1 gallon	4.5l	12°F	−11°C
3½ gallons	16l	15°F	−9°C
4 gallons	18l	28°F	−2°C
5 gallons	23l	40°F	4°C
		50°F	10°C
Area		55°F	12°C
Square Feet		60°F	15°C
6 square feet	0.56m²	65°F	18°C
14 square feet	1.3m²	70°F	21°C
100 square feet	9.29m²	75°F	24°C
1,000 square feet	92.9m²	80°F	26°C
		85°F	29°C
Cubic Measure		120°F	48°C
Cubic Feet		131°F	55°C
0.3 cubic feet	0.008m³	140°F	60°C
1.3 cubic feet	0.03m³	158°F	70°C
16 cubic feet	0.4m³		
32 cubic feet	0.9m³		

INDEX